JAPAN BEYOND
THE KIMONO

DRESS, BODY, CULTURE

Series Editor: Joanne B. Eicher, *Regents' Professor, University of Minnesota*

Advisory Board:

Djurdja Bartlett, *London College of Fashion, University of the Arts*
Pamela Church-Gibson, *London College of Fashion, University of the Arts*
James Hall, *University of Illinois at Chicago*
Vicki Karaminas, *University of Technology, Sydney*
Gwen O'Neal, *University of North Carolina at Greensboro*
Ted Polhemus, *Curator, "Street Style" Exhibition, Victoria and Albert Museum*
Valerie Steele, *The Museum at the Fashion Institute of Technology*
Lou Taylor, *University of Brighton*
Karen Tranberg Hansen, *Northwestern University*
Ruth Barnes, *Yale Art Gallery, Yale University*

Books in this provocative series seek to articulate the connections between culture and dress which is defined here in its broadest possible sense as any modification or supplement to the body. Interdisciplinary in approach, the series highlights the dialogue between identity and dress, cosmetics, coiffure, and body alternations as manifested in practices as varied as plastic surgery, tattooing, and ritual scarification. The series aims, in particular, to analyze the meaning of dress in relation to popular culture and gender issues and will include works grounded in anthropology, sociology, history, art history, literature, and folklore.

ISSN: 1360-466X

PREVIOUSLY PUBLISHED IN THE SERIES

Helen Bradley Foster, *"New Raiments of Self": African American Clothing in the Antebellum South*
Claudine Griggs, *S/he: Changing Sex and Changing Clothes*
Michaele Thurgood Haynes, *Dressing Up Debutantes: Pageantry and Glitz in Texas*
Anne Brydon and Sandra Niessen, *Consuming Fashion: Adorning the Transnational Body*
Dani Cavallaro and Alexandra Warwick, *Fashioning the Frame: Boundaries, Dress and the Body*
Judith Perani and Norma H. Wolff, *Cloth, Dress and Art Patronage in Africa*
Linda B. Arthur, *Religion, Dress and the Body*
Paul Jobling, *Fashion Spreads: Word and Image in Fashion Photography*
Fadwa El Guindi, *Veil: Modesty, Privacy and Resistance*
Thomas S. Abler, *Hinterland Warriors and Military Dress: European Empires and Exotic Uniforms*

Linda Welters, *Folk Dress in Europe and Anatolia: Beliefs about Protection and Fertility*

Kim K. P. Johnson and Sharron J. Lennon, *Appearance and Power*

Barbara Burman, *The Culture of Sewing: Gender, Consumption and Home Dressmaking*

Annette Lynch, *Dress, Gender and Cultural Change: Asian American and African American Rites of Passage*

Antonia Young, *Women Who Become Men: Albanian Sworn Virgins*

David Muggleton, *Inside Subculture: The Postmodern Meaning of Style*

Nicola White, *Reconstructing Italian Fashion: America and the Development of the Italian Fashion Industry*

Brian J. McVeigh, *Wearing Ideology: The Uniformity of Self-Presentation in Japan*

Shaun Cole, *Don We Now Our Gay Apparel: Gay Men's Dress in the Twentieth Century*

Kate Ince, *Orlan: Millennial Female*

Ali Guy, Eileen Green and Maura Banim, *Through the Wardrobe: Women's Relationships with Their Clothes*

Linda B. Arthur, *Undressing Religion: Commitment and Conversion from a Cross-Cultural Perspective*

William J. F. Keenan, *Dressed to Impress: Looking the Part*

Joanne Entwistle and Elizabeth Wilson, *Body Dressing*

Leigh Summers, *Bound to Please: A History of the Victorian Corset*

Paul Hodkinson, *Goth: Identity, Style and Subculture*

Leslie W. Rabine, *The Global Circulation of African Fashion*

Michael Carter, *Fashion Classics from Carlyle to Barthes*

Sandra Niessen, Ann Marie Leshkowich, and Carla Jones, *Re-Orienting Fashion: The Globalization of Asian Dress*

Kim K. P. Johnson, Susan J. Torntore, and Joanne B. Eicher, *Fashion Foundations: Early Writings on Fashion and Dress*

Helen Bradley Foster and Donald Clay Johnson, *Wedding Dress Across Cultures*

Eugenia Paulicelli, *Fashion under Fascism: Beyond the Black Shirt*

Charlotte Suthrell, *Unzipping Gender: Sex, Cross-Dressing and Culture*

Irene Guenther, *Nazi Chic? Fashioning Women in the Third Reich*

Yuniya Kawamura, *The Japanese Revolution in Paris Fashion*

Patricia Calefato, *The Clothed Body*

Ruth Barcan, *Nudity: A Cultural Anatomy*

Samantha Holland, *Alternative Femininities: Body, Age and Identity*

Alexandra Palmer and Hazel Clark, *Old Clothes, New Looks: Second Hand Fashion*

Yuniya Kawamura, *Fashion-ology: An Introduction to Fashion Studies*

JAPAN BEYOND THE KIMONO

Innovation and Tradition in the
Kyoto Textile Industry

JENNY HALL

BLOOMSBURY VISUAL ARTS
LONDON • NEW YORK • OXFORD • NEW DELHI • SYDNEY

BLOOMSBURY VISUAL ARTS
Bloomsbury Publishing Plc
50 Bedford Square, London, WC1B 3DP, UK
1385 Broadway, New York, NY 10018, USA

BLOOMSBURY, BLOOMSBURY VISUAL ARTS and the Diana logo are trademarks
of Bloomsbury Publishing Plc

First published in Great Britain 2020

Cover design by Adriana Brioso
Cover image: Fabric design *"chrysanthemum and waves"* (*kiku to nami*) by Pagong.
© Kamedatomi Co. Ltd. Photo by Jenny Hall

A catalogue record for this book is available from the British Library.

A catalog record for this book is available from the Library of Congress.

ISBN: HB: 978-1-3500-9541-0
PB: 978-1-3500-9542-7
ePDF: 978-1-3500-9540-3
eBook: 978-1-3500-9543-4

Series: Dress, Body, Culture

Typeset by Newgen KnowledgeWorks Pvt. Ltd., Chennai, India
Printed and bound in Great Britain

To find out more about our authors and books visit www.bloomsbury.com
and sign up for our newsletters.

For Carolyn Stevens

who is a constant inspiration

CONTENTS

ILLUSTRATIONS AND VIDEOS

Figures

Diagrams

Tables

Videos

ACKNOWLEDGMENTS

I would like to express my deepest appreciation to the many people who have contributed to the completion of this book. First, to all of the informants who took part in my research; without their time, effort, and enthusiasm this book would not have been possible. In particular, I would like to thank the CEO of Kamedatomi Co. Ltd., Kameda Kazuaki, designer Kuwayama Toyoaki and business manager Miyamoto Kazutomo of Kyoto Denim, and designer Wakabayashi Takeshi and PR manager Hashimoto Maki of Sou Sou for the generous time they spent explaining their industry and allowing me access to their world. I also owe a debt of gratitude to Professor Yūzō Murayama from Doshisha Business School for introducing me to valuable contacts, as well as giving me helpful information.

I owe my sincerest gratitude to Professor Carolyn Stevens and Dr. Jeremy Breaden whose mentorship has been vital to me throughout the stages of this research. They both consistently provided me with valuable guidance and feedback, as well as encouragement and support. They also imparted big picture perspectives and challenged me to become a more rigorous scholar. I would also like to thank the anonymous readers of my manuscript, whose advice and suggestions have been invaluable in improving my work.

I am deeply thankful to all of those who helped me with Japanese translations. In particular, thank you to Toshiyuki Nakamura, Ema Shin, and Keisuke Yamaoka. This book would not have happened without the insight of David Templeman, who inspired me to pursue this topic of enquiry, and who encouraged the germination of the initial idea.

Finally, to my family and friends, a heartfelt thank you for your unconditional source of encouragement and belief in me. My parents have provided me with support and encouragement. My friends Sally McLaren and Albie Sharpe not only provided my accommodation in the heart of Nishijin during my fieldwork but also encouraged and supported me throughout my research. Thank you to Kara Rasmanis for her belief in me, and her technical assistance. A special thank you to Charlotte Smith and Owen Jones who provided feedback for many ideas, and were always reassuring and empathetic listeners. A huge thank you to my husband, Keisuke Yamaoka, for giving me the time and space to research, for financial support, translation advice, constant encouragement, and intellectual stimulation. And thank you to my son, David, who has showed me anew how to be curious about the world.

NOTE ON TRANSLITERATION

In this text Japanese words have been romanized using the modified Hepburn Romanization system, and appear in italics. Japanese words that are already a normal part of the English lexicon (e.g., Tokyo) appear according to their regular English usage.

Japanese names are presented in the order of family name first, personal name second, as is Japanese linguistic custom. However, I have followed individual preference for the transliteration of names of Japanese authors of English-language works. I have also followed individual preference in romanization of personal names, such as Yohji Yamamoto.

HISTORICAL DATES

Major Japanese historical periods referred to in this book:[1]

Jōmon	*c.* 8000–300 BCE
Yayoi	*c.* 300 BCE–300 CE
Nara	710–84
Heian	794–1185
Kamakura	1185–333
Muromachi	1336–573
Edo (Tokugawa)	1600–867
Meiji	1868–911
Taishō	1912–25
Shōwa	1926–88
Heisei	1989–2019

1
DRESS TO DESTRUCTION

"You cannot ride a bicycle or drive a car while wearing a kimono," stated Wakabayashi Takeshi, an apparel designer for the Kyoto-based textile design company Sou Sou. His statement struck me as important so I included it as I gave a paper at an academic conference; yet, a North American scholar challenged it, maintaining that she often wore a kimono and rode a bicycle (Hall 2015: 60). This difference of opinion illustrates the gaps in how people view the "correct" way to wear a kimono (as well as the correct way to ride a bicycle!) (ibid.). If a woman is wearing a kimono in the "correct" mode of postwar convention[1]—it is difficult to ride a bicycle or drive a car. The body is wrapped tightly in a tubular style, secured by under-sashes as well as with the wide *obi* (kimono sash); the well-overlapped fold makes taking large steps almost impossible. Throwing a leg over a bicycle would dislodge these overlapping folds and pedaling would be restricted. The *obi*, as knotted in a typical style such as the *taiko musubi* (drum bow), is enhanced by stiffeners and would be uncomfortable and become crushed against the back of the seat while wearing a seat belt and driving a car (ibid.). Whether or not these activities are possible while wearing a kimono, however, is not the issue. Rather, it is this perception of what can and cannot be done in a kimono that is important. This is significant because I believe that Wakabayashi's statement lies at the heart of both the decline in *wafuku* (a term meaning Japanese clothes, including kimono) and the reinvention of *wafuku* (ibid.).

It is evident from the statement above that Japanese designers' views about the suitability or otherwise of the kimono for contemporary life vary greatly and it is this that is driving the reinvention of the kimono. As an example of this reinvention, another designer, Kameda Kazuaki, uses his family's Taishō-era kimono patterns to make contemporary clothing under the brand-name Pagong, for his company Kamedatomi Co. Ltd., which is sold in Kyoto. I stumbled upon one of Pagong's branches in Gion by chance. I was wandering the narrow laneways in the historic district of Gion Shimbashi, heading towards the little bridge over Shirakawa, when I noticed a colorful *noren* fluttering over the sliding doorway of a newly timbered shop. The outside aesthetic was clean and fresh, and a mannequin wearing a bright aloha shirt stood on the front step. The patterned fabric grabbed my attention—*uchiwa* fans decorated with golden carp, intertwined with lavender and peach dragonflies overlapping each other across a background of swirling blue and white water. I stepped into the tiny shop and gazed at the tops and shirts lining the walls up to the ceiling. Printed on silk or extremely fine cotton were pale pink cherry blossoms, yellow peonies, sky blue chrysanthemums, green and orange mandarin ducks, golden Japanese carp, and tan swallows flying across indigo irises.

The Pagong sales assistant was keen to explain the processes of production and the historical provenance of the patterns, fueling my interest and appreciation even more. After several years of being a customer at Pagong and then discovering other thriving companies in Kyoto that were also using heritage industry techniques to create contemporary goods, I deemed that these designers' success conflicted with media reports[2] about the decline of traditional textile production in Kyoto. Weren't these companies perpetuating the use of traditional skills and designs? I felt that to understand what was really happening in the traditional textile industries, these companies needed to be included as examples of how the industry was actually changing and growing.

Kyoto designers (and their consumers) are adapting and adopting *wafuku* to create a new vehicle for expressions of Japanese culture. The term "*wafuku*" is generally used as a counterpart to "*yōfuku*," which was coined in the Meiji period (1868–1912) to denote Western[3] dress (Milhaupt 2014: 125). The reinvention of *wafuku* exemplifies the relationship of the past and the present in the Kyoto textile heritage industries. In addition, such designs, as a new representation of cultural identity, counter the widespread perception that these heritage industries are in decline (Hall 2015: 61). The reality is more complex than a simple decline in demand for kimono. Designers and consumers are redefining *wafuku* while retaining its "traditional" image. This book addresses the key question: "how are designers and consumers making *wafuku* suit contemporary everyday life?" Figuratively, how are they making kimono ride a bicycle? (ibid.).

This chapter presents historical and contemporary analytical frameworks for two important concepts used for my research; in particular, the concepts of "tradition" and "fashion" both overseas and in Japan. I problematize these concepts to unpack certain assumptions about them and show how Japanese conceptualizations of them do or do not match these assumptions. For example, I demonstrate that Japanese emic concepts of tradition differ from those of other cultures in that they include the possibility of reinvention and change. I also illustrate how Japanese designers and people in Japanese society more widely use these concepts to reinterpret Japanese clothing from the past and their preferred readings of the present. Both the production and consumption of textiles are bodily practices. Therefore, I argue that a sensory analysis of contemporary Japanese fashion is useful because the body is the site through which we perceive and experience the world, and clothing acts as a receptacle for conceptualizations of our individual and cultural identities.

Kyoto as a Field Site

To understand the contemporary production of *wafuku*, I conducted ethnographic fieldwork consisting of interviews, participant observation, textual analysis of advertising material, and statistical analysis of government and textile associations' production data. During the primary period of fieldwork in late 2012, I interviewed contemporary Kyoto designers who use traditional methods and design elements to create cutting-edge fashions, with subsequent follow-up interviews from 2013 to 2016. To fully comprehend the designs and techniques these companies are using, I explored the production-side of the industry, namely kimono- and *obi*-making companies. Therefore, my research included specific companies and workshops operating within Kyoto involved in creating kimono or *obi*, or contemporary equivalents. The kimono industry is highly complex because of the system of division of labor; it is unusual for one company to complete all aspects in the production process. To address this complexity, I explored a range of companies across the industry including industry associations, wholesalers, weavers, dyers, finishers, and retailers. I learnt about these companies through a range of methods, such as exploration of the streets, word of mouth, publications, and internet searches. I interviewed heritage industry artisans including those working for Nishijin manufacturers (Nishijin is a district located in northwest Kyoto that is renowned for its woven brocade), *yūzen* (a rice-paste resist method of dyeing), *shiborizome* (Japanese tie-dyeing), and *tsujigahana* (a method that combines *shiborizome* with embroidery, hand painting, and the application of gold and silver foil) artisans, weaving gallery managers, contemporary Kyoto designers who use traditional methods and design elements to create innovative fashions, and Kyoto retailers selling such items. In order to address issues of sensory ethnography (discussed below), I took part in a tea ceremony while wearing a kimono, undertook workshops in Nishijin weaving, *tsutsugaki yūzen* dyeing, and *shiborizome* dyeing, attended Jidai Matsuri (the Festival of Ages), observed domestic and foreign tourists wearing traditional and contemporary apparel, and during my fieldwork, I stayed in the heart of the weaving district of Nishijin. I also conducted video tours of designers' workspaces and photographed finished items to provide sensory experiences for the reader that take them beyond the written format of my research. While my main focus was on textile artisans and designers,[4] my interviews also included experts in auxiliary fields, such as a *nihongami* stylist (one who specializes in traditional hair arrangements), a professor at a business school in Kyoto who teaches business strategies to those involved in the heritage industries, a samurai armor reproduction specialist, a long-standing participant in Jidai Matsuri and owners of a kimono recycling atelier.

I focus on the active use of kimono as related to contemporary design and craftsmanship to analyze the way kimono are worn on the body, how garments are experienced as well as interpreted, and how this experience in turn affects production and consumption (Hall 2015: 62). Sensory ethnography is a useful frame with which to examine these ideas because it refocuses the ethnographic enquiry to include not just traditional inputs that contribute to textual writing but also all of the senses in data collection methods and writing: for example, how the tactile qualities of textiles affect the design process, the importance of visual observation in passing on tacit knowledge, or aural characteristics of workplace environments and their influence on the succession of skills (ibid.). Sensory ethnography can give us information that language cannot, such as kinaesthetic or bodily learning. It is a particularly good fit with the Japanese arts because not only do many of them concentrate on and influence the sensory experience, but they are also taught through experiential practices called *kata*, discussed in more detail below, that rely on employment of all of the senses (ibid.). In addition, the textures of fabrics, the exact colors of a kimono, or the sound, rhythm, and noise level of a power loom are easier to understand if they are experienced with all the senses. Of course, the textual paradigm's limitation is that the sensory experience must be related via text in this format. Readers are relying on the ethnographer's ability to then translate those perceptions and sensory experiences into the written word. In academic writing, smells and tactile qualities can only be described using words, and tactile and visual qualities can be represented through images. Not only are these qualities filtered through the ethnographer's own descriptive capabilities but also through the ethnographer's personal senses and cultural paradigms. The body is not a passive recipient of information taken in through the senses, but it actively perceives information through a culturally constructed sensory paradigm. Just as we learn to "see," so we learn to acknowledge and utilize other senses that are a socially recognized part of our cultural environment. As Classen puts it, "Sensory models are conceptual models, and sensory values are cultural values" (1993: 136). Howes expands on this, opportunely using weaving as an example:

> For example, the tactile qualities of a weaving, which may be of immense importance to the culture concerned, are excluded when the work is analyzed in terms of its visual aesthetics and reproduced as a photograph or drawing. The visual image is retained and may be tremendously powerful in itself, but all the invisible threads that tie it to a larger cultural tapestry of textures and scents and sounds are snipped off. (2003: 35)

This statement lies at the heart of my research methodology and I have attempted to include this wider cultural tapestry. However, I concede as Howes does, that writing about the senses is necessarily bound by the limitations of language; while the inherent subjectivity of written forms of communication and the difficulty of expressing the sensory paradigm remain problematic, there is no other medium that has the permanency and fixedness of the written word.

In addition to the problem of writing, it is challenging for the foreign scholar to represent cultural interaction in a way that expresses the indigenous culture's ways of thinking and perceiving in terms that locals might find acceptable. Ethnographers are constantly trying to close the gap between an ethnographer's experience and the informant's experience. In order to bridge this, Pink suggests thinking ethnographically about the senses from a self-reflexive and experiencing body, an approach that sees the sensory as embedded in the ethnographer: "Indeed, the task of the sensory ethnographer is in part to invite her or his reader or audience to imagine themselves into the places of both the ethnographer and the research participants represented" (2009: 42). This was one of my goals and why I undertook various *taiken* (personal experience activities) during my fieldwork.

The Senses in Japan

Historically, many of the Japanese arts concentrated on a combination of sensory experiences—for example, *kadō* (the way of flowers or *ikebana*) (visual and tactile), *sadō* (or *chadō*, the way of tea) (taste, visual, tactile, olfactory), *shodō* (calligraphy, the way of writing) (visual and tactile), and *kōdō* (the way of incense) (olfactory and tactile).[5] In calling for an increased awareness of the other senses, we must acknowledge that visual presentation plays a significant part in Japanese culture—there have been numerous studies of such areas as food presentation, gift wrapping, and more recently, popular culture such as *manga*. In her seminal work, *Wrapping Culture* (1993), Joy Hendry discussed how presentation in Japan embodies several layers of politeness. The function of wrapping—objects, the body or even words—is to refine the object within. The importance of wrapping is not merely to decorate an object, but to influence the object itself. This is also true of many of the Japanese arts—they influence the senses in such a way as to alter the character and behavior of the individual enacting them. As Kondo points out regarding tea ceremony, the practitioner represents his or her mental state by an action such as ritual ablution—crouching at a basin and then entering the tea room signifies humility, and "performing these actions is as good as having the right attitude, for it should induce the right attitude" (2005: 206). In addition to this, "in drinking the aesthetic infusion, one partakes not only of the tea and of the qualities it embodies, but of the care, the grace and the selflessness that went into its preparation" (ibid.: 207).

Practice is crucial for the transmission of Japanese culture. The conventional method of teaching the traditional arts in Japan is through mimicry and repetition, about doing rather than discussing. This is referred to as *kata*, a ritual-like process of training that is found across the arts in Japan, including martial arts, flower arranging, calligraphy, tea ceremony, and dance. Yano defines *kata* as "the isolable elements by which an art form may be taught through observation, imitation, and repetition" (2005: 195). The master artisan passes on tacit knowledge through this style of training, and the trainee learns through mimicry and repetition of the recognized forms, and through trial and error.

Through my fieldwork I saw the sensory aspect of learning crafts many times over. For example, in a *tsutsugaki yūzen* (handmade rice paste-resist dyeing) workshop held at the Australian Academy of Design in Melbourne, the artisan Kobayashi Shumei was keen for students to touch, smell, and act in the production process. The workshop notes stated, "Do not be afraid to make mistakes. I would like you not only to watch me work, but to *use your own five senses* to create a piece" (2011: introduction, emphasis added). It is clear from steps in his production process that all five senses are integral to the creation of a work. When Kobayashi makes *umezome* (plum dye) using a technique dating back to the early Muromachi period (1338–1573), he tastes the dye for tannin to ascertain its strength. He likened much of the process to cooking, and also pointed out that many of the by-products could be consumed. The importance of sensory perceptions for the textile industry is reiterated by Hirose Yuichi, 36-year-old president (and ex-Olympic surfer) of Hirose Dye Works in Tokyo, who also likens the making of dye to cooking (Okazaki 2015: 38).

The senses not only play a major part in the production of Japanese arts but also in the way Japanese designers think about design, as Hiramitsu (2005) found when she was researching the clothing designs of Issey Miyake. Hiramitsu notes Miyake "designs a garment from within where the human body touches the fabric" (ibid.: 36). In fact Miyake himself linked this way of thinking about clothing design to the kimono, stating, "I learned about space between the body and the fabric from the traditional kimono … not the style, but the space" (Piotti 2014: 218). The design process is intertwined with the prospective product's existence as an embodied object and as a sensory object. Designers constantly address the interplay between imagination and function, and therefore must constantly consider the senses in this process. This is a dialectical process, because, as Mauss noted in his essay "Techniques of the Body," "the gait will vary according to whether the clothes are sewn or draped" (2006: 99). Miyake must consider not only how his designs will feel on the wearer but how they will work on the body as it moves through time and space. Kobayashi must think about how his sensory perceptions of taste, vision, and touch will interact with his imagination to bring about his textile creations. Sensory ethnography best explores these aspects of Japanese design. However, ethnographic fieldwork should include, but not be limited to, a sensory approach because the way in which people perceive information about the world is through the senses, and these senses are culturally constructed. As Classen says, "When almost every other aspect of human bodily experience—from the way we eat to the way we dress—is now recognized as subject to social conditioning, it is surprising that we should still imagine that the senses are left to nature" (1993: 5).

Tradition in the Textile Industry

My research focuses on contemporary Japanese textile designers who are using "traditional" techniques to create garments because their work constitutes a link between static and innovative cultural expressions. "Tradition" is a term that has been much debated in anthropology and other disciplines, and the topic is frequently debated in Japanese studies (Bestor 1989; Brumann & Cox 2010; Vlastos 1998). In attempting to understand what "tradition" means to Japanese designers and Japanese consumers, it is necessary to explore the terminology that is associated with it—concepts that are loaded with meanings which often prove interchangeable in practice. The term "tradition" itself comes packaged with value-laden assumptions that can, on closer examination, be challenged, but a crucial aspect of the issue is that the validity of assertions of "tradition" is not necessarily important to participants. With respect to artisans and their relationship to tradition, the discourse of tradition is still often used to validate and authenticate material objects or cultural practices, whether or not core assumptions such as age or originality, are verifiable. This book aims not only to explain how these particular traditions in Japan are constructed but also describe how participants use the discourse of tradition to construct culture, and how the discourse of tradition translates across cultures. For example, casual observers tend to think of Japanese material culture as falling into two opposing categories: the unchanging exotic samurai of the past versus the hyper-technological world of popular tropes such as Nintendō's Super Mario. But what of cultural representations that lie between?

In their discussion of boundary textiles in Latin America, Demaray, Keim-Shenk, and Littrell record some primary questions pertinent to tradition and textiles; "When we speak of traditional textiles, are we referring to designs, colors, fibers, the means of production or all of these elements from the past? How can we determine when a 'tradition' began? How long does a design, color, fiber, or technology have to persist to be considered traditional? How do these concrete elements relate to their meanings for producers and the consumers?" (2005, n.p.). Such questions highlight the complexity of the concept of tradition, a complexity that stems from the ambiguous and subjective terms interconnected with it, such as "old" or "original," but also from the fact that stakeholders invoke a variety of elements in its application. For example, when questioned about what tradition (dentōteki) means, many of my informants attempted to pinpoint a length of time, citing a hundred years as a potential age for textile techniques to be considered traditional. One designer told me that tradition is "simply something which continues for a long time, lasts one hundred or two hundred years. One hundred years has meaning." Therefore, their definition of tradition included aspects of age, continuity, and permanence. However, at the same time my informants recognize that techniques in the industry have undergone, and are continually undergoing, change. A young Kyoto kimono designer responded that "even though we say techniques are traditional, they have new thinking, some parts are old, some are new." Traditions are not fixed or static, they change and evolve over time, and it is societal recognition of a material object, ritual or technique that earns it the label "traditional." In addition, societal ideas about what constitutes "tradition" are contested, and designers' and artisans' definitions may not correspond with those of consumers. As Edensor points out, "Rather than being ossified and archaic, traditions are continually *reinvented* in a range of different contexts" (2002: 6).

Tradition and Cultural Nationalism

The kimono has been adopted as the national costume of Japan and is therefore upheld as an example of Japanese traditional culture. Tradition is often used in this way to promote group membership, especially the nation state, and is therefore cited when discussing national symbolism such as costume, ceremonies, and cultural heritage. As Stinchecum states, "The invention of a tradition, or cultural invention, becomes necessary to form a new group identity vis-à-vis the 'other'" (2010: 126). Japanese national dress is a prime example of this cultural invention because, as mentioned above, in the Meiji Era the term *yōfuku* was coined for Western dress, and used as a counterpart to *wafuku*, "before *yōfuku* there could be no *wafuku*" (Dalby 2001: 66). There were other forms of clothing worn throughout Japanese history, but it is the kimono that has become the recognized symbol of Japanese apparel, and thereby one of the most commonly portrayed vehicles that communicates traditional Japanese values. The word "kimono" is an abbreviation of *kirumono* (literally "thing to wear") but it has come to represent *kosode*—the ankle-length robe with flowing sleeves that the world now recognizes as Japanese dress (Milhaupt 2014: 20). It was during the Meiji Period the kimono was increasingly identified as Japan's national costume (ibid.: 21). The Meiji government declared that its goal was to Westernize Japan, constructing a cultural distinction between Japan as "traditional" and the West as "modern." Japanese men were encouraged to adopt Western-style dress (*yōfuku*) and close-cropped hair; they were "made into models for function and Western rationality" (Goldstein-Gidoni 1999: 355). In contrast to this, women were encouraged to wear kimono, and in 1872 the government introduced sumptuary laws banning women from having short haircuts, measures that served as "a symbolic message sent to Japanese women to become repositories of the past and of traditional values" (ibid.: 355). Thus, men and the masculine were associated with "modernity" and women and the feminine were associated with "tradition." For several decades, Japanese citizens (men, in particular) came to live what Edward Seidensticker dubbed a "double life" (*nijū seikatsu*), "switching as appropriate between a suit-wearing, meat-eating, Western-style persona and a kimono-wearing, rice-eating and increasingly nostalgic Japanese soul" (Seidensticker 2010: 101).

By establishing *wafuku* in opposition to *yōfuku*, the kimono in particular has been cast in the "unchanging exotic samurai of the past" category. The unchanging form of kimono means it is also assumed to be "traditional" because, to outsiders, it appears to have remained the same throughout history. However, this view of kimono does not take into account trends in pattern design or mode of wearing, further discussed below. And, in any case, adhering to the kimono form does not necessarily guarantee a garment's acceptance as an authentic kimono, as I illustrate in Chapter Four.

The city of Kyoto is also cast in the unchanging samurai role, culturally constructed as the seat of Japanese tradition, with the local government, prefectural government and many of the residents happy to perpetuate this image of the city as the seat of tradition. Of course, there is much historical evidence that can be drawn on to support this view. The city has 1,600 temples and 400 shrines, and some of the few remaining active geisha quarters in Japan. There are seventeen properties, listed as the "Historical Monuments of Ancient Kyoto," that are recognized as World Heritage sites (UNESCO World Heritage Centre 1992–2016). However, Kyoto is also a modern city, with wide boulevards and contemporary buildings, home to 1.4 million residents (Kyoto Prefecture 2010). According to the Kyoto Foreign Investment Promotion Committee, Kyoto is a center for IT and related high-tech industry, with the head offices of Shimadzu, Nintendo, Kyocera, Omron, Horiba, Murata Manufacturing, Rohm, and NEC based there (KIC 2014). It also has a high concentration of universities.

The textile industry forms part of Kyoto's cultural identity of tradition, and as a result even Japanese often assume the city is conservative, unchanging and staid. For example, Yamagata-based kimono stylist Akira Times dislikes Kyoto because he thinks it is only concerned with "preserving old culture and making money from it," something he terms "Kyoto sickness" (Cliffe 2017: 102). This image of formality and conservatism is enhanced by the official recognition of Kyoto's cultural heritage. "Traditional" crafts of Kyoto are officially supported by Kyoto Prefecture's Division of Textiles and Crafts, in the Department of Commerce, Labor and Tourism. According to the Kyoto Prefecture website, local crafts that meet three criteria are designated with the title "Kyōmono[6] Traditional Crafts"; they are primarily handcrafted, they employ traditional techniques, and predominantly traditional materials or designs are used (Kyoto Prefecture 2011). The Japanese Ministry of Economy, Trade and Industry (METI) currently recognizes three main traditional techniques being used in the Kyoto kimono industry as "officially designated traditional craft products" (METI 2013): Nishijin *ori* (weaving), *kanoko shibori* (a specific form of tie-dyeing), and *Kyō-yūzen* (Kyoto-style rice paste-resist dyeing). This state recognition of Kyoto kimono techniques verifies them as worthy of preservation for the nation but belies the evolving nature of traditions. These techniques are being retained through innovations in technology and production processes that reduce costs and make the items more affordable (Hall 2015: 63).

However, cultural identity is not constructed by the state alone. Kyoto people, and the wider Japanese public, use the expression *Kyō no kidaore* to describe Kyoto locals' passion for clothing, including kimono. *Kidaore* means dress to destruction: Kyoto locals have the reputation for spending their money on clothing and fashion rather than on other necessities such as food.[7] How we dress and represent ourselves is integral to our cultural identity, but dress is more than merely a visual representation of self. Not only do clothes embody memory and knowledge of cultural practices, but they can also convey traditional morals, expectations, and roles. The concept of *kidaore* highlights the importance of dress and textiles for Kyoto people; Kyoto is considered by Japanese to be the cultural heart of Japan, thereby illustrating the wider significance of the textile and fashion industry.

In addition, in the past decade there has been a grassroots increase in interest in the kimono in both Kyoto and nationwide (Sasaki 2009), demonstrated by the popularity of kimono *taiken* (kimono experience) among the public as well as by kimono-wearing social groups and second-hand kimono stores. And, as will be discussed in Chapter Four, kimono *taiken* in Kyoto comes packaged as, and is undertaken by participants with an expectation of, a kimono-wearing experience in the context of a nostalgic "traditional" Kyoto. I surmise that this increase in kimono *taiken* has been in part spurred by the current economic recession and influenced by a concurrent rise in nationalism in the global sphere more generally. The rise in "banal nationalism," or "the routine and familiar forms of nationalism" (Billig 1995: 7), emphasizes tradition, cultural heritage, and nostalgia for past eras. Therefore it is not surprising that an accompanying expression of cultural nationalism is taking place in the form of rising popularity in the national dress, the kimono. Of course, interest in kimono is not automatically an expression of nationalism. Individuals wear clothing for many different reasons and, as I demonstrate in the following chapters, there are many other factors that are contributing to the kimono's reinvention and revival. Such factors include digital technologies that are helping to decrease productions costs, social media aiding artisans in connecting directly with customers and alternative contexts for wearing kimono. Periods of political and economic instability are not new or unique to Japan. However, when a country is insecure about their political and economic identity in the world, cultural identity comes to the fore as an issue (Kosaku 1992), and this can occasion a refocus on tradition and traditional culture. Nevertheless, the adoption of digital technologies and the influence of social media on the Kyoto textile industry is evidence that Kyoto is not the unchanging exotic samurai of the past nor the hyper-technological world but something in between.

Tradition and Authenticity

How the discourse of tradition translates across cultures has been a key question for many scholars, artists, and conservators and many rely on the UNESCO World Heritage organization for guidance. Since its formation in 1972, UNESCO has held a succession of conventions to incorporate new definitions regarding intangible heritage that accommodate cross-cultural perceptions.[8] These conventions have highlighted a number of key issues regarding the concept of tradition that are useful for my discussion. While many UNESCO projects concerned the preservation of tangible heritage such as Cambodia's Angkor Archaeological Park, Australia's Great Barrier Reef, and Italy's Venice and its lagoon, the conventions also argued for the protection of intangible heritage, such as weaving and dyeing techniques, and claimed that they could be regarded as "traditional." The discourse of "tradition"—and the notions of "authenticity" and "legitimacy" that are inextricably linked to it—can be applied to intangible heritage, and Japanese ways of thinking about tradition differ from those in the West. Bound up with ideas of Shinto and Zen Buddhism, and the ephemeral nature of the world, renewal and decay, Japanese thinking regarding "tradition" intrinsically includes revitalization, adaptation, and change, which departs from the Western focus on preservation. It is possible that these philosophical and spiritual principles have some impact on Japanese views of tradition as opposed to those in the West, but in reality what is important to the participants in the process is the aura and perception of tradition, rather than the actual facts regarding age, authenticity, and originality.

French philosopher Jean Baudrillard noted that the quest for authenticity arises from an obsession with certainty concerning four characteristics: origin, date, author, and signature of a work (1996: 76). Applying the term "original" to textile artisans is problematic (as it is for *ukiyo-e*) because the means of textile production are distributed among so many individuals that it becomes difficult to ascertain who the creator is: the *shitae-shi* (design sketcher), *sobyō-shi* (specialist who copies the design outline onto the cloth), *norioki-shi* (the person who applies the paste-resist), *hikizome-shi* (the person who applies the dye), and so on. In fact, apart from exceptional precedents such as Ogata Kōrin (1658–1716), most kimono from the late Edo and Meiji periods were produced by anonymous craftspeople who specialized in certain stages of a kimono's production or in a particular form of weaving or dyeing (Milhaupt 2014: 183).

The Greek root for "authentic" means "self" or "oneself" and therefore implies that a work is "authentic" if created by a recognized and legitimate builder/designer/artisan (Jokilehto 2009). As noted above, a sole designer or artisan is problematic for Japanese arts. In addition, where does that leave traditions such as Japan's famous Ise Shrine, which has been rebuilt every twenty years since the eighth century (ibid.)? In this case, authenticity arises from the unchanging tradition of building and the newness (and cleanliness) of the materials, rather than the standing structure itself. The essence of the tradition is in the act of replacing the object.

The resulting document from the UNESCO conference of 2004, the *Yamato Declaration on Integrated Approaches for Safeguarding Tangible and Intangible Cultural Heritage* makes these important definitions: that intangible cultural heritage is defined as the knowledge, skills, and artifacts that communities pass on through generations and recognize as part of their cultural heritage that provides them with a sense of identity and continuity; because intangible cultural heritage is "constantly recreated," the term "authenticity" is not relevant in identifying and safeguarding it (2004: 1). No one would argue that Ise Shrine is not "authentic"; the authenticity of cultural heritage that is constantly recreated lies in the continuity of cultural practice, and this authenticity is validated by the community's belief in the heritage. Newness and renewal do not necessarily rule out tradition or authenticity, despite the implied signification. Reisinger and Steiner's discussion concerning object authenticity in tourism is pertinent because they also argue that "authenticity" is not a useful term. They propose using other terms such as "genuine," "real" or "true" to describe objects or performances. However, these terms are equally problematic—how do we evaluate "genuine" or "real"? As they point out, part of the issue concerns whether or not objects are what they appear to be or claim to be, and whether or not they are made or performed by locals according to traditions. In the case of Ise Shrine, these issues are undisputed, but, as I discuss in Chapter Five, the case of Nishijin woven goods is more complex because of contemporary practices of outsourcing and technological innovation.

Authenticity is also linked with legitimacy in that something authentic is implicitly reliable or trustworthy. At the 1994 UNESCO Nara Conference on Authenticity, it was determined that the notion of authenticity should remain constant, but the sources of information that provide the legitimacy for that authenticity could vary. Jokilehto explains, "For example, in an ancient historical monument, such as the Parthenon of Athens, the sources of information would be fundamentally based on the material authenticity, while in the case of the Ise Shrine, these would be based more on cultural continuity, and thus on the immaterial aspects of the heritage" (2009: 129). However, Bestor points out that tradition is valued in "the eye of the beholder, as much as anywhere" (1989: 264). This constructivist approach to authenticity reflects fluidity and negotiability rather than a concrete truth (Reisinger & Steiner 2006: 70). However, most traditions, even invented traditions, have some historical basis (some fact, concept, or knowledge that is rooted in history) and need such qualities to claim their legitimacy, even if they are then contested.

Writing about a "traditional" *shitamachi* (neighborhood) in Tokyo, Bestor notes how an "ahistorical past" is used to legitimize the present (1989: 11). This strategic employment of "tradition" to suit certain goals has been noted by other scholars of Japan in regard to areas such as sumo (Thompson 1998), martial arts (Inoue 1998), and even Japanese national cultural identity (Harootunian 1998; Hashimoto 1998; Robertson 1998). Hobsbawm and Ranger's edited volume, *The Invention of Tradition*, documents numerous Western examples of this phenomenon, demonstrating that the evocation of tradition to achieve certain goals is a widespread strategy. This theme of the strategic employment of "tradition" reappears in Chapter Five when discussing marketing of contemporary *wafuku*.

In the UNESCO definitions quoted above, it is the term "recreate" that signals a main shift from the preservation/conservation approach used for tangible cultural heritage prior to 2004 in terms of World Heritage, but it can be argued that all tradition is "recreated." Inherent in tradition's link to a long-established past is the concept of transmission to future generations, and in the handing down process, heritage, either tangible or intangible, must be recreated in terms of legitimacy, authenticity, age, and permanency.

Innovation in Tradition

Fantasy writer and satirist, the late Sir Terry Pratchett highlights the core issues regarding the re-created nature of traditions in his book *The Fifth Elephant*: "This, milord, is my family's axe. We have owned it for almost nine hundred years, see. Of course, sometimes it has required a new handle, new designs on the metalwork, a little refreshing of the ornamentation … but is this not the nine-hundred-year-old axe of my family?" (Pratchett 1999: 405). This then begs the question, if something is based on tradition, on past techniques, how does innovation affect authenticity and legitimacy? It is difficult to say how much something can be altered before it ceases to be perceived as "tradition" but it is definitely a graded judgment and dependent on the participants' perceptions (as will be seen in Chapter Two regarding digital *yūzen*). In the Japanese textile industry, the introduction of various fabrics such as silk (c. sixth century CE) and cotton (late fifteenth century CE), the development of dyeing techniques such as *tsujigahana* (stitch-resist tie-dyeing) (1570s), paste-resist *yūzen* (1680s), and *kata yūzen* stenciled dyeing (1881), and the development of chemical dyes (late Meiji period) could all be described as innovations (The Japan Craft Forum 1996). Often, the introduction of new techniques that streamline the production process are viewed by society as somehow cheating or equaling a loss of authenticity. This can actually instigate a reaction against the new techniques, and a return to what society deems as "traditional" practices. But as my research regarding digital *yūzen* shows, Japanese emic concepts of tradition include ideas of innovation and change that can render such innovations authentic.

Brumann found this to be the case with local perceptions of "tradition" with regard to Kyoto architecture. Over the last decade, interest in Kyoto's historical town houses (*Kyō-machiya*) has resulted in renovation projects and "a point on which almost everyone agrees is that *machiya* require *saisei*[9] and this is a divergence from conventional architectural preservation and its emphasis on 'freezing preservation' (*tōketsu hozon*), i.e. retaining the physical structure as unaltered as possible" (2010: 159). Brumann noted that the word locals from Kyoto use when discussing their plans to restore *Kyō-machiya* is *saisei* rather than *hozon* (preservation) (ibid.: 154). Therefore local people's ideas about retaining traditional architecture involve innovation through the process of regeneration, which incorporates new, or at least "younger," elements. Many of the *Kyō-machiya* that are restored are repurposed (part of a gentrification process)—while living in the Kansai area I visited several examples including Café Bibliotic Hello!, Kyoto Nama Chocolat Organic Tea House, and the Manzara-tei restaurant chain.

In his study of *Kyō-machiya*, Brumann also found, when questioning individuals on their motivations to revitalize the *Kyō-machiya*, that they did not necessarily equate age with tradition; less than 20 percent of his questionnaire respondents gave the fact that *machiya* are old (*furui*) as their motive for preservation, whereas more than 75 percent were motivated by houses being traditional (*dentōteki*). Brumann concluded that "rather, it is an ongoing connection of things past to the present, with the perspective of further evolution in the future, that is the motivational focus" (2010: 162). It is evident that newness (associated with cleanliness, both spiritual and physical) is valued in Japan. Rent for accommodation is calculated with regard to the age of the building (newer buildings command higher rent) and apartments are usually completely gutted and refurbished before they are rented out again (the cost passed on to the renter in the form of a "gift" of money in the Kansai region). Until the past ten years or so, second-hand shops were virtually non-existent in Japan, and perfectly functional items (including electrical goods such as televisions, rice cookers, and ovens) were simply thrown away (part of the Bubble economy's discourse to encourage consumers to consume hyperbolically).

Japanese clothing, however, presents a more complex example. Slade points out that a kimono had a longer life than most Western clothing because the structure of the kimono meant that overall styles did not change as much (2009). Furthermore, one size could fit all and therefore kimono could fit successive generations. Fashion trends did not affect its overall structure, but were more closely linked with how the kimono was worn (how much the neckline overlapped, how tightly or loosely the robe was wrapped around the body, or what other components were matched with it). Therefore tradition, as linked to concepts of continuity and permanence, are an integral part of kimono culture. Slade notes that since the mid-Tokugawa period there had been many used-clothing shops in Edo, and that individuals began stealing clothing to sell in the 1720s because used clothing was in such demand: "By the eighteenth century, wholesalers of used clothing emerged; and the volume of trade was huge. The standardization of the kimono made this trade much more vibrant than the trade in used clothing in Europe and America; when you can fit into anything on display, the opportunities for consumption greatly increase" (2009: 56). Kimono have always been reused and recycled and "these notions are inherently embedded in traditional kimono culture" (Okazaki 2015: 151). Kato Yoshihiro, manager of Kyoto dressmaking and kimono making company Fuji Koubou, states,

> A kimono should *never* be thrown out—if there is no daughter, pass it on to your son's wife or a relative! Also you can wear them for decades, even if your body shape changes. When they are wrecked you can make them into a futon or a cushion. In that regard, the price-performance of kimonos is actually quite high. (cited in Okazaki 2015: 152)

The concept of continuity, in terms of permanency and durability, and its connection to traditional Japanese clothing is particularly evident in the case of *boro* ("rags") that farmers of the Tohoku region reused to make practical garments (Hall 2018a: 289). This form of recycling occurred from ancient times well into the twentieth century (Figure 1.1). They made clothes, futon covers, bags, shoes and rope by stitching, patching or braiding together scraps of fabric (ibid.). They sometimes reused the same material through four generations (Koide & Tsuzuki 2008: 108). Tanaka Chūzaburō, an Aomori-born folklore researcher, began collecting and documenting *boro* from the mid-1960s, travelling throughout Aomori Prefecture (Hall 2018a: 289). When describing an Aomori funeral, Tanaka said, "When someone died, the relations all cried as they fought over who got the kimono" (ibid.).[10]

Tradition and *Kata*

Exploring the Japanese concept of *kata* with respect to its reliance on imitation raises the question of whether or not we can view any practices handed down this way as innovative. While this form of teaching, based on specific patterns or *kata*, may appear to stifle creativity, innovation can occur in two ways: by accident, "as part of the human element of imperfection" (Yano 2005: 195); or deliberately "but predicated upon the accumulated privilege of years of practice,

Figure 1.1 An example of *boro* from Tanaka Chūzaburō's collection in the AMUSE museum, Asakusa, Tokyo. Photo: Jenny Hall.

replication, and stature within the arts organization" (ibid.). During the 1993 Ise Shrine renewal, one of the carpenters complained that he was not allowed to use his creativity, "being obliged to make an exact replica" (Jokilehto 2009: 128). The current Japanese law on the protection of cultural heritage (*Bunkazai Hogohō*) regarding "living traditions" and "intangible cultural heritage" requires "that the traditional knowledge and skills be transmitted exactly as they have been learnt. It is also accepted that, however, in the implementation, the individual craftsperson may use his/her creative capacity, and not simply prepare a replica" (ibid.: 130).

It is the idea of continuity, the transmission "from generation to generation" that provides the legitimacy to tradition, but, as mentioned above, there is also room here for innovation and creativity. A Swedish musicologist at the 2004 UNESCO conference pointed out that in order for a musician to play a piece by Brahms, as the composer originally intended it, musicians can look at various notes from the nineteenth century, but Brahms himself was keen for musicians to interpret the music for themselves and therefore did not leave detailed instructions on how pieces should be played. Therefore we cannot always define "authenticity" in performance because "a certain freedom of interpretation should be seen as part of the idea of musical performance" (Jokilehto 2009: 126). In the same way that musicians read notation, textile designers read the fabric and adjust their processes accordingly. *Tsutsugaki*[11] artisan, Kobayashi Shumei pointed out that "to touch and know the consistency of the fabric is important" in creating a work as every fabric has a different quality (personal communication, April 17, 2011). In a similar vein, fashion designer Yohji Yamamoto talks of *nuno no hyōjō*—"the expression of the cloth" (Kondo 1992: 181), using it to describe how the fabric tells him what to create.

When young Japanese designers use techniques of production such as *yūzen* (dye-resist methods) that date back to the Edo period[12] (1603–1867) or earlier, it is important to consider how their current knowledge of such techniques has been transmitted from generation to generation. Mimicry and repetition are the conventional methods of teaching the arts in Japan (and elsewhere) but, as Yano illustrates in her examination of the popular music genre *enka*, the patterned formulas or *kata*, which constitute the teaching process, are more complex than repetition alone. It is important for the student to copy their teacher's work as precisely as possible and repetition is the key to embodying that knowledge, as "working on the external through kata transforms and defines the internal" (Yano 2002: 26). Australian textile artist and weaver Mirka Rozmus draws a useful parallel between learning a musical instrument and making textiles, citing the importance of "physical and muscular memory" as important to both music and weaving (Otowa 2009: 14).

The master, therefore, "perfects kata to the point where it vanishes" (Yano 2002: 26) as the "creative goal of kata-training is to fuse the individual to the form so that the individual becomes the form and the form becomes the individual" (ibid.: 26). Intrinsic in this process is the Japanese concept of *kodawari. Kodawari* is "'fastidiousness,' 'a personal passion to pursue something,' 'disciplined dedication,' or 'obsession' with something" (White 2012: 67) demonstrating the depth of knowledge needed to master a technique or process through the practice of *kata.* But, as Yano explains in regard to *enka*, while it is important to adhere to particular *kata*, once techniques have been mastered to the extent suggested above, the skill and depth of knowledge of the techniques enables the artist/singer/performer the ability to introduce elements of individual style and produce something new. Therefore,

> kata becomes not merely a distillation of one individual way of doing things but a historic panoply of teachers past and present, embedding the doer and the doing in a thick diachronic context. Kata at once establishes, constructs, and verifies a relationship with the past. (Yano 2002: 25)

Kata clearly "places emphasis on technique, on the process of doing" (Yano 2002: 25). *Kata* holds ritualistic and symbolic functions—in Japan, *kata* is a rite of passage that the student must pass through in order to obtain credibility and be accepted as a master of an art. These artisans receive training in their craft through *kata*, and the main purpose of *kata* is to copy or imitate the master craftsperson. As Yano explains, "Kata relies upon repetition as the very means by which expression emerges, historically embedded and validated. Authenticity here does not dwell within the singular moment or as individual authorship, but accrues over time amidst a group context" (2005: 193), so it is actually replication that creates and legitimizes authenticity of a skill, an idea which will remerge in Chapter Five.

Fashion

An analysis of contemporary Japanese textile designers and the apparel they create ultimately involves a discussion of fashion in wider society, its meanings and its cultural significance. The study of fashion has proved a problematic issue among scholars because of its connection to vanity and excess, which leads many to view it as trivial and therefore having no merit as a scholarly subject. This section addresses some of these issues, arguing that fashion is important because of its role in social and cultural practice.

Fashion's Inferiority Complex

Fashion, and the fashion industry, is often viewed by intellectuals, the media, and the general public as superficial and frivolous. Anna Wintour, editor-in-chief of US *Vogue* magazine, bemusedly alludes to this attitude in the documentary, *The September Issue* (Cutler 2009), stating that her older brother works with housing people in need, her sister supports farmers rights in Latin America, and her younger brother is political editor of the *Guardian*, so she thinks "they are very amused" by her occupation. Even Wintour's daughter, Bee Shaffer, says of the industry, "It's a really weird industry to me" and "I would never want to take it too seriously" (ibid.: 2009).

At the high end of the contemporary industry, the seemingly impractical nature and exorbitant expense of *haute couture* elicit criticism, but fashion merits academic attention because the way we dress is about identity, about how we see ourselves and the impact of society on the individual creation of self through dress. Fashion is bound up with issues of body image, cultural and ethnic identity, religion, gender, group membership, exclusion and inclusion, class, and social status. Dress "is, before almost everything else, the repository for conceptions of individual and collective identity" (Slade 2009: 4). Not only is it a repository, it is one of the means by which "bodies are made social and given meaning and identity" (Entwistle 2000: 7).

Fashion is made by and for bodies: "It is produced, promoted and worn by bodies. It is the body that fashion speaks to and it is the body that must be dressed in almost all social encounters" (ibid.: 1). This focus on the body supports my argument that contemporary Japanese fashion should be analyzed with close attention to sensory issues, as the body is the site through which we perceive and experience the world. Fashion is about bodily practices and should be studied as such because "dress in everyday life is about the experience of living in and acting on the body" (ibid.: 5). This includes the production as well as the consumption of fashion—a gulf that sociologist Joanne Entwistle claims has not yet been bridged by social theory (ibid.). Moreover, fashion in its wider context is intertwined with economics, politics, and culture in complex ways. Not only has it been a driver for economic and technological advancement, it also illustrates human creativity, something which anthropologists, such as Jared Diamond (1992), believe sets us apart from other life forms.

Clothing, Dress, and Fashion

In scholarly research, often the use of terms such as clothing, dress, and fashion vary depending on the discipline: anthropologists tend to use "dress" and "adornment," sociologists and social/cultural historians use "fashion," and historians use "costume" (Entwistle 2000). There is generally a lack of consensus or consistency in the use of terms, but there is some agreement on defining "fashion" as a *system* of dress. This fashion system can be defined as "a particular set of arrangements for the production and distribution of clothing" (ibid.: 45).

No doubt motivated by fashion's implied whimsy and extravagance, many scholars of fashion have attempted to clarify the difference between "fashion" and "dress." Invariably they then proceed to use the terms interchangeably because both "fashion" and "dress" are concerned with adornment of the body. Part of the problem with trying to separate "dress" and "fashion" lies in the fact that when we start to unpick the elements of each, we find that the differences between them disappear. They both include elements of aesthetics, taste, judgment, and meaning, and are context-dependent. The main point of differentiation set down by many scholars (Bourdieu 1984; Davis 1992; Entwistle 2000) is in the temporal nature of fashion as compared to dress, but dress also changes. I believe that the real difference lies in the rate of change that is *implied* by the term "fashion," as I will explain below.

"Clothing" can be defined as a covering for the body. Early scholars such as Carlyle (2008 [1831]) and Veblen (2008 [1899]) see clothing as incorporating three functional aspects: modesty, protection, and decoration—and these functions drive early analyses (Edwards 2011) and therefore shape how we view clothing and fashion today. Carlyle believed that "the first purpose of clothes … was not warmth or decency, but ornament" (2008: 102) because he argued that warmth could be found in the vegetation or landscape. In addition, Carlyle states that "among wild people, we find tattooing and painting even prior to [c]lothes" (2008: 102). While Carlyle includes body adornment in the category of "clothes," Johnson and Foster distinguish it from "dress." They usefully characterize clothing as a more limited category, and "dress" as a broader term that encompasses cosmetics, jewelry, nail polish, hairstyles, and bodily adornment such as scarification, piercing, and tattoos (2007).

Veblen, writing in the late nineteenth century, believed that individuals used clothing primarily to gain advantage and impress others. He wrote that "our apparel is always in evidence and affords an indication of our pecuniary standing to all observers at the first glance" (2008: 257), making an interesting point regarding consumption in the late nineteenth century that still holds true today. Because of this association with self-image and status, fashion is also often vilified as a "conspicuous waste of goods" (ibid.: 257), but it is no more "guilty" of waste than any other form of consumption (such as homes, furnishings, food culture or art). One of the reasons fashion is singled out for criticism could be that it is merely more immediately visible than other forms of conspicuous consumption.

While other scholars, such as Entwistle (2000), have provided comparable ways of looking at "fashion," Kawamura's cogent argument that "fashion is not a material product but a symbolic product which has no content substance by/ in itself" (2005: n.p.) is compelling because it addresses the indefinable qualities inherent in "fashion." She argues for a distinction between clothing as a tangible material object and fashion as a cultural symbolic object, a belief system. Fashion (an "immaterial object") cannot be easily separated from clothing (a "material object") because "clothing and dress are the raw material from which fashion is formed. Fashion is intangible whereas clothing is tangible" (Milhaupt 2014: 24). Fashion as a belief is manifested through clothing; "People are wearing clothes, but they believe or wish to believe that it is fashion that they are wearing and that they are consuming fashion and not clothing. That belief is born out of the socially constructed idea of fashion which means a great deal more than mere clothing" (Kawamura 2005: n.p.).

Kawamura believes that dress cannot be considered fashion, or, more precisely, "in fashion," until it has been adopted and used by a large proportion of people in a society, but this can be viewed as a circular argument, as the object has to be labelled as fashion before it reaches a wider stage of consumer acceptance. Entwistle agrees: "Fashion therefore refers not just to the production of some styles as popular or elite, but also to the production of aesthetic ideas which serve to structure the reception and consumption of styles" (2000: 48), resulting in something akin to Bourdieu's concept of *habitus* (1984). The *habitus* is a conceptual way of explaining the relationship between social structures and individual agency. Bourdieu believed that embodied dispositions, such as taste, were produced by particular conditions of a class through education (including both formal and informal learning). In regard to dress, Entwistle sees this as "a practical negotiation between the fashion system as a structured system, the social conditions of everyday life such as class, gender and the life as well as the 'rules' or norms governing particular social situations" (ibid.: 37).

Kawamura, however, is arguing for a difference between "dress" and "fashion," one that recognizes that both terms need to be contextualized to understand their meanings. The term "fashion" has the concept of mutability embedded within it, whereas "dress" does not. We can "dress up," "dress down" or "dress casually," but none of these necessarily mean we are dressed "fashionably." Or as Bourdieu simply put it, "Fashion is the latest fashion, the latest difference" (1993: 135). Entwistle seeks to clarify the connection between dress and fashion thus "fashionable dress is dress that embodies the latest aesthetic; it is dress defined at a given moment as desirable, beautiful, popular" (2000: 1). In regard to Japanese dress, the kimono has not changed its shape for hundreds of years but the way it is worn and the coloring and fabric patterns are the aspects that have changed over time with fashion trends. This was evident in my research of brands such as Pagong, whose designers are following the current trend for nostalgia by using "retro" Taishō era kimono patterns for contemporary clothing, but updating them with a twenty-first century color palette (discussed further in Chapter Three).

In today's society, Veblen's utilitarian view (i.e., "elegant dress" is considered "wasteful consumption" but "protection of the person" is not [2008: 263]) is evidenced in everyday consumer attitudes as well as by fashion designers themselves (Davis 1992). Japanese designer Yohji Yamamoto expresses the desire for protective functionality in the Wim Wenders documentary, *Notebook on Cities and Clothes*:

> At the beginning of the nineteenth century, and if you are born in a not very rich country, the winter is really winter for you, it's very cold so you need a thick coat on you, then this is life, this is real clothes for you, this is not for fashion. That coat is so beautiful because you feel so cold and you can't make your life without this coat … and I feel strong jealousy—if people can wear my things in that way then I could be so happy. (cited in Wenders 1989)

Davis dubs this "antifashion" stance "utilitarian outrage," which "castigates the wastefulness, frivolity, impracticality and vanity associated with fashion, with its changes from season to season, with the invidiousness it occasions and the fickleness it induces" (1992: 168–9). This utilitarian view has also been referenced in the wider media by parodies of the fashion industry such as *The Devil Wears Prada* (Frankel 2006).

The utilitarian view prioritizes bodily protection, comfort, and modesty over other functions of clothing such as adornment and decoration; fashion is seen as going beyond practicalities to something unnecessary, excessive, and whimsical, and it is this notion along with the constant need to consume new styles and trends that creates the urge to critique fashion, which in turn creates a need to defend it. Many well-known thinkers, such as the French philosopher Jean Baudrillard, have taken the subject seriously, suggesting that fashion is a significant form of resistance against the industrialized world's quest for utilitarianism. He recognized that "the universal denigration of fashion results from its futility and artificiality, qualities that constitute a taboo in a utilitarian society" (Slade, 2009: 11). Even American fashion designer Elizabeth Hawes illustrates this in her critique of the fashion industry in the 1930s, *Fashion Is Spinach*,[13] stating that "fashion persuades millions of women that comfort and good lines are not all they should ask in clothes" (1938: 6–7). More recently, Edwards makes a similar point, stating that we "quite clearly do not dress according to function or need alone" but that "utility still remains and motivates many of the less fashion-conscious groups and individuals" (2011: 16).

But, as Entwistle points out, making a distinction between "fashion" and "dress" does not solve this issue because the two are not mutually exclusive: the choices made in getting dressed can be aesthetic as much as "functional" (2000: 43). Furthermore, what is considered "functional" or "practical" is culturally specific. Cliffe makes this salient point in regard to kimono,

> Western dress was sold to Japanese on the grounds of modernity and practicality. However, being told that western clothing was more practical would not mean that one suddenly experienced one's own clothing as impractical. Kimono had been practical for Japanese for over a 1,000 years. (2017: 47)

It is clear from this statement, and the history of kimono, that cultural constructions of functionality and practicality change over time, and therefore the boundaries about what is considered wasteful, frivolous or vain also change. As already stated above, even among Japanese designers, views about the suitability or otherwise of kimono vary greatly.

Another oft-quoted early scholar of fashion, German sociologist Georg Simmel[14] (1858–1918), wrote that "fashion does not exist in tribal and classless societies" (1957: 541); this statement was made in a modernist environment which privileged the rise of capitalism over other social theories. Simmel felt that it was only with the development of a class system, where the masses began to emulate the elites, that fashion could come about: "The elite initiates a fashion and, when the mass imitates it in an effort to obliterate the external distinctions of class, abandons it for a newer mode—a process that quickens with the increase of wealth" (1957: 541). Fashion is therefore seen as connected to modern capitalism (which creates distinct classes), the result of the so-called trickle-down effect. This is, however, a narrow understanding of fashion, prejudiced by the rise of the ready-to-wear fashion industry at the time. This trickle-down view of fashion ignores the fact that fashions are not "dumbly followed" but can trickle-up as well (Edwards 2011: 17). Examples of street fashion influencing couture in the West include Katharine Hamnett's designer ripped jeans and Vivienne Westwood's punk collections (ibid.). In the Japanese context, the Edo townspeople and the women of the pleasure quarters set fashion trends, such as the aesthetic ideal of *iki* (Yamamoto 1999: 7), a kind of "urbane chic" (Milhaupt 2014: 126) of subdued hues, fine patterns, restrained eroticism—a combination of restraint and dandyism (Ikegami 2005). Some interpret *iki* as a return to the earlier aesthetic of *wabisabi*, but it is a much more complex concept which can be used to describe a person's posture, a way of wearing a kimono, pronunciation of some words, certain facial expressions, a style of walking, gestures, certain colors and patterns, and even some styles of singing (Yamamoto 1999: 4). This demonstrates that fashion trends are not only initiated by the upper class.

In addition, to base the development of fashion on class alone is to exclude all of the other factors that influence changes in dress, such as gender, ethnicity, religion, and social status. A broader view includes fashion as a visual expression developing from the dialectical relationship between the human desire for conformity as well as differentiation that occurs within any society (Cameron 2000). The development of the fashion industry has become more pronounced with the development of capitalism (as have all the subsets of consumer industries such as home décor, electronic equipment, automobiles, appliances, and toys), but it is problematic to argue that the fashion industry is predicated upon, or is not extant outside of, capitalist societies. Ethnocentrism has meant that Western scholars such as Simmel, Bourdieu, and Veblen tend to view fashion as a primarily Western phenomenon because they exclude fashion from the developing world (Edwards 2011: 12). Theories that distinguish fashion as primarily a modern phenomenon linked to the development of consumer capitalism can be challenged by "the prevalence of complex designs in dress prior to capitalist development and the universality of styling in dress according to social values, tastes and systems across time and space" (ibid.: 12). Even Kawamura, a Japanese national who focuses on fashion research methods, has fallen into the trap of privileging the rise of the Western fashion system, positioning Paris as the birthplace of fashion and deeming the fashion system a result of capitalism.

A focus on the functional aspects of fashion disregard the fact that adornment and decoration serve to fulfil many purposes that are no less important to us than bodily protection, comfort or modesty. There is a self-conscious relationship between the body and attire, where customers "cease to buy things not just because they like the colour or the fit but because somehow in their heads it equates with something that somebody else has told them that they might want to *be*" (Edwards 2011: 161). Erving Goffman's now classic book *The Presentation of Self in Everyday Life* is a useful starting point for thinking about the relationship between body and attire, because, like fashion, the presentation of self is framed as the interplay between the external environment (that imposes rules and norms) and the internal (how the external is experienced and transformed by individuals) (1959). Entwistle relates this concept to dress, stating that "dress in everyday life is always more than a shell, it is an intimate aspect of the experience and presentation of the self and is so closely linked to the identity that these three— dress, the body and the self—are not perceived separately but simultaneously, as a totality" (2000: 10).

This aspect of the self, expressed through dress, encapsulates emotion and memory, as well as serving to negotiate culturally specific contexts. This may involve aspects of conformity and differentiation, but it also involves a more multifaceted mix of elements that can include what Goffman terms "sincere" or "cynical" intent (1959: 18). As Davis explains, dress provides "a kind of visual metaphor for identity and, as pertains in particular to the open society of the west, for registering the culturally anchored ambivalence that resonates within and among identities" (1992: 25). Dalby believes that sincerity plays a larger role in Japanese dress, stating "Western tradition tends to characterize clothing as facade—a wolf in sheep's clothing is anything but sheepish. In Japan, clothing and wearer merge" (2001: 4). The embodied aspect, the physical experience of wearing clothing, can affect the mental state of the wearer (mentioned above and discussed further in Chapter Four). However, ascertaining the sincerity of apparel is highly problematic. Furthermore, the intimacy of the relationship between the body and clothing transcends cultures, even if particular cultures feature specific means of expressing this intimacy.

Craik believes that "clothes construct a personal *habitus*" because they are "technical devices which articulate the relationship between a particular body and its lived milieu" (1993: 4). It is this relationship—this embodied aspect of attire—that has largely been ignored in fashion discourse, but it is a crucial element that influences the adoption or rejection of fashion by individuals and societies. Undoubtedly, dress and fashion involve aspects of taste and aesthetics, but "clothes in everyday life are not like art, nor do they pretend to be: clothes in everyday life take on the form of the body and in doing so get crumpled, creased, ripped and so on" (Entwistle 2000: 71). Edwards notes that "clothing in particular is often rather meaningless when hanging on rails and piled on shelves in shops," and that it is "the imagining of what something is like to *wear* that really gets the pulse racing" (2011: 35). As a barrier between the body and its environment, dress is the meeting place of public and private, it "is both an intimate experience of the body and a public presentation of it" (Entwistle 2000: 7). Mackie has highlighted the barrier aspect of clothing in reference to Lolita culture, where the frills prevalent in such clothing obscure the shape of the body and act as "an especially dense border between the body and the outside world" (2009).

Fashion as Cultural Practice

The fixity or static quality of "dress" is contrasted with "fashion" as temporary, rapidly changing, up-to-the-minute (associated with modernity); in other words, "dress" is unchanging, or slow to change and is thus often associated with "tradition," national costumes or military dress. Scholars have attempted to distinguish "fashion" from "dress" using the temporal nature of the former, the "restless change in fashion" (Veblen 2008: 271), as the point of differentiation, implying that clothing is a static category. Entwistle believes that traditional dress does change, but such change is "not driven by the logic of regular and systemic change characteristic of fashion in the west" (2000: 47). This "change for change's sake" is the point of differentiation for Entwistle (ibid.). But by treating fashion as a mark of civilization, "other codes of clothing behaviour are relegated to the realm of costume[15] which, as 'pre-civilized' behaviour, is characterized in opposition to fashion, as traditional, unchanging, fixed by social status, and group-oriented" (Craik 1993: 4). Craik provides examples of changes in "traditional" clothing such as the newly designed clerical robes necessitated by the ordination of women in Australia. She states, "While acknowledging that not all clothing is fashion, all clothing systems have at least a distant relationship with fashion systems and stylistic conventions" (1993: 2). Edwards goes further, stating that "fashion is becoming less about clothes and more about images, magazines and media reports on what's hot or who wore what where" (2011: 161). This changing nature of how "fashion" is practiced illustrates that it may be more useful to see fashion as not a product of modernity, but a cultural practice that has been around for centuries, albeit in different forms and in different regions.

Fashion is a cultural practice that changes over time, but it is also possible for styles to become entrenched. In postwar Japan, Liza Dalby noted how the kimono had become static and fixed to the "samurai-turned-bourgeois" style, with even less room to move in both physical terms and in compliance with accepted conventions of wearing it (2001: 126). Although samurai only made up 6 percent of the population, theirs was the dominant ideology and after the Meiji Restoration, Japan underwent a process of "samuraization" (Iwabuchi 2009: 50), which included the construction of the kimono as the national dress. Prior to this, the kimono was reserved for the upper classes and for special activities such as festivals. Dalby explains that two-piece clothing was for labor, for everyday, was low class and rural and that kimono was for leisure, festivals, was high class and urban. However, in "the nineteenth century, kimono was native, two-piece foreign" and "in the modern period, kimono was for women, two-piece was for men" (2001: 165).

The two-piece clothing Dalby refers to was an ensemble such as *jinbei* (a short jacket that crosses left over right with a tie fastening, and loose-fitting shorts or trousers) or *noragi* (regional work clothing) that was typically comprised of two pieces: a *haori* (a short jacket) and *mompe* (loose-fitting trousers that come in at the ankle). The physical restrictions imposed by the kimono, its association with the upper classes, and its elevation to that of Japanese national dress resulted in the more formal kimono (and its mode of wearing) being the one that has persisted. Dalby admonishes that "even as kimono academies urge women to find ways to squeeze kimono back into everyday life, the stiffness of the mode they promulgate undermines their efforts, aesthetically and functionally" (ibid.: 136). There are strict standards of what is and is not acceptable, aligned to age, status, and social situation. This is because "kimono today and the right way of wearing them are redolent of the ever-present issue in Japan of being authentically Japanese" (ibid.: 126).

Japanese Fashion: A Pre-Industrial Example

Japan provides an excellent example of how the fashion industry operated in pre-industrial society. In the eighth century, textile industries were already formally organized and operating under government sponsorship (Woodson 1997). A systemized practice of fashion was operating as early as the Heian period (794–1192). Evidence for this includes sumptuary regulations imposed in the early eleventh century restricting the number of kimono that women could wear to five layers (Wada 1996: 180). Prior to this some noble women had been known to wear up to forty layers, suggesting that there was a competitive aspect to dress at the time; to wear many layers was to be "in fashion." Sei Shōnagon, a lady of the imperial court who lived from the mid-900s to 1017, wrote the *Makura no Sōshi* (Pillow Book). In it, she describes the apparel of various court officials—the term "color" in Heian literature referred not to a single color, but to a fashionable layering of robes to produce specific colored patterns, known as *kasane no irome* (Monden 2014: 154). Author of *Genji Monogatari* (*The Tale of Genji*), and Sei Shōnagon's contemporary, Murasaki Shikibu also described women's fashions of the period throughout her book *Murasaki Shikibu Nikki* (*The Diary of Lady Murasaki*). As Bowring states with regard to Murasaki's diary, clothing and fashion "were close to a fetish in court circles" and this concern was "a major indicator of character and style, one of the ways in which a lady-in-waiting could make her mark and show her individuality" (2005: n.p.). Bowring notes that according to Murasaki's diary, women also added false hems or cuffs to the sleeves of mantles and jackets "to accentuate the main point of appreciation" (ibid.: n.p.). Murasaki describes the apparel of those around her in detail, indicating the importance of dress as an appropriate sign of status, but the following shows that it was also important as an expression of self-identity: "They suddenly realized how, although each one of them had tried to show some originality, those of a common age are bound to have common tastes. There was a strong atmosphere of rivalry" (Murasaki 2005: n.p. [*c.* 1008]) expressed through such details as embroidery on jackets, and silver thread and foil applied to clothing and fans. Practices within this fashion system, which focused on layering of kimono and a close alignment of apparel with nature and the seasons, was limited primarily to the imperial court, but awareness of fashion as expressive of cultural ideals of beauty as well as class and status was extant throughout Japan.

One scholar of traditional fashion in Japan is Kawakami Shigeki, an expert in Japanese textiles from the Muromachi and Edo periods. He chronicles the changing fashion trends of *kosode* (now called *kimono*) by analysing the Kyoto National Museum collection. Kawakami notes that the fashion trends can be seen not in the shape of the *kosode* (which "continued unchanged for the following four centuries"[16]) but in the decorative compositions (1997). Dalby confirms that "pattern and color date a kimono more surely than its shape" (2001:18). Originally decorations were created through weaving, but this proved restrictive so "a new dyeing technique,[17] was created out of necessity during this period, and the *kosode* designs reflected the aesthetic and techniques of the period at their best" (ibid.: 22). Even in this early period, a relatively high turnover of fashion trends, such as decorative motifs, is evident (ibid.: 23).

These fashion trends were not limited to the nobility—published catalogs of *kosode* designs such as the *Shinsen Ohiinagata* (newly compiled pattern book, first published in 1667) demonstrate that trends were important in other social classes as well. Kimono pattern books (*kosode moyō hinagatabon*) have been published continuously in Japan since 1666 with approximately 170 or 180 books published between that year and 1820 (Milhaupt 2014: 46). They provide evidence of a sophisticated system of production, distribution, and consumption (ibid.: 25) by serving as kimono makers' manuals, consumer catalogs (wealthy patrons rather than the majority of the population), and fashion plates or advertisements (ibid.: 32). In addition, *ukiyo-e* of fashion leaders (*kabuki* actors and courtesans) provide important information about popular styles and also reveal possible collaborations between artists, publishing houses, and the textile industry—for example, in Utamaro's woodblock series "Contemporary Beauties" prints include prominent logos of kimono vendors such as Echigoya, Matsuzakaya and Daimaru (ibid.: 32–4).[18]

An analysis of the kimono pattern book designs attests to their complexity and to their role in expressing an individual's personality, taste, and culture—for example, one pattern in the *Shinsen Ohiinagata* (Asai 1667: 16) shows a *kosode* with a design incorporating the figures of two large hats (*kasa*) and a heron (*sagi*) (Figure 1.2). Merging these two words results in the Japanese word for magpie, *kasasagi*, which alludes to Tanabata, the annual Japanese star festival. According to legend, the weaving princess, Orihime, and her cowherd lover, Hikoboshi, were banished to opposite sides of the Amanogawa (the Milky Way, or "heavenly river") as punishment for laziness. Magpies build a bridge across the sky once a year on July 7 so that the lovers can meet. Kawakami explains that,

Figure 1.2 *Shinsen Ohiinagata* image showing a *kosode* with a design incorporating the figures of two large hats (*kasa*) and a heron (*sagi*).
Source: National Diet Library Digital Collections.

"these motifs were not meant to be seen simply as descriptive ones, but to be enjoyed as witty designs with imaginative interpretations" (1997: 27). Milhaupt notes how a kimono reflected not only a wearer's taste but also their knowledge of poetry, stating that "these garments challenged the viewer to decipher and identify the poetic allusion presented" (2014: 38). This kind of intertextuality (Mackie 2010) was found in many aspects of kimono and kimono making:

> Certain parts of the kimono, such as sleeves and collars, are saturated with significance and have developed webs of metaphor connecting literature, aphorism, and daily life. When we take seriously the proposition that clothing is woven of meanings as much as it is of fiber, its structure can provide a dimension of understanding that greatly illuminates a purely historical chronology of changing modes of dress. (Dalby 2001:13)

In Japanese society, fashion communicated social position, rank, and status and therefore also posed a threat to political power if individuals dressed outside their status or rank. Japan already had a history of sumptuary laws from the Heian period that codified dress (I discuss sumptuary laws in more detail later in the chapter). In order to consolidate its power, the Tokugawa Bakufu established *buke sho-hatto* (Laws for the Military Houses) in 1615, which further prescribed conduct and dress (Kawakami 1997). Then in the mid-Edo period, the shogunate sought to increase political control of the rising merchant class by introducing sumptuary laws regarding their attire, which included bans on elaborate hair combs, parasols, silk kimonos, and a ban on the "selling of peculiar things to hit the public fancy" (Durston 2005: 20). Another scholar of Japanese social history, Ikegami Eiko, describes how in the early Tokugawa Period (1603–1868) marginalized people, both as individuals and collectives, used fashion to express their discontent with the increasing restriction of social mobility between the ranks during an era of relative peace—during the earlier Warring States Period (1467–1600), warriors had been able to move up the ranks by proving themselves through military prowess. Young men, who became known as *kabukimono*, expressed their frustration with the increasingly rigid political regime by subverting the government's sumptuary laws. In the late sixteenth to early seventeenth century, groups of young men from the fringes of the samurai class—typically *ro'nin* (master-less samurai), low-ranked, and servants of samurai—deliberately wore ostentatious, offbeat clothing, imported velvet collars, and flamboyant long swords. As Ikegami says, "They spread their message of discontent and non-conformity primarily by affecting specific fashions in dress and behaviour" (2005: 262).

The production and distribution of apparel during the Edo Period supports the idea that a complex fashion system was in operation. The seat of the imperial court and Japan's capital from 794 to 1869, Kyoto, is also the traditional home of Japanese textile production. At the end of the Genroku Period (1688–1704), considered the Golden Age of the Edo Period, artisans had difficulty keeping up with demand, especially in the newly invented *yūzen* dyed fabrics. This may also have been a response to political machinations at the time as "one stimulus to the development of *yūzen* was that Edo authorities were setting limits on the degree of luxury allowed to *kosode*" (the earlier word for kimono) (Milhaupt 2014: 21). The labor-intensive *shibori* tie-dyed kimono was banned during the period but *yūzen* could be used to obtain a similar look. Dalby suggests that it was at the end of the seventeenth century that the "fashionable mind" first appeared in Japan that is the equivalent of today's consumer mentality, with commercial establishments arising that catered for this desire to be "au courant" (2001: 44). This is supported by the establishment of Echigoya in 1673 (prior to this they did home visits), who catered for the mass market, had fixed low prices, and accepted cash only (Ikegami 2005). In 1697 there were seventeen major kimono stores in Edo, but by 1735 there were sixty-three (ibid.), illustrating the increase in commercialism and the rise of the merchant class. It is also confirmed by the widespread existence of pattern books, the Edo period's fashion magazines, a hundred years prior to western Europe (Cliffe 2017: 37). In addition, the Japanese language supports the idea that a fashion system had been in operation in the country for a long time. This is borne out by expressions such as *ryūkō* and *imamekashii* (both terms meaning fashionable) that had been in use for centuries before the introduction of the English word "*fuasshon*" in Japan (Milhaupt 2014: 24).

Historically, fashion in Japan has acted as a cultural code to communicate class, rank, and status—and this was not only confined to the upper classes (Ikegami 2005). The color and type of fabric of a kimono and *obi* could reveal class and rank. Liza Dalby explains this codification of color, noting that certain colors, textures, and fibers were reserved for aristocratic ladies, but that these "were allowed only occasionally to individual ladies of lower rank as a mark of imperial favor" (2001: 249).

Even a woman's *kanzashi* (decorative hair ornaments) expressed a woman's social standing. These kinds of social distinctions were emphasized further with the introduction of numerous sumptuary laws in the Tokugawa period, some of which included: the exclusion of non-samurai from wearing silk (though some other classes were allowed to wear *tsumugi*—a low quality silk made from the floss of wild silk cocoons or from the leftovers of a cultivated crop); the exclusion of silk as used for sumo wrestling; and the reservation of the colors *murasaki* (purple) and *kōbai* (pink-red dye obtained from the safflower) for the samurai class (Ikegami 2005). These sumptuary regulations demonstrate the state's struggle to maintain and control the social hierarchy during a period of great economic change.[19] The symbolic power of the state became embodied in the clothing individuals wore and how they styled their hair—it was not only clothing but also body adornment such as teeth blackening, footwear, hair style, and hair ornaments that signified an individual's occupation, status, and rank.

In present-day Japan, a kimono still signifies much about its wearer, even "a decision to wear kimono is not casual" (Dalby 2001: 126), although this is changing, as evidenced by a proliferation of rental kimono shops, discussed in Chapter Four. The type of kimono and the way it is worn communicates age and status, but it also tells something of the person's nature, class, and upbringing. Dalby explains that young ladies reveal these personal attributes not just by the kimono they choose on certain occasions, but by how they wear their kimono: "The ideal Young Miss is innocent, reserved, obedient, and cheerful. Her kimono, when worn properly according to modern *wafuku* convention, should express this" (2001: 220). Age and life stage is readily perceived in the following ways: "The extent of pattern coverage on formal kimono is a good indication of the wearer's age. The waist-deep florals, butterflies, and swirls gambolling upon a Miss's *furisode* drop down to upper-thigh level on a formal kimono for a Missus. From there, pattern slowly sinks toward the hem in a subtle progression that whispers a woman's age" (Dalby 2001: 222). Kimono can also reveal a woman's marital status—a single woman wears *furisode* (a kimono with long sleeves), while a married woman wears kimono with shorter sleeves. Once a woman is married, she will not wear *furisode* again, but an unmarried woman can continue to wear the longer sleeves, although as she reaches her 30s she may choose to wear ordinary-length sleeves even if she is not married. Dalby states that a 30-year-old unmarried woman is still considered by some a "social anomaly" (2001: 220). However, in 2013, more than a decade after Dalby's publication, the mean age of first marriage was 29.3 years old for women, making this way of thinking outdated (MIC 2015: 19). In addition, women have been known to subvert expectations regarding their attire in terms of kimono color and design.

Fashion throughout much of Japanese history has provided a codified communication of status, class, and rank, but it has also been shown to mold and refine the body within. While the kimono in twenty-first century Japan continues to play this role to an extent, contemporary *wafuku* often subverts these traditional aspects both through intertextual referencing in fabric-pattern design and through the contemporary body's experience of apparel in today's context (discussed further in Chapter Three). In the twenty-first century, Kyoto designers continue to link the present with the past by using traditional designs and manufacturing methods. By combining contemporary functionality with these long-established designs and technologies, they produce innovative fashion while aiming to incorporate a "feeling" or "essence" of Japanese design in the product that says something about the relationship between people and things, the process of production and consumption.

Book Outline

The following four chapters comprise of descriptions and analyses of my interviews with and observations of designers/manufacturers, retailers, and consumers. In Chapter Two, I describe the techniques and skills used to create Japanese clothing, namely kimono- and *obi*-making companies, because I argue that change and innovation primarily occur in these technical processes. Heritage techniques can constrain design because of fixed ideas about design as well as practical limitations of production processes, or they can enable designers to create new products within the paradigm of "tradition" and acceptable notions of "Japanese" clothing culture. Contemporary designers who utilize traditional kimono-making techniques or motifs are thus able to draw on the deep contextual meanings of kimono design, production, and consumption, and to market their goods in the context of these meanings. The heritage techniques also play a part in design because the designers are concerned with sensory perceptions other than what the garment might look like on the body—such as comfort, which includes breathability, flexibility, and so on—making the design process intertwined with the prospective product's existence as an embodied object and as a sensory object. For example, designers consider how it feels for the wearer, the spaces created between the body and the fabric, or the unique qualities of the material. Kyoto is still seen as the "authentic" source of the craft's expertise and knowledge both in Japan and overseas, and so my main focus in Chapter Two is the Kyoto area that fosters this artistic and retail community.

In Chapter Three, I feature case studies on three Kyoto companies to illustrate how heritage industry techniques are being used to create contemporary apparel. These three companies, Pagong (Kamedatomi Co. Ltd.), Sou Sou, and Kyoto Denim, were chosen because they illustrate the reinvention of *wafuku* particularly well and in a variety of ways. Through these case studies, I show that these companies are making the kimono "ride a bicycle" in a figurative sense by retaining certain traditional techniques of production and by creating suitable apparel for contemporary lifestyles.

Chapter Four explores the blurring of boundaries between "traditional" and "modern" by considering the wider implications of Japanese kimono fashion on society through the practice of "cosplay" (costume play) of fashion *taiken* (a sensory experience). I problematize the concept of fashion authenticity in a newer aspect of contemporary everyday use of kimono, and show how consumers are blurring the lines between "tradition" and present-day apparel through imagined communities and performativity. This is important because it demonstrates what is occurring at the retail/consumption end of the textile industry, as opposed to in design and manufacturing. This analogy of fashion *taiken* with cosplay illustrates how wider society is making kimono "ride a bicycle" through their reconceptualization of *wafuku*. This in turn feeds back into the industry through a notional (and literal) loosening of the kimono, a garment which was worn according to a strict standardized format in the postwar period in accord with Japan's desire to rebuild their cultural identity.

Chapter Five looks more closely at the mechanics of innovation and change in this "traditional" Japanese industry and shows that innovation has occurred within all aspects of the Kyoto textile industry supply chain: design, production, distribution, and marketing. In design and production, we can see efforts to make *wafuku* more congruent with contemporary lifestyles and middle-class budgets. In regard to distribution, I detail the unexpected consequences of new technology on long-held historical monopolies of distribution, and illustrate how companies are using a variety of methods to market their *wafuku* products. And in the case of promotion and retail presentation, Japanese marketers of consumer goods (like those in other media-rich countries) have realized that, in the present advertising "visual jungle," "multisensory marketing" is the way to appeal to the modern consumer (Howes 2005b: 287–8). Shops and items in shops exude scents, objects are designed for their tactile qualities, and advertising appeals to shoppers' "inter-sensual logic" (ibid.: 292). Kyoto textile retailers are savvy to such concepts but often have a unique take on them, for example, collaborating with confectioners or incense manufacturers, and selling the resulting products in their retail outlets, or manipulate them to appeal to customers in culturally specific ways.

Conclusion

This book engages with questions of tradition, authenticity, and innovation with reference to Japan's enduring symbol of culture, the kimono. But it is also about the sensory experience and thus includes images and videos to assist the reader to approach the study of kimono in a variety of ways. While I acknowledge that we do not really see the things pictures represent in a "true" sense (see Pettersson 2014: 279) I think these images, both static and moving, help the reader understand what is happening because "when we view images that represent other people's sensory experiences, then we are better placed to imagine what these might be like" (Pink 2009: 110).

Such issues regarding cultural heritage and identity mentioned above are of concern to all states and nations in the global arena. An examination of the Kyoto textile industry demonstrates the often conflicted expectations of artisans, community members, and nations regarding issues of tradition, authenticity, and cultural identity. Artisans must navigate through these expectations while at the same time maintaining their own values and satisfying their own creative imaginations. Daliot-Bul has argued that since 2002 the Japanese government has promoted the production of a "Japan Brand" as "one that resonates with the emerging global image of 'Cool Japan'" as part of their Japanese Intellectual Property Strategy (2009b: 247), but that this has ultimately failed because it merely "resorts to a familiar and conservative self-exoticizing discourse" (ibid.: 253). I maintain, as Daliot-Bul does, that such strategies fail to grasp the fact that the creation of cultural identity and images surrounding it are market driven. Kawamura states, "Fashion always reflects the prevailing ideology of a society" (2012: 4) but in the twenty-first century this must include the interplay of local, national, and global society. One such market appears to be that of an emerging imagined global community of artisans and craftspeople. This has been termed a "transnational craftscape" (Kawlra 2015). I return to this discussion in Chapter Six.

While it is true that many of the artisans I interviewed commented on the decline in demand for kimono in Japan, this statement is by no means the only external factor affecting production in the textile industry. By looking at companies that are using traditional techniques to produce contemporary clothing, I show that the industry is complex, and that there are a number of contributing factors including the invention of new products that employ heritage industry skills, innovations in production, new distribution patterns, and changing attitudes and tastes among consumers. These factors are allowing the industry to adapt and change, and enabling the kimono to "ride a bicycle."

In this chapter I have explored two key concepts that underpin my analysis: tradition and fashion. Both of these concepts are integral to a discussion of the Kyoto textile industry (as will be seen in subsequent chapters), especially companies using heritage techniques to produce contemporary apparel. I have embedded the discussion in Kyoto's history as this city is recognized by Japanese and international visitors as the historical (and therefore "traditional") heart of Japanese culture, especially textile culture, where citizens "*kidaore*": dress to destruction. Third-generation kimono *yūzen* factory owner, Kameda Kazuaki, explained the importance of fashion for Kyoto people like this: "Kyoto people will eat poorly while wearing good clothing. This is the case now. Even if I only eat *ochazuke* (tea over rice) I want to wear good clothes. If I have any spending money, I'm thinking about the shoes or pants, the shirt that I want" (Kameda 2012). Most people I met interpreted "*kidaore*" in this way. However, Miyamoto Kazutomo, a young partner in the jeans design company Kyoto Denim, told me the expression has many meanings. He said that most people today assign a negative meaning to it, believing it indicates obsession and excessive consumption but he prefers to think about the clothes' life span:

> During a kimono's life span, first it might be worn for a ceremony, or important event, and then if it gets stained, the mother washes it and remakes it for her daughter to wear, and then it is used to make futon, *zabuton* [floor cushions], cloths and dusters. Its final life stage is to be burnt and the silk ashes are used for plant feed. If you use the clothes fully, the full life span, then that's *kidaore*. In this case it has a really good meaning. *Kidaore* doesn't have a bad meaning. This generation only knows the negative meaning of *kidaore*. But originally this meaning was more common I think. This was the real meaning of *kidaore*. (Hall 2018a: 289)

This way of thinking also supports the notion of permanency and frugality in Japanese fashion discussed earlier in the chapter, as opposed to an image of over consumption and waste. A kimono maker assigned a similar meaning to the expression. He told me,

> If you have a lot of fish, then you eat lots of fish, if you have lots of fruit, you eat lots of fruit, you don't waste it. If you have some imperfect kimono material, you wear it or you give it to your family to wear. Other people say that Kyoto doesn't have many raw materials, unlike the rest of Japan, so we had to be good at making things. Kyoto people make kimono, they don't stop. Kyoto makes the most kimono. (Personal interview October 19, 2012)

These alternative meanings seek to distance "fashion" from its frivolous image and give it a more utilitarian stance but these concepts are not mutually exclusive—fashion can be both frivolous and practical. However, such conflicting interpretations highlight the importance of clothing and textiles for the people of Kyoto. The industry is integral to Kyoto's cultural identity and thereby to the people's cultural identity. It is the "traditional" aspect of the industry, the long history and continuation of the crafts—that is, constantly referenced to prove the authenticity of this cultural identity, while at the same time this label of "tradition" allows for revitalization and change. The main stakeholders in the industry rely on the national cultural heritage argument for their claims of authenticity. However, as I discuss in Chapter Five, these claims for authenticity demonstrate the often shaky foundations on which cultural identity is based, foundations of cultural nationalism.

This focus on authenticity and cultural identity in turn relies on the idea of "tradition." This chapter has problematized "tradition" to demonstrate the complexity of issues of historical tradition in the contemporary art scene. In terms of the kimono today, art historian and Japanese textile expert, Terry Satsuki Milhaupt makes an apt point that "extant kimonos, as well as the shifting meanings of the word itself, chronicle cultural developments, reflect shifts in aesthetic tastes and denote social identities. As such, the kimono and its meaning have changed with the times—it is anything but 'traditional'" (2014: 23). Therefore, we can see in the Japanese context how difficult it is to apply concepts such as "tradition" and "authenticity" to real-life examples. One of the most important points to come out of the UNESCO conventions is that "interpretations of authenticity and their application should be attempted within the specific cultural context" (*Yamato Declaration on Integrated Approaches for Safeguarding Tangible and Intangible Cultural Heritage* 2004). I suggest that this phrase "the specific cultural context" is important because application of the discourse of tradition is bounded by how participants apply and utilize terms in local settings to legitimize and frame their cultural heritage, rather than prove concrete facts about it.

"Fashion" is also a term that requires cultural contextualization, as can be seen by the alternative meanings of *kidaore*. In contemporary Western society "fashion" is a term loaded with meanings, many of them casting the industry in a negative light—mass consumption, wastefulness, superficiality, conceit, and expense, and this is also the case with some interpretations of *kidaore*. By placing fashion in opposition to "function" (in a utilitarian sense), scholars have neglected fashion's important role in both socialization and representation of the self. In the case of Japan, the problem of applying a utilitarian view of fashion is highlighted by both Kameda's view of *kidaore* as being core to his economic priorities and Miyamoto's view of fashion as fulfilling its full economic and utilitarian function.

Therefore, Japanese dress offers a valuable non-Western case study in demonstrating the role of fashion in society. Historically, Japanese dress has served as a vehicle not only to communicate socioeconomic status but also to express other kinds of personal information about the individual to society through visual means. It shows fashion's interconnectedness with all aspects of social life, including its function as a political tool and as a driver of technological and economic change. The "trickle-up" and "trickle-down" effect is readily evident in Japan, both historically as evidenced by conformation to or flouting of sumptuary laws and in contemporary Japanese society through the adoption of kimono as national dress and a way of authenticating Japaneseness. However, fashion also needs to be analyzed in terms of lived experience. Not only is fashion a visual means of representing self, but it also affects the body directly, and it is this interplay between body and fashion, the sensory negotiation between self and society, which has been overlooked in the study of fashion.

2
CREATING KIMONO

Historically, ethnographers limited their descriptive fieldwork to geographical areas where their chosen subjects lived and often represented the field site and its residents as autonomous entities. However, in reality this is not the case and in fact what can be deemed a "community" has come into question. The development of the internet in particular has highlighted to ethnographers, anthropologists, and social theorists that the physical reality is less important than the social connections between individuals who view themselves as part of "imagined communities" (Anderson 2006 [1983]). While textile production occurs in other geographical locations in Japan, my fieldwork interviews are limited to Kyoto because this city is deemed by Japanese people to be the heart of the textile industry in Japan and is also the historical center for textile production.

However, in a complex, postindustrial, postmodern world, limiting research to one geographic area is not realistic—the web of wholesalers, materials suppliers, and artisans stretch to other regions and even other countries and the imagined community interacts globally. The wider connections that Kyoto designers and artisans have with other commercial entities demonstrate that they are not operating in a cultural silo. This book thus includes these connections—both artistic and economic—that Kyoto artisans are making with a globalized Japan (the primary market for their products), and this will be further examined in Chapter Five. However, Kyoto is still seen as the "authentic" source of the craft's expertise and knowledge, and so my main focus in this chapter is the Kyoto area that fosters this artistic and mercantile activity.

Kyoto's link with textiles can be dated as far back as the Kofun period (250–538 CE), when a Korean named Hata and his clan of silk weavers settled on the Kyoto plain (Dusenbury 2010). *Nishijin-ori*, a collective term for silk cloth from the Nishijin district of Kyoto, traces its roots back to this clan (The Japan Craft Forum 1996). An official weavers' guild was established in the city during the Heian period (794–1185) (Woodson 1997: 15); due to the patronage of shogun's such as Toyotomi Hideyoshi (1536–1598) and the increasing wealth of the merchant class in the Edo period (1600–1868), textile production experienced a boom in production and sales (The Cultural Foundation for Promoting the National Costume of Japan, 2014b). Those involved in the Kyoto textile industry are now some of the most powerful families of modern Japan—for example, the precursor of the Mitsukoshi department store, Echigoya, founded in 1673, was a small family textile business that was the first to sell at fixed prices (Ikegami 2005). Given this history, the legitimacy of Kyoto as a center for textiles can be easily sustained.

Surprisingly, the current textile industry statistics do not appear to support Kyoto's image as the seat of Japanese textiles. Of thirty-nine nationally recognized traditional woven textiles, Kyoto is home to only one (Dentō kōgeihin sangyō shinkō kyōgai 2015). Okinawa produces eleven in comparison. In terms of dyed textiles, Kyoto produces four of the recognized eleven in the country, and under the category of "other textiles" (such as embroidery, braided cord, and so forth), Kyoto produces two of the four (ibid.). However, artisans I spoke to told me that across the traditional craft industries, Kyoto has the biggest concentration of artisans and this is supported by the statistics. Out of 218 Officially Designated Traditional Craft Products, Kyoto is home to seventeen (METI 2013), which, if calculated on a prefectural basis, means that Kyoto produces 36 percent of Japan's total Officially Designated Traditional Craft Products. These figures do not include output and nor do they account for Kyoto's long history of textile production and its perception as the traditional focus of textile production.

The traditional textile industry in Kyoto is made up of Nishijin *ori* (woven textiles), *Kyō-kanoko shibori* (tie-dyed textiles, also called "fawn-spot tie-dyeing"), *Kyō-yūzen* and *Kyō-komon* (dyed textiles), *Kyō-nui* (embroidery), *Kyō-kumihimo* (braided cords), and *Kyō-kuromontsukizome* (black dyeing for wedding and mourning kimono). The prefix "Kyō" before each term refers to Kyoto, and reinforces this location's primacy in the artistic tradition. Table 2.1 gives an indication of the size of these crafts in comparison with several other traditional industries in the region. According to these figures, the textile crafts make up the bulk of the traditional crafts in Kyoto. Originally, as with many traditional Japanese arts, the stages of textile production were segregated and a specialist performed each step. This is still true to a certain extent today, with designers outsourcing the more traditional techniques such as *shibori* tie-dyeing or *kumihimo* (braiding) to older experienced artisans, but because of this historical legacy even the companies that specialize in weaving or *yūzen* (paste-resist dyeing) will outsource specialist skills such as pattern design, paste application, or steaming, as will be explained in more detail below. Today's design companies are relatively small-scale and often operate with less than a dozen staff members. They also tend to express the desire to stay small and produce for the domestic market. However, this is slowly changing, with the internet enabling these studios to gain increased exposure to international markets and easier methods of exporting than ever before.

The field site proved a multi-sensorial experience, and work places varied from rooms in individual's houses to factories to venues that appeared

Table 2.1 *Traditional Crafts Registered by the Law for the Promotion of Traditional Crafts (dentōteki kōgeihin sangyō no shinkō ni kansuru hōritsu) (enacted May 1974)*

Craft		Production	No. of Businesses	No. of Employees	Production Value (million yen)
Nishijin Textile	Weaving	Kimono, Obi belt, tapestry	653	6,000	47,746
Kyoto Yūzen Dyeing	Dyeing	Kimono cloth	846	5,164	28,575
Kyoto Fine- Pattern Dyeing	Dyeing	Kimono cloth			
Kyoto Fawn Spot Tie-dyeing	Dyeing	Kimono cloth, Obi belt	94	1,760	2,200
Kyoto Black Dyeing	Dyeing	Formal Kimono	171	342	750
Kyoto Embroidery	Other Fiber Craft	Kimono cloth, Obi belt, ornaments	40	300	100
Kyoto Kumihimo Braids	Other Fiber Craft	Obi strap	10	50	75
Kyoto Kiyomizu Ware	Pottery and Porcelain	Dish, vase	273	990	3,534
Kyoto Lacquer Ware	Lacquer	Dish, furniture	Unclear	Unclear	1,000
Kyoto Joinery	Wood	Ornaments for tea ceremony and incense	13	29	185
Kyoto Household Buddhist Altars	Buddhist Altars and Accessories	Household Buddhist altars	Unclear	Unclear	90
Kyoto Buddhist Paraphernalia	Buddhist Altars and Accessories	Statue of Buddha, accessories	Unclear	Unclear	2,810

Kyoto Stone Carving	Stone	Garden ornaments, millstone	8	17	180
Kyoto Art Dolls	Dolls	Dolls for boys' and girls' ceremonies	38	230	330
Kyoto Folding Fans	Miscellaneous Crafts	Folding fan	Unclear	Unclear	100
Kyoto Round Fans	Miscellaneous Crafts	Round fan	Unclear	Unclear	25
Kyoto Art Mountings	Miscellaneous Crafts	Mountings	Unclear	Unclear	2,275

Source: KIC Report (2009), Kyoto Foreign Investment Promotion Committee.

no different from modern day offices. I used the local *de-rigueur* mode of transport—the bicycle—and often found myself pedaling down narrow back streets in residential areas to homes that contained workshops. The artisans in particular worked in designated rooms in their houses and weaving workshops consisted of high-ceilinged rooms (to accommodate the looms) tacked on to houses. While weaving in Kyoto is associated with the district of Nishijin, other techniques linked with kimono making such as *shibori* (tie-dyeing), *shishū* (embroidery), and *yūzen* (paste-resist dyeing) are executed across the city.

The Nishijin district remains the most cohesive and active of Kyoto's textile neighborhoods (see Diagram 2.1). The district's social structure and dynamic provide insights into the lives of many of the artisans that work with the designers I researched. In her comprehensive book on Nishijin weavers, *The Silk Weavers of Kyoto*, Tamara Hareven explains,

> Nishijin is the name for three interrelated entities: the district of Kyoto west of the Imperial Palace, in which silk-brocade weaving has been carried out for five centuries; the production process, which is complicated and requires the finest weaving skills in Japan; and the unique product—the brocade used for priestly garments and for *obi* (sash for the kimono) that are worn on the highest ceremonial occasions, such as weddings, the tea ceremony, Noh plays, and traditional festivals (2002: 25).

The Nishijin district is located in Kamigyōku, in the northwest of Kyoto city, and encompasses the area from Kitayama-dōri[1] in the north to Marutamachi-dōri (toward the south), and Nishioji-dōri in the west to Karasuma-dōri (toward the east). The district was established in 1477 after the Onin Civil Wars, when weavers returned to Kyoto from their safe haven in Sakai (Osaka) (ibid.). According to the Nishijin Textile Center website, after the end of conflict, one group settled north of Shinmachi-Imadegawa and became known for producing *nerinuki* (a fabric that was woven with raw silk as the warp threads, and scoured silk as the weft, making it lustrous) (Nishijin Textile Center 2004). Another group settled in the Omiya area in a former military camp (*Nishijin* literally means "western camp"), and began producing twill-weave cloth (Hareven 2002: 26). The Omiya group became famous nationally for producing Nishijin *ori*, woven brocade, and in particular for making *obi*. The Nishijin Textile Center (Nishijin Ori Kaikan), run by the Nishijin Textile Industrial Association (Nishijin Ori Kōgyō Kumiai), a cooperative organization of Nishijin textile manufacturers, lies at the heart of this district. Residents identify themselves as Nishijin people (*Nishijin no hito*) representing "a tradition of family-based craftsmanship and industry that has been embedded in the community for centuries" (ibid. 2002: 26). As Moon states, Nishijin *ori*

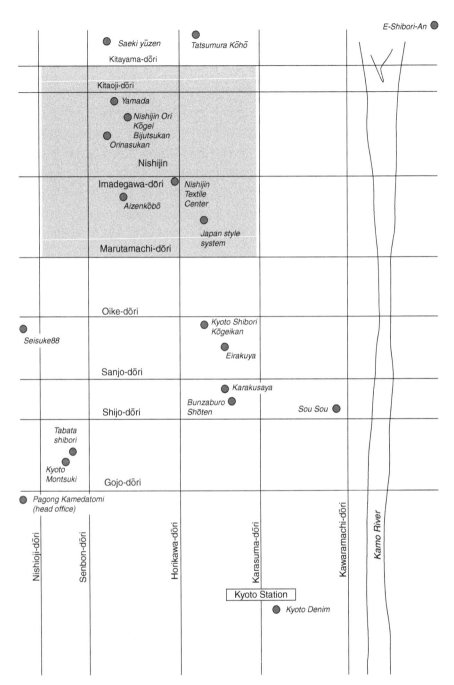

Diagram 2.1 Map of Kyoto indicating the Nishijin textile district and the main companies I researched. Most of the locations given on this map are production sites with the exception of Karakusaya, Eirakuya (Head Office), Bunzaburo Shōten, and Kyoto Denim, which are retail outlets.

claims to materially embody the most sophisticated handicraft technology of weaving to be found anywhere in the world, representing the unique Japanese aesthetic—the delicate seasonal sensibilities, concepts of colour and design, cultural sentiments related to religious festivals, beliefs, and so forth. Thus the claim that Nishijin weaving is one of the most valuable cultural heritages of the country and needs to be preserved and continuously re-produced seems to be legitimate to many Japanese concerned with culture, tradition and history. (Moon 2013: 73)

My accommodation during fieldwork was at a friend's house in the heart of Nishijin. The previous owners of the house were *obi* weavers, and the large room built on the back of the house still contained looms at the time my friends purchased it in 2007 (the looms were removed before occupation). The building was an *obi*-making factory until my friend moved in and sometimes, as she wrote in an email, "gold or silver thread drifts down from the beams in the back room where the looms used to be" (personal communication, September 2012). Weaver's workshops in Nishijin are easy to distinguish because of these high-ceilinged rooms and because of the loud "clickety-clack" noise of the looms that emanate when they are in operation.

The house was located on the corner of a very narrow street, one that was too narrow for cars but that are common in neighborhoods in Japan. From the house I could hear the rhythmic thumping of looms from a building at the end of the street. They stopped every so often, then started up again, and could be heard from 8:00 a.m. to 6:00 p.m., Monday to Saturday. Now many *obi* workshops are closing their doors, but at the beginning of the eighteenth century—the industry's height—Nishijin must have been noisy and lively, with the feeling of being at the center of the world of textile production. It is estimated that there were seven thousand weaving machines and tens of thousands of employees during this period (Nakaoka et al. 1988). Now the district is sleepy, and the workshops around the area have not been updated or renovated. If they are sold, they are knocked down and new houses are built or they are simply left empty.

Here, the business of weaving kimono and *obi* flourished, withered, and struggles today. Hareven documents the changing nature of the Nishijin landscape since the 1980s, where once "the planning and production of cloth [were] integrated within this traditional neighbourhood" to the area now becoming "a hunting ground for real estate developers, who have been transforming Nishijin's historical streetscapes into a hodgepodge of poorly designed, modern commercial buildings" (2002: 29–30). Despite this, on certain streets it is still possible to experience Nishijin corporeally through the noise and vibrations of looms and threading machines, which gives us an idea of what the area would have been like in the past (visit https://www.youtube.com/watch?v=83eAzytumCo for a video walk around Nishijin).

Nishijin affected my senses especially in terms of its soundscape, but a focus on other aspects of textile production highlight different sensory experiences, such as the unique smells (and tastes) of dyeing fabric, or the physical movements of weaving. It is important to document these sensory experiences not just to understand the context of the field site, but also in order to understand the impact of these experiences on the artisans themselves, and in particular the impact on the future of the industry. I illustrate this impact as I outline the main textile-making techniques used in creating kimono and *obi* below, before introducing designers who are incorporating these techniques into their contemporary products.

Fabric and Fibers

My primary research focus was the dyeing process, but in the interests of understanding the process in its entirety, I offer a brief explanation of the elements that make up the fabric used for dyeing. Silk and sericulture techniques are believed to have been introduced to Japan from China in the fifth or sixth centuries (Slade 2009). As early as the sixth century an Imperial Weaving Office (*Oribe no Tsukasa*) is recorded in the government documents, the *Taihō Ritsuryō* (The Code of the Taihō Era), so it is evident that weaving was well established in Japan at this time (Nakaoka et al. 1988). Until the sixteenth century, the main woven fabrics used for clothes were silk, ramie, flax, and hemp. Silk was primarily used by the nobility, as dictated by the sumptuary laws outlined in Chapter One, but practical issues such as activity also determined the fabric used for various clothing—for example, a *haori* (jacket worn over a kimono) would be made of silk if intended to be worn for practicing *ikebana* or *chado* but not if intended to be worn while laboring. So status and activity influenced the choice of fabric and both of these would have had a direct sensory impact—the feel of certain fabrics such as silk or hemp on the skin would have been a sensorial reminder to the wearer of their status, and the stiffness/suppleness and delicacy/durability of the fabric would have dictated what actions could be undertaken while wearing certain apparel. Conversely, as Woodson (1997) points out, dress worn for status impact might not be practical in terms of sensorial comfort. Woodson gives the example of a background painting for the Lotus Sutra in which a washerwoman wears a short indigo tie-dyed sleeveless summer garment over a white wrapped skirt while her mistress "seems overwhelmed by her *jūnihitoe* on one of Kyoto's notoriously hot, humid summer days" (ibid.: 16).[2]

It was not until the seventeenth century that Japanese weavers learned how to weave silk fabrics that are now most often used for kimono such as *chirimen* (silk crepe), *tsumugi* (pongee, a soft thin cloth made of raw silk), *rinzu* (woven damask), or *ro* (silk gauze). Prior to this, these weaves had been imported from China, and even during the first half of the Edo period, the "most prized cloth, such as that produced by the famed Nishijin weavers of Kyoto" was woven mainly of silk thread imported from China (Tsurumi 1990: 15). But in the mid-eighteenth century domestically produced silk was embraced by Nishijin weavers, stimulating domestic sericulture production, and by the 1830s, silk thread was spun all over Japan, primarily by women (Tsurumi 1990). Different regions in Japan became renowned for different fabrics, often influenced by environmental conditions, for example Oitama *tsumugi* from Yamagata Prefecture, Ojiya *chijimi* (ramie crepe) from Niigata Prefecture, Miyako *jōfu* (ramie) from Okinawa Prefecture, or Nishijin *ori* from Kyoto.

With increased access to foreign markets from the Meiji period onward other natural fabrics became popular for kimono such as *asa* (linen) or *yōmō* (wool). The type of cloth used depends on the activity, formality, and the intended season for wear—woven patterns such as *kasuri* (Japanese ikat) and dyed repeat patterns are considered informal, as are bast fibers (woody fibers obtained from the stems of certain plants) such as ramie. Only reeled silk fabrics such as silk crepes like *chirimen* and satin weaves like *rinzu* are used for formal kimono, with satin typically being used for spring kimono, gauze for summer, crepe for autumn, and damask for winter (Dalby 2001: 235). Casual *obi* can be made of *chirimen*, *tsumugi*, *habutae* (light-weight silk fabric often used as lining), twill, satin, gauze weaves, cotton, or wool while a formal *obi* is usually brocade or tapestry weave, the unspoken rule being that the more highly patterned, the more formal the *obi*. The Tango peninsula, located in the north of Kyoto Prefecture on the Sea of Japan, supplied Kyoto with plain white *chirimen* silk crepe for kimono during the Edo period and nowadays *chirimen* is still produced there.

Of the main companies I researched, only Kamedatomi Co. Ltd. (brand-name Pagong) uses silk in its contemporary designs for aloha shirts, but for its other products, it uses a fine weave cotton. Contemporary clothing company Sou Sou also uses cotton for the majority of its products (including kimono), in particular cotton from the Ise Peninsula in Mie Prefecture. Ise cotton has been popular since the Muromachi period because of its high quality but the development of man-made fibers and the move to Western clothing during the Meiji era lead to a decrease in demand, so now only a few Ise cotton manufacturers remain (Sou Sou US 2016a). Sou Sou favors the Usui Fabric company's cotton in particular because of its specific qualities: they claim it is light, warm, and wrinkle resistant. Kyoto Denim uses denim made from Madagascan cotton manufactured in Kurashiki, Okayama Prefecture. The company states that the factors that affect a cotton's quality include the country of origin, the type of cotton flowers, and the climate, and that these all affect the price significantly (Kyoto Denim 2014–15). Kyoto Denim claims that Madagascan cotton is the finest cotton in the world but extremely rare, especially in Japan. The reason the company selected this cotton, according to its website, is because it "aimed for the texture of the fabric to resemble kimonos, so we chose thin, long-staple cotton" (Kyoto Denim 2015).

For kimono in particular, man-made materials are becoming more common, and there are a number of reasons for this trend. Hareven discusses the Japanese government's bid in the 1980s to protect domestic silk production by adding high tariffs to imported Chinese silk thread (2002). Nishijin manufacturers were therefore unable to take advantage of cheaper foreign supply chains and have shifted to polyester to keep costs low. *Obi* are typically woven of silk thread using a range of methods to obtain an embroidery-like quality but Yamasaki Sayo, a demonstration weaver at the Nishijin Textile Center, told me that very little silk thread is produced in Japan anymore. At the Nishijin Ori Museum of Art (Nishijin Ori Kōgei Bijutsukan) factory, the weaver for the gallery also told me that Japanese silk thread is becoming difficult to obtain, and therefore they now source it from Brazil, a fact corroborated by other artisans in the industry. Obviously, the government could not halt this decline in domestic silk production. The government also could not stop the decrease in the numbers of Nishijin handloom weavers, and in fact Hareven states that neither the national nor prefectural governments made any attempts to protect their industry but it was also the Nishijin manufacturers' practices, not just market forces, that contributed to the decline in local weavers (ibid.). The manufacturers began to outsource weaving to the Tango peninsula in order to save costs, because they could pay Tango cottage weavers less than those in Nishijin. In fact, approximately 50 percent of the woven material used for Nishijin *obi* that is officially designated and labelled as Nishijin *ori* by the Nishijin Textile Industrial Association is outsourced to Tango in the north of Kyoto Prefecture and another 10 percent is outsourced to China and Korea (I discuss this aspect of the industry in more depth in Chapter Five) (Hareven 2002: 47; Yamada personal interview 2012).

Polyester *chirimen* is also made on the Tango peninsula and recently polyester kimono have increased in popularity largely because they are much more affordable than those made of natural fibers. *Chirimen* is used to make bags, *furoshiki* (the traditional Japanese wrapping cloths used to carry or gift wrap items), and other accessories as well. Manufacturers' fabric and material choices are important in the context of sensory experience and the construction of authenticity, as discussed in Chapter Five regarding what constitutes a kimono. From the consumer's perspective, wearing a polyester kimono does not feel or sound the same as wearing silk, and it is not considered as authentic as a silk kimono by aficionados.

In recent years environmental and sustainability issues have also become a factor in fabric choice decisions. Some companies have developed products using recycled materials to differentiate their brands. For example, *furoshiki* (wrapping cloth) company Karakusaya keenly promotes their range of polyester *furoshiki* and "eco-bags" made of recycled PET bottles. The manager at Karakusaya, Otsuka Miyuki, told me the polyester *furoshiki* were popular because they could be folded up and put in the pouch provided and when taken out they were not creased. They can also be machine washed. *Furoshiki* have seen a resurgence in the last decade and are now being marketed as a way to reduce waste and avoid the layers of disposable plastic and paper that accompany almost every purchase in contemporary Japan. As an example of this innovative "return" to tradition, in 2006 the Japanese minister of the environment, Yuriko Koike, created the *"mottainai furoshiki"*[3] made of a fiber manufactured from recycled PET bottles and presented it at the Senior Officials Meeting on the 3R Initiative (reduce, reuse, recycle) held in Tokyo in March 2006 (Ministry of the Environment 2006).

Designers also consider maintenance in their choice of material for a kimono. One of the problems of silk kimono is cleaning—they are very difficult to clean and only specialist cleaners know how to clean them, which involves unpicking all of the seams and resewing them after cleaning (a polyester kimono is washable at home in comparison). Despite this, silk is dubbed the "queen of fibers" by Japanese people because of its texture, feel, luster, and the beauty of its color. Pagong urges customers to dry clean their silk aloha shirts as washing can weaken the silk fibers. Other fibers, such as cotton, are more easily cleaned but cotton has a different kind of maintenance issue—starch. According to my informants, regular cotton becomes harder the more it is washed, something I have been unable to verify. But Sou Sou claims that the cotton they use is different from other cotton because the thread is lightly twisted and then hardened with natural starch before it is woven; as it is washed the starch comes out and the clothing becomes softer as "the thread tries to return to its original cotton form" (Sou Sou US 2016a). Sou Sou also highlights the traditional production processes of the company it sources cotton from—Usui Fabric Company's looms have been passed down from generation to generation and they use a traditional weaving method; only 40 feet (12 meters) of cotton is produced each day by twenty weavers. This kind of care and attention to traditional techniques fits with Sou Sou's own brand philosophy (discussed in further detail below).

As can be seen from the discussion of fabric and fibers above, it is difficult to separate these from processing techniques. Therefore, further discussion on fabric use will be taken up in the dyeing technique sections below.

Materials—Dyes

Prior to the Meiji period, natural pigments were used to dye fabric, and this proved a highly sensory experience as mentioned in Chapter One. As early as the Heian period natural dyes were made from boiling or fermenting ingredients such as plant fibers, and therefore a dye pigment (*some-iro*) was named after the material used to create it. For example, extracting dye from plum trees involved boiling the trunk of the tree for several hours and a typical method of ascertaining whether or not the dye was strong enough was to taste it for the tannin content (Kobayashi 2011). The names of many of the colors came from either the plant's dyeing properties such as *umezome* (plum dye), and *kuwazome* (mulberry dye) or from the color of its blossom such as *sakura-iro* (cherry blossom color), and *momo-iro* (peach color). As Woodson (1997) notes, obtaining dyestuffs required knowledge and experience in sourcing and extracting pigments, dyeing fabrics, and yarns, and fixing colors with mordants. During the Edo period, the main colors used were reds, purples, blues, greens, yellows, browns, greys, and black (ibid.: 18). Some ingredients such as sappanwood chips, used to create red dye, were imported from India through Dutch traders (ibid.: 18). Blue, brown, and grey were used without restriction among all classes, presumably because indigo and tannins from various kinds of wood (for browns and greys) were readily available in Japan. Dye is particularly important because color combinations and intensities are characteristics through which artisans and studios can be identified.

The seven traditional textile industries in Kyoto, mentioned above, include *Kyō-kuromontsukizome* (black dyeing for wedding and mourning kimono). Due to the intensity of the hue, black is one of the most difficult colors to dye cloth and in Japan, as in Europe, the complexities of achieving deep blacks pushed up the price of black clothing. Arakawa Toru, the fourth-generation president of black dyeing company, Kyoto Montsuki, stated that *kuromontsuki* (black formal kimono that includes the family crest) is the most expensive form of clothing in Japan today. Kyoto Montsuki has been dedicated solely to *kurozome* (dyeing fabric black) since 1915. In 1978 the company invented a ground-breaking dyeing technique resulting in what it dubbed *junguro* ("pure black") and its dedication to its craft prompted the Imperial household to order their costumes (*omizome*) for the 1989 funeral ceremony of the Shōwa emperor from them. Today Kyoto Montsuki dyes black fabric for kimono for *geiko* (a geisha is called a *geiko* in Kyoto), *maiko* (apprentice geisha), and *sumōtori* (sumo wrestlers) as well as black kimono and black formal Western-style mourning attire for the general public. It also dyes attire for *kurogo*—the stage assistants that wear black during kabuki and *bunraku* (Japanese puppet theater) performances—and *sumizome* (daily wear—literally "black ink dye") for monks. Plus, since 2009 it has launched a new range of products under the label "BL-WHY" of *kurozome* denim (see Figure 2.1).

The reason dyeing fabric black is difficult is that there is not one pigment that can achieve a deep black—the fabric must be dyed first with other colors such as madder, indigo, or tea leaves (this is called "bottoming"—*shitazome* in Japanese) and then finished with black oxide. There are various grades of black, and blacker fabric is considered higher quality. If a black pattern is created on a black background, different fibers (including paper) and thread types are used to achieve the subtle difference needed for the pattern to be seen. Kyoto Montsuki performs bottoming many times to create the necessary depth of black, so the black oxide needs plenty of dye and becomes expensive. Historically, dyeing

Figure 2.1 BL-WHY black denim jeans by Kyoto Montsuki, 2012. Design © Kyoto Montsuki Inc. Photo: Jenny Hall.

over and over to get a deep black made the material stiff and rough so "it is said that the cloth made of the black oxide finish would not be cut with a sword" (Kyoto Montsuki Co. Ltd., n.d.: 5).[4]

Ai-iro (indigo blue dye, also called "Japan blue," made from the Japanese indigo plant, *polygonum tinctorium*) is another color associated closely with Japanese textiles, and in particular it is used for making *samue* (traditional monk's working clothes), but these days it also colors place mats, tablecloths, *noren* (split entrance curtains), and wall hangings. It is still used by Japanese artisans today but it is becoming rare to encounter goods dyed from natural indigo and there are many reasons for this. Utsuki Norito at Aizenkōbō, a Kyoto indigo-dyeing workshop in business for three generations, said that now only five farmers in Japan grow *polygonum tinctorium*, the plant used in Japan to produce *aizome* (indigo dye)[5]. It is also difficult to turn the plant fibers into a dye pigment because the process is complicated and messy—the fibers must be fermented for a week at a certain temperature and the dye bath fed with wheat husk powder, limestone powder, lye ash, and *sake*. I noticed the smell of the fermenting indigo as soon as I walked into Aizenkōbō—it was stored in big jars out in the courtyard and there was an acrid odor and a metallic foam floating on the surface of the dye, known in Japan as *ai no hana* (indigo flowers). Utsuki indicated that even his skin constantly smells of it. He said historically indigo dyers tasted the dye to ascertain its readiness but these days because they add ash and slaked lime they cannot taste it, so he gauges the fermentation process by temperature, pH testing, and by color and smell. In addition, indigo requires the fabric to be soaked in the dye and dried several times to achieve depth of color—cotton and linen are soaked fifteen to twenty times and silk is soaked forty to forty-five times. The dye solution becomes weaker the more it is used, which is how the paler colors are achieved. These factors discourage many young artisans from learning natural indigo dyeing techniques. However, Utsuki did point out some advantages in using natural indigo—the color does not run when washed and it is said to be an insect repellent. For this reason, historically it was used to dye *heri*, the fabric edging used on *tatami* mats, which were commonly infested with *dani* (mites). He also claimed that the "eggplant blue" was impossible to achieve using chemical pigments.

Chemical pigments were introduced into Japan in the Meiji period with a *Some Dono* (Dyeing House) established in 1875 to train Kyoto artisans in chemical dyeing techniques (Nakaoka et al. 1988). Synthetic dyes are now the main dyes used in Japanese textile production because they are more colorfast (see Utsuki's comment above—natural indigo dye is obviously an exception to most natural dyes) and it is easier to gauge the resulting color, but mixing them is still not an easy process. The dyes are measured and mixed by hand, and, if the powdered pigments are altered by even a few grams, it might result in an unsuitable color for the color scheme that will affect the whole dye batch. A kimono pattern can involve more than twenty different colors, so the color selection process is key to the success of the design. How do you explain the exact shade and tone of a color, or how it will react with a certain type and weight of fabric? To achieve this kind of knowledge, the practitioner must draw on their senses and spend a considerable amount of time practicing (Hall 2018a: 300). In addition, if the amount of coverage intended is large, the dyer must estimate and make enough to cover it because the same color cannot be recreated. This might not be so crucial for some designs where variations in the color of a flower's petals, for example, might add to the charm. A kimono is usually a one-off creation, so as long as there is enough dye for a consistent background color for one garment, that is sufficient, but for a company creating contemporary apparel that intends to make several of the same item, large quantities of dye need to be mixed and coded as there may be several dozen containers of mixed dye. Mixing up quantities of chemical dyes is messy and is often not an activity that young Japanese artisans are prepared to do, even though it might be an easier task than creating natural dyes. As a result, the number of artisans in Kyoto with this skill is in decline.

Kyoto Montsuki maintains that an important part of dyeing is the water quality—the company has an abundant underground water source in its factory, indispensable for dyeing (Kyoto Montsuki Co. Ltd., n.d.). A good-quality water source has been also noted as crucial by *yūzen* artisans who historically washed their dyed fabrics in Kyoto's Kamo River. Minerals in the tap and well water can affect the dye reaction, preventing the dye from fully bonding to the fiber, so the quality of the water is important. In addition, abundant water is a crucial aspect of the dyeing process. When natural dyes were used this was probably not so detrimental to the environment, but with the adoption of chemical dyes it becomes highly problematic (Hall 2018a: 290). As a comparison, sports manufacturer Nike asserts that dyeing one kilogram of fabric (approximately five T-shirts) takes 100–150 liters of water (Laskow 2012). Dye factories must treat that waste water, as well as any water polluted by other processes of textile production such as bleaching, before disposing of it. This kind of wastewater often ends up in rivers (ibid.). Kyoto artisans are allowed to wash their fabrics in the Kamo River once a year at an event held every August called the *yūzen nagashi jitsuen* (*yūzen* washing performance) (Hall 2018a: 290). The practice of washing excess dye from the fabrics in the river was common before pollution laws forbade it in the late 1970s, but now a final wash of the fabric serves to remind the industry of the historical importance of the river for them (ibid.).

An alternative dyeing method has developed in recent years with the advent of the inkjet printer. I interviewed three companies in Kyoto that were designing using computer graphics—called CG (*shī- jī*) design in Japan—and using an inkjet printer to print onto fabric: Mori Makoto designs *furisode* (long-sleeved kimono), especially for *seijin shiki* (the coming-of-age ceremony); Kawabe Yūnosuke designs a range of products from the 2004 Olympics Japanese synchronized swimming team's suits to *yūzen* camouflage wear; and Seisuke88 primarily makes bags and accessories based on Meiji-period designs.

Inkjet printing allows the artisan to avoid the messy and difficult task of mixing up dye pigments and avoid so much water wastage. It also enables designers to print small or large batches, and reproduce more of exactly the same fabric design. But most importantly it gives the designer direct control over the colors—in Kyoto the processes of production have always been divided between specialists, as detailed below, so this is a significant change—they no longer need to rely on other professionals to interpret their designs, but they are still reliant on the ability of their computer software color management system to faithfully color-match their on-screen shades.

There are two main types of dyes used in textile inkjet printing: pigment inks or dye-based textile inks. Each has their advantages and disadvantages, these are ink stability, versatility with fiber types and pre- and posttreatments for wash properties (e.g., colorfastness and stain-resistance treatment). Dye-based inks include acid dyes for silk, nylon, and wool, disperse dyes for polyester, and reactive dyes for cotton and rayon. Kimono designer Mori Makoto uses both acid dyes (which require steaming after printing to set the colors) and reactive dyes to print his *furisode* designs because he uses two different inkjet printers.[6] Although pigment inks do not require such posttreatments, they are less stable, they tend to cause nozzle clogging, have lower color density, less vibrant colors, and a smaller color gamut—all reasons why they have not been so widely adopted (Fu 2006). Takahashi Seisuke, producer of brand Seisuke88, pointed out that hand printing or screen printing primarily use a maximum of fifteen different colors because to create a new screen for each color takes time and labor, but inkjet printing has about forty thousand different colors that can be easily used. I give a more detailed explanation of digital designing and printing below.

Technology

As discussed in Chapter One, *saisei* (revival, revitalization) is built into Japanese concepts of tradition. As with the introduction of weaving technology from Korea to Japan, the adoption of chemical dyes, inkjet printing, and automated looms are seen as part of this revitalization of a "traditional" industry and therefore becoming part of the tradition itself. Of course, cultural adaptation is a part of any cultural history, and Japanese culture "is the result of centuries of cultural hybridization," with the seventh and eighth centuries being one of the country's great "borrowing" eras (Monden 2008: 38). Cultural hybridization is something Japanese have always done extensively, making use of various techniques and discarding others, while at the same time imbuing objects with their own renegotiated cultural meanings. This concept of tradition as including revitalization and change spans the textile industries in Kyoto; *yūzen* designer Kawabe Yūnosuke put it like this: "We think of tradition as a constant thing, as with our thinking about *yūzen*, but in fact it is always evolving and innovating" (Japan Style System Co. Ltd. 2015). These innovations had a huge impact not just on cost and speed of production but also on the bodily experience of artisans, as I illustrate below. This is particularly evident in the weaving industry during the past 150 years and the *yūzen* dyeing industry in the past 20 years.

Orimono

Weaving (*orimono*) is primarily the construction of cloth, but it is also the art of creating patterns on fabric as it is woven on the loom (rather than adding patterns after the fabric is woven by dyeing, printing, or stitching) (Hall 2015: 64). There are four main types of looms in use in the kimono industry today: the treadle loom (a more traditional loom with no automation), the jacquard (a semiautomated system where a punch card controls the warp threads), the power loom (which uses a power source to drive mechanical parts), and the digital loom (computerized control of the warp and weft) (ibid.). These looms are described in detail below, but all have the same basic function: to hold the warp threads in place while the weft threads are passed through a "shed" (tunnel) of warp threads in which some are raised and others lowered to allow the weft to go under or over them (Schoeser 2012). The pattern and texture are determined by the sequence of the warp-thread positions (Hall 2015: 64). Extra wefts can be inserted that run the full width of the fabric, or only where additional color is required, to create more complex patterns. In Kyoto, much of the weaving performed locally since the late Meiji period has been not to make kimono cloth but done to create *obi* (Nakaoka et al. 1988) and more recently contemporary items such as bags, neck ties, and interior furnishings, but the looms used are identical for kimono making (Hall 2015: 64).

Takabata — Treadle Looms

Prior to the Meiji era, two main kinds of loom were used in Japan — the *takabata* (treadle loom) and the *sorabiki-bata* (draw loom). A *sorabiki-bata* required two people, the weaver and an assistant to manage the figure harness (which is used to control each warp thread separately). It was very similar to the Western draw looms used in the seventeenth and eighteenth centuries, except that the assistant sat on a high stage called a *sorabiki* (literally, sky machine), rather than beside the loom (Nakaoka et al. 1988). This is important because traditionally it was women or young boys who were the assistants, acting as "human jacquards" (Hareven 2002: 42) (probably because they weighed less) and men worked the main part of the loom because it took a lot of strength to operate. The introduction of the jacquard made the *sorabiki* obsolete, and women were then free to become weavers in their own right.

On a treadle loom, the weaver controls the warp threads using foot pedals, while threading the weft shuttle across the fabric; there is no mechanic action. The wooden loom operates as an extension of the body (Hall 2014: 173), and the weaver develops a rhythm, beating the warp threads tightly after each slide of the shuttle — tap tap slide, tap tap slide — it sounds like a drum punctuated by the squeaks of the foot pedals moving the warp. The pace is slow and frequently interrupted by necessary alterations and adjustments such as rethreading the shuttle or pulling the completed fabric through the cloth roller.

Watching, listening, and feeling the vibrations of the looms is a different experience from actually weaving the material oneself. At the Nishijin Textile Center, a tourist showcase for Nishijin *ori* housed in a large modern building on Horikawa-dōri, I participated in *ori taiken* (literally a "weaving personal experience"). The center is a large modern multistorey building with a runway for kimono fashion shows on the first floor, a retail area surrounded by artisans demonstrating their skills on the second floor, and a museum on the third floor. I was set up in front of a handloom (see Figure 2.2) on the second floor and given the basic instructions for weaving a simple silk scarf, including three basic movements — passing the shuttle from side to side between the warp threads, pulling the beater forwards to tighten the threads, and pressing the floor pedal to change the warp for the next pass of the shuttle. At first it felt a bit like driving a car, because one's arms and legs need to be coordinated at the same time as they perform different kinds of actions. I used my right foot for the pedals — right foot down, pass the shuttle from right to left and tighten it with the beater,

Figure 2.2 Handloom at the Nishijin Textile Center. Photo: Jenny Hall.

then left pedal down and pass back from left to right. I was doing two different patterns—a loose one and then a tight one, to create lines or stripes in the fabric. The weaver was instructing me and told me to pass the shuttle fourteen times (each side had seven rows). You could establish a sort of rhythm, but this was interrupted as you had to stop to move the fabric round the cloth roller, and change the shuttle spindle when it ran out. Adding more thread required weaving the end of the thread into the thicker section of weaving, and then starting the new shuttle in the same section. The most difficult thing was to maintain the regularity of the weave and to get the weave tight/loose enough along the edges to make the edge of the scarf straight. Of course, this was weaving at its most basic—a weaving structure called *hira-ori* or plain weaving, in which the warp threads and weft threads cross each other alternately, but I could imagine that these repetitive actions would become muscle memory with practice. Eventually, the weaver would not have to consciously think about it; as Kenneth Kensinger wrote about Peruvian Cashinahua weavers, "Her hands know" because "they are the conduit by which the knowledge entered the body" (1991: 40–1).

There are three main weaving structures and all woven textiles are made using a combination or variation on these: *hira-ori* (plain weaving), *aya-ori* (twill weaving; crossing points of warp and weft form a diagonal), and *shusu-ori* (satin weaving; crossing points of warp and weft are positioned at regular intervals, with the warp being thicker than the weft) (Yanagizawa 2011). Nishijin artisans use highly complex combinations, involving threading different colored warps in, using multiple shuttles, creating multilayered pieces, and using threads that have been pre-dyed with a pattern.

Today, weavers might also use a jacquard (*jakādo* in Japanese) in conjunction with their handloom, a device first imported from France in 1873 (Kobayashi 1998). A jacquard is an attachment that can be added to a handloom or a power loom to control the warp threads. Even weavers such as Tatsumura Kōhō (discussed below), who is famous for recreating ancient textiles from fragments using traditional methods, employs a treadle loom with a jacquard attachment (see Figure 2.3).

Figure 2.3 A treadle loom at Tatsumura Kōhō that includes a jacquard at the top. Photo: Jenny Hall. First published in *Thresholds 42: Human*, p. 172 (2014).

Jacquard

The jacquard weaving process begins with a rough sketch that is transferred to a piece of graph paper, specks of color applied box by box to form a blueprint chart (see Figure 2.4). This chart then dictates the colors of yarn to be dyed and the accurate order of the stringing of the loom, so the combined warp and weft will match the originally conceived design: the chart is crucial to the process. The jacquard board is perforated with holes according to the chart (Figure 2.5) that the jacquard reads and translates to the loom by raising and lowering the warp yarn. The adoption of the jacquard was significant because it meant that a weaver did not have to remember the entire sequence of treadlings that make up a pattern, or keep track of where they were in the sequence because the jacquard did this for them (Hall 2014: 173).

One form of Nishijin weaving that still does not utilize the jacquard is *tsuzure-ori*, or "fingernail weaving," a kind of tapestry. Originally from China, it is a brocade in which the loom operator places a picture of the intended piece (rather than a blueprint) under the warp threads as a guide, and must push down hard on the foot pedals to bunch the warp threads (Hareven 2002: 11). The weaver must keep track of the pattern carefully and this form of weaving is particularly hard on the eyes (Hareven 2002: 135).

Tatsumura Kōhō is a fourth-generation weaver of the Tatsumura Textile Company, founded in 1907. The company specializes in the restoration of

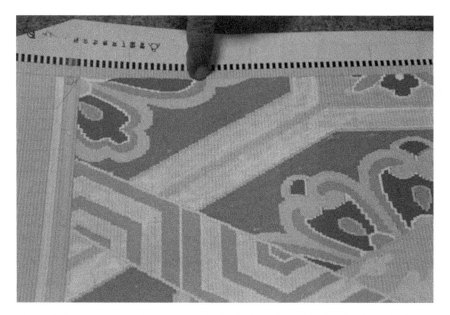

Figure 2.4 Graph paper with a pattern design indicated by dots. Photo: Jenny Hall.

Figure 2.5 A jacquard punch card. Photo: Jenny Hall.

ancient textile fragments (in particular fragments from Kyoto National Museum, Tokyo National Museum, and the Shōsōin repository), weaving of traditional Nishiki (brocade) works, theater stage drop curtains, and commemorative woven pieces. Tatsumura Kōhō's great grandfather, Tatsumura Heizō I (1876–1962) restored seventy ancient textile fragments dating from the seventh and eighth centuries, found in nearby Nara's Hōryūji Temple and the Shōsōin repository (tied to the Imperial Household Agency), and devised nearly thirty weaving techniques. He also believed in learning from the past and managed to recreate the weaving techniques of the complex warp-faced compound weave that was invented in ancient China and lost around the Tang Period (618–906 CE) (Kobayashi 1998).

Tatsumura Kōhō believes that the high precision and skill required to weave his company's fabric, and the high quality produced, justifies the fabric he produces being distinguished from ordinary silk goods (*kinu orimono*) by giving it the label *nishiki* (meaning "brocade"—a combination of the *kanji* for silk and the *kanji* for gold).[7] Each piece must pass through the hands of more than seventy different craftsmen during the process of production. The company's website states that "the work of Tatsumura Kōhō can be compared to that of a conductor who gathers together craftsmen like musicians in an orchestra, to complete each musical piece" (Koho Tatsumura Corp. n.d.).

The pieces are woven in layers, creating a three-dimensional effect. Tatsumura says that power looms are efficient and help to reduce production costs, but that "multi-colored complex and finely detailed weaving can only be done on a handloom"—by which he means a treadle loom with jacquard attachment (ibid.). He feels that "in the world of weaving, one of the most important aspects is the visual-textural feeling of the cloth" (ibid.). Other weavers who opt for handlooms rather than power looms offer the same opinion—that there is something textually different about fabric woven on a handloom that cannot be created on a power loom. At the Orinasukan in Nishijin weavers also shun the use of power looms in favor of handlooms. The Orinasukan is a museum and weaving workshop dedicated to *obi* and Noh costumes. There are fourteen handlooms in the workshop where ten weavers work making *obi* with between 800 and 4,800 warp threads. Nojiri Shūichi, a weaver with a fifty-year career, said that the *obi* he was weaving measured 10 meters in length and would take him thirty months to complete.

The textile industry workplace includes a gendered workforce that has responded to changes in production over the years. Change and innovation has occurred at many junctures over the past 1500 years since the Hata clan moved to Kyoto from Korea. The introduction of the jacquard and power loom also had a significant impact on the division of labor in the industry, especially for women, who had previously done auxiliary tasks but not played a main role in this industry. Diagram 2.2 gives an idea of some of these major changes in the Nishijin weaving industry since the Edo Period and their impact on the workforce (including women). These changes are of interest to my case studies because they demonstrate how workers are organized, and give some glimpse of what happens in the "*ura*" (behind the scenes in the business) as opposed to in the "*omote*" (public side of the business), which was not always visible during my interviews.[8]

Power Loom

The power loom was already widely used in Japan by the late 1880s, but Nishijin weavers did not adopt it at first because it was not seen as suitable for Nishijin textiles. It could not be used to weave ikat (*kasuri* in Japanese—a type of weaving in which patterns are created by resist-dyeing the warp or weft threads prior to weaving) or complicated figured fabrics. Nakaoka et al. (1988) point out that for Nishijin kimono and *obi*, treadle looms that enabled the weaver greater scope to use their handiwork skills, were more suitable. A power loom is defined as any form of loom that includes mechanization. That is, the shuttle, shedding (the raising of the warp threads to create the "shed" for the shuttle to pass through), the battening of the weft threads, and the taking up of the roll of completed fabric are mechanized and driven by a power source rather than by hand. In fact, Nishijin power looms are not the same as industrial mechanical looms used elsewhere because the type of brocade produced in Nishijin needs additional skills and craftsmanship than ordinary industrial weaving; Nishijin power loom weavers must still operate shuttles by hand to achieve the intricate designs and

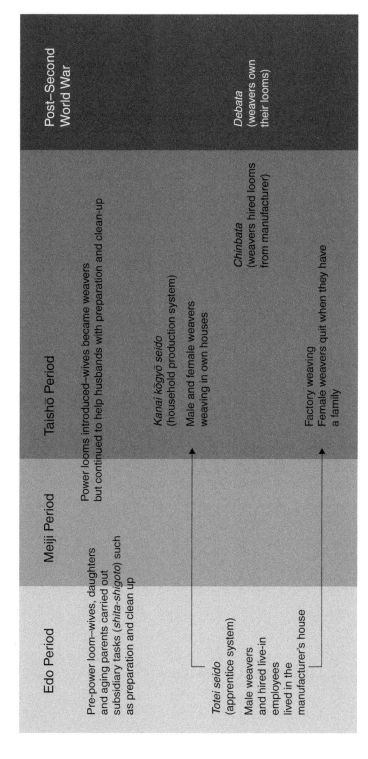

Diagram 2.2 Changes in the division of labor in Nishijin from the Edo period to post–Second World War.
Source: Adapted from Hareven (2002: 51–7).

Figure 2.6 A woven copy of a Canaletto from the Nishijin Ori Kōgei Bijutsukan showing the *bokashi* effects that can be obtained by a digital loom, 2012. Photo: Jenny Hall.

one weaver must operate one loom as opposed to one weaver operating several industrial looms as occurs in Europe (Hareven 2002). However, handlooms persist and "a significant characteristic of Nishijin has been the coexistence of various forms of production and of old and new technology" (ibid.: 45). Those who persist using the handlooms, such as Tatsumura Kōhō, believe that his products are superior because they are hand woven, but as Hareven points out, it can just as easily be argued that "technological improvements in the power loom enable weavers to produce color and texture effects that are similar or even superior to those of the handloom" (ibid.: 44–5). Hareven gives the example of complicated *bokashi* designs—gradations of colors shading into each other— "like in an impressionistic painting" in a wider range of colors that can be woven on the power loom (ibid.: 45) (see Figure 2.6). In addition, the power loom was three times as fast as the handloom in terms of production (ibid.: 57).

The impact of the power loom must have been tremendous for weavers, in terms of both speed of production and work environment. Prior to its introduction, weavers would have been able to work at their own pace, with the clacking of the wooden looms as their soundscape. With the power loom, the pressure to keep up with the machine's pace, the intense noise it produced and the smell of the oiled machine would have been overwhelmingly different (Hall 2014: 174). The introduction of the power loom in other countries such as Scotland was followed by riots and strikes by handloom weavers (Clark 1997). In addition,

Figure 2.7 A typical weaving factory in Nishijin. Photo: Jenny Hall.

typically Nishijin workshops are small, and the power looms are larger than most treadle looms so the workspace becomes even more cramped when the latter are replaced by the former (Figure 2.7).

To give some idea of the impact of the power loom on working conditions of weavers, it is useful to consider other areas of the textile industry during the same period. The introduction of power looms was accompanied by Western-style machine production such as mechanized silk and cotton reeling. The Meiji government began to establish large silk and cotton mills in the 1880s, pushing to modernize and urging citizens to "reel for the nation" (Tsurumi 1990: 5). This took a lot of adjustment for those who had been involved in silk production in cottage-style situations—for a start they were not used to working with so many other people from other areas of the country, nor with working set hours. Initially many workers who started at the mills were from samurai or ex-samurai families who had had their stipends drastically cut under the Meiji regime, necessitating family members to go out to find work (*dekasegi*). In her comprehensive account of female textile workers in the Meiji Period, Tsurumi notes that at first, conditions in the government mills were relatively good: at the Tomioka silk mill in Gunma Prefecture (established in the Meiji era and designated a UNESCO World Heritage Site in 2014), trainees worked nine to twelve hours per day, had regular rest breaks, Sundays off, lived in a spacious dormitory, and had a satisfactory food supply (1990: 30–1). However, as the mills cut costs to compete with foreign prices, conditions deteriorated which reflected a general trend across industries in the economic downturn of the 1880s. By the turn of the century, of the larger mills in Osaka, Tokyo, and Nagoya that still had dormitories, conditions were very bad, with chronic overcrowding. Typically, there was one *tatami* mat per person but in the worst cases there were twenty women (including child workers) to an eight *tatami* mat room, day and night shifts shared bedding, there was no clean bath water, and they were insufficiently fed on bad quality rice (ibid.: 133). Shifts were supposed to be twelve hours but often workers had to complete machine maintenance and prep materials, which could result in up to eighteen hours of work per shift (ibid.: 142). Machines were kept running during official break periods so at least some, if not all, workers could not take a break and often had to eat at their machines. The factories were not well ventilated, and were freezing in winter and extremely hot in summer with noise and dust at unbearable levels. As Tsurumi states regarding a typical cotton mill, "In roving and spinning sections especially, cotton fluff flew about everywhere, getting in eyes, noses, mouths, and ears, entering the pores of the skin exposed to it. In constant motion, spinning machines made such a loud clamor that operatives had to scream to make themselves heard … After a few years, workers became partially deaf" (ibid.: 141).

Although working conditions today have improved (see the weaver's comments below) and new technology has eliminated some of the complicated production processes in weaving such as manually feeding the shuttle back and forth, there are still health and safety issues for weavers, particularly in areas such as aural health. At the workshop depicted in Figure 2.7 I noticed weavers who were wearing hearing aids—additional confirmation that the power and digital looms affect weavers' hearing. I never saw a weaver wearing ear protectors or any kinds of protective clothing beyond an apron or overalls. When I asked Yamada,[9] a third-generation Nishijin-based *obi* manufacturer, about hearing loss, he told me that the weavers "get used to" the noise and said that babies that grow up having been surrounded by the noise while in the womb only cry when the looms stop (Hall 2014: 174). These health risks and the work environment's effect on the senses play a role in discouraging younger people from entering the weaving industry. Murayama Yūzō, now a professor at Doshisha University Business School and director of the school's Innovative Globalization of Kyoto's Heritage Industries program, grew up in a Nishijin textile making family. His father was a manufacturer, producing dark indigo summer crepe, and he described his family home as "a kind of factory—behind there were two or three textile machines so I kind of lived with those machines." He told me he decided not to take over his family's business, citing the following reasons: "I looked at my mother working and she had such hardship. She had to sit down every day and do really small things. I didn't like that. I helped her to do that kind of detailed work but I didn't want to do that kind thing for good" (personal interview September 18, 2012. Professor Murayama's family business shut down in the 1970s because neither he nor his brother wanted to do that kind of work.

Digital Loom

Manufacturers started to use digital looms in the 1980s (Hareven 2002). A digital loom is a power loom in which the jacquard design component has been computerized (Hall 2015: 64). The designs are put onto a 3.5 inch floppy disk (eliminating the need for punch cards) that is placed in a disk drive attached to the power loom. Thus follows the design as dictated by the computer data. It is notable that the ICT used in digital weaving is stuck somewhere in the 1990s rather than using a USB drive or Wi-Fi connection to transmit information. Yamada explained that it is too expensive to change the looms to a more current technology, especially when he uses over thirty looms. He also believes that the weavers are too old to understand how to use USB drives but I was unable to verify his claim. The youngest weavers Yamada employs are 45 years old, and the oldest are 80 years old, with the average age being between 60 and 70 years old.

Yamada produces *mofuku obi* (mourning *obi*) and more casual and colorful *fukuro obi* at his Nishijin-based company (ibid.). His company does not dye thread or fabric, but designs and coordinates weavers in the Tango Peninsula to produce the *obi.* Designs are done on a computer in-house and the digital blueprint chart is now sent via e-mail attachment (until January 2013 the designers posted their designs to the weavers on a 3.5-inch floppy disk but designers must now seek new alternatives as the floppy disk manufacturer ceased production—an issue bound to have a large impact considering his comments above). Yamada said that only 20 percent of *hataya* (weavers) currently use this method (ibid.: 64–5). He said that to outsource the designs to a *monya-san* (*obi* pattern designer) would cost between 30,000 and 50,000 yen per design but creating designs in-house using e-design is "free"—it only requires time (ibid.: 65). His son creates the designs using Adobe Photoshop—it takes him about five or six hours per design. So the traditional *obi hataya* are limited financially in the number of different designs they can produce[10] but Yamada can make hundreds of different designs (ibid.). And the weavers Yamada employs use digital looms so the production time is much faster than traditional methods—about two to three days as opposed to two to three months (ibid.). (Visit https://www.youtube.com/watch?v=qTMoy7KU4ZY&amp=&feature=youtu.be to view and hear a digital loom in action.)

The weaver at the Nishijin Ori Kōgei Bijutsukan factory uses a digital loom to weave *maru-obi* (a double-sided *obi*, which is one thick strip of cloth that will be folded down the center). The multiple shuttles are operated by a power source and the jacquard pattern is computerized so the weaver's first task is to check that the machine is turned on and operating correctly. Aside from that she must also prepare all of the weft threads for the shuttles by winding them onto spools (a machine is used for this), thread the loom warp threads that involves thousands of silk threads that are thinner than human hair, rethread shuttles when they run out of thread, ensure the new shuttle thread is taken into the weaving pattern, and maintain the machine. I asked her about working conditions and if they had changed over the forty-nine years that she has been weaving.

> Now I work Monday to Friday from 9.00 am to 5.00 pm and get public holidays off, but in the past I worked longer hours and had less days off. The busiest period was about 30 years ago, during the bubble economy. Now the neighbourhood is quiet compared to then—Nishijin was noisy with the sound of weaving machines. The machine is so noisy! My hearing has become worse because of it. All of the weavers using these machines have bad hearing and suffer from hearing loss. And the factory is hot in summer and very cold in winter. Young people do not want to do this kind of work—it is noisy and hard and the demand for kimono is decreasing. The machine drips oil on me, staining my clothes so it is dirty work and I do not get to wear the beautiful things that I make. The women at the gallery [that displays her goods] are wearing beautiful kimono, aren't they? But I don't have a chance to wear them. (Hall 2014: 175)

Considering the conditions and assembly line-like environment of her job—including social alienation and boredom that must result from doing repetitive tasks—the weaver's resentment is not unexpected. She stands all day, overseeing the operation of the machine, the noise of which continues with few breaks during work hours (visit https://www.youtube.com/watch?v=mCm33 wTA2uc&feature=youtu.be to see and hear her digital loom in operation). Her criticism serves as a contemporary example of similar resentments by workers (often expressed in song) of the late nineteenth century (Tsurumi 1990).[11]

As we have seen, to create a pattern or design using weaving is a complicated process. It traditionally involved many skilled artisans in the production process to create the pattern, transfer it to a blueprint chart, string the loom with the correct colors, and for the weaver to keep track of exactly when to insert new colored threads in the weft. Dyeing, although potentially not as precise depending on the technique used, made the process of transferring pattern to fabric much more direct.

Shiborizome

Shiborizome (tie-dyeing), a technique that has existed for over a thousand years in Japan, is the Japanese collective term for all forms of dye-resist using stitching, pleating, binding, folding, clamping, twisting, or wrapping to create patterns across the fabric (Hall 2015: 66). There are various kinds of shibori, for example: itajime shibori, a shaped-resist technique made by sandwiching cloth between two pieces of wood; nui shibori, in which a running stitch is used to gather the cloth; and *kumo* (spider) *shibori*, whereby cloth is pinched and bound in sections, resulting in spiderweb-like designs (ibid.). *Kanoko shibori* (literally "fawn-spot tie-dyeing," because the tiny tie-dyed dots are said to look like the spots on a fawn's back) is the most revered form of *shibori* in Japan (ibid.). It is the most difficult form of *shibori* because minute sections of cloth must be tied in rows, each one even and tight (ibid.).

At the Kyoto Shibori Museum (Kyoto Shibori Kōgeikan) I learned *itajime shibori* using woodblock shapes and pinching folded silk gauze fabric between them before dyeing. First, I folded the fabric in half and then back on itself, then again, like an "accordion" into a triangular shape. I put a wooden heart-shaped block on each side and clamped it (estimating where exactly to put the other block). Once it was folded and clamped, the material was dipped into the dye for three seconds at a time. I checked the color and penetration by pulling open the leaves a little and then redipped it if necessary. In a two-dye project that created a third color, I did the blue dye first, then undid the clamp and moved the wooden block (at this point the fabric had a white heart with blue surround) so that it overlapped the original heart, re-clamped it, and dyed it red, washing it in water after each dip. The parts of the cloth that had been exposed to both dyes became purple. I re-dipped one of the corners into red dye and the other corner into the blue dye for further depth of color. Then, the fabric was washed and dried leaving a subtle pattern in pale shades.

Yoshioka Kenji, the manager at the Shibori Kōgeikan, explained the process of making a kimono using *shibori* methods. First a person does a sketch, knowing the available techniques. Then a stencil of it is made and holes punched out so that *aobana*, a fugitive (or nonpermanent) blue dye made from the dayflower (*Commelina Communis*—also known as spiderwort) or *tsuyukusa* in Japanese, can be used to transfer the pattern onto the silk. The *aobana* will later be washed out of the material. After that it is tied according to the pattern—it can be stitched around (to make, e.g., a flower), gathered and pulled tight, and the resulting bulb covered in plastic and tied (*bōshi shibori*, which results in the desired shape having an undyed center), or pinched and tied, or gathered in lines to create a rippled effect. Several people will be involved in making one kimono, and artisans specialize in each *shibori* technique.

On a second visit to the Kyoto Shibori Kōgeikan, Tanigaki, a *shibori* artisan and teacher working at the museum taught me *kumo shibori*, a technique used to create a spiderweb-like pattern. The shapes had already been threaded and some of the more complicated sections had already been tied for me. Tanigaki explained that the outcome would be affected depending on how the fabric was wound and gathered, and each piece of *shibori* was influenced by the skill and creativity of the artisan. For this *shibori* I used the tool as well—a metal loop on a wooden base that the artisan sits on to keep it steady, and hooks the ends of the threads onto so it can be pulled tight. I started by taking a shape, already marked on the fabric by threads, pulled the ends of the threads through the hook, then smoothing out the shape, pinching the halfway point with my left fingers and gathering the fabric back onto that. Next, I had to select the top thread and release it, pulling it all the way through so that the fabric gathered was at one end of the thread. Then I wound a section of fabric in toward the hook, making it go around the fabric twice at the base of the design, then slowly winding it along so that it spiraled up and formed a cone. Near the top, Tanigaki showed me the technique of pinching the finger and thumb of my right hand, placing it on the thread and pushing down; after looping the thread around, I could put my pinched fingers on the top of the cone and the thread would tie off on it. I did that for each flower-shape. Then to create the lines of dots in the design, I had to use both hands to gather the fabric back onto itself so it concertinaed along the thread, pulled the little material tag down onto it, and release one thread to tie it off once around and pull it down well, angling the material slightly away from me to get it tight, then wrapping it twice around (visit https://www.youtube.com/watch?v=cgKEIsVBcz8&feature=youtu.be for Tanigaki demonstrating this whole process using the *shibori* tool). Once all of the tying was complete, the whole piece of material went into warm water to ensure that the dye would take evenly (*jire*), before being immersed into the dye vat. It had to be moved and swirled around in the dye vat for ten minutes before it was rinsed and dried. The threads could then be removed to reveal the completed piece. The fabric is usually steam ironed (*yunoshi*) as the final process but this does not completely flatten the fabric—there will still be small bumps where the fabric was bound tightly, creating a texture unique to *shiborizome* (Figure 2.8a–d).

Tabata Kazuki does a range of *shibori* in his home workshop in the southwest of Kyoto, including *Kyō-kanoko shibori*, *itajime shibori*, *bōshi shibori*, and *nui shibori*. In his *tatami*-matted workroom on the second floor there is a bench fixed to the end wall with hooks that are used to secure the thread for tying. Tabata learned *shibori* from observing his father and is now certified by METI as a traditional craft artisan (Hall 2015: 67). He dyes cloth using *Kyō-kanoko shibori*

Figure 2.8a Silk tied for dyeing. Photo: Jenny Hall.

Figure 2.8b The cone-shaped ties of *kumo shibori*. Photo: Jenny Hall.

Figure 2.8c The piece of *shibori* after dyeing but before the ties have been removed. Photo: Jenny Hall.

Figure 2.8d The completed piece of *shibori*. Photo: Jenny Hall.

(his main specialty) for traditional apparel like kimono and *yukata* (ibid.). He told me that to complete the fabric for one kimono using this method takes two hundred thousand ties (Figure 2.9a and b).[12]

He also works for contemporary apparel manufacturers such as design studio Sou Sou. The products he dyes for Sou Sou are important examples of *wafuku* designed for contemporary lifestyles. They include Sou Sou's *tenugui* (cotton hand towels), "flying squirrel" caplets, t-shirts, and *furoshiki* (wrapping cloth) bags (ibid.). He ties the fabric in his workroom and dyes it by hand in his backyard. Tabata told me that the chemical dyes smell unpleasant and sometimes attract

Figure 2.9a An example of Tabata's *kanoko shibori*, 2012. Video still: Jenny Hall.

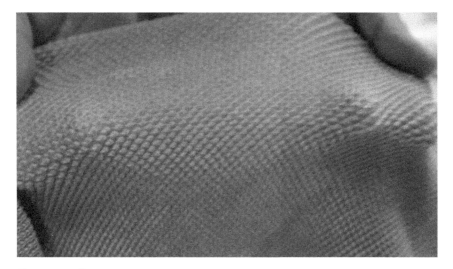

Figure 2.9b Tabata's *kanoko shibori* stretched to show the tiny dots. Video still: Jenny Hall.

mosquitoes. His neighbors complain about this and also about the noise he makes with his mallet when he is tightening ties. He cannot do it late at night, and he also pointed out that older artisans struggle with this kind of work because it is physically demanding and labor-intensive (Hall 2015: 68). He must dye in all weather, even if it is very cold, including washing the material, and he often gets callouses on his hands from tying, especially if he does many in one day or if the fabric is thick, such as material used for winter clothing. He often posts on his Facebook page that he has just completed tying a batch of fabric, and this could amount to several thousand ties for one order.

In contrast, Katayama Kazuo designs and sells *shibori*-dyed scarves and accessories with a very different feel at his shop, Katayama Bunzaburo Shōten (Figure 2.10). He has been designing *shibori* for ten years but does not do the *shibori* himself—rather, he outsources the tying to China, and then the items are shipped back to Kyoto for dyeing (Hall 2015: 68). His products are either silk or polyester; he began producing the latter because he said customers insisted they wanted to be able to wash them. His adaptation of *shibori* exaggerates the tying aspect of the technique and the pieces are not steam ironed.

The result is three-dimensional sculptural works and Katayama uses these sculptural characteristics to design scarves, necklaces, bracelets, lampshades, and some clothing (ibid.). When asked what the difference between Japanese and cheaper Chinese *kanoko shibori* was, Tabata said it was to do with the uniformity of the ties, the rows, and the height of each knot. According to The Cultural Foundation for Promoting the National Costume of Japan website (Minzoku Ishō Bunka Fukyū Kyōkai[13]), most of the tying work for *kanoko shibori* is done in Korea today because of a skills shortage in Japan (2014a: n.p.) but this outsourcing appears to be shifting to China. The globalization aspect of Kyoto textile production will be examined in more detail in Chapter Five.

Figure 2.10 A *shibori* scarf from Katayama Bunzaburo Shōten, 2012. Design © Bunzaburo. Photo: Jenny Hall. First published in *New Voices in Japanese Studies*, Vol. 7, 2015 (The Japan Foundation, Sydney).

Tsujigahana

Tsujigahana (meaning the "intersection of flowers") originated from the middle of the Muromachi period (1338–1573) and was practiced until the beginning of the Edo period (seventeenth century) before dying out completely due to an increase in popularity of other techniques, in particular *yūzen* which proved simpler and allowed more freedom of expression as well as more control over the final result. There is controversy about the definition and the origin of the term *tsujigahana*. Little is known about the artisans who created it and the techniques are shrouded in mystery because there is almost no recorded information about them. However, according to my informant Fukumura (discussed below) in the postwar period, artisan Kubota Itchiku, known as Itchiku (1917–2003) decided to revive *tsujigahana*. Because of the lack of information, Itchiku struggled to recreate the techniques. For example, *nerinuki*, the fabric originally used for *tsujigahana*, was no longer being woven so he substituted *chirimen*, and he used synthetic dyes rather than natural. Eventually he developed his own version of the technique and dubbed it "Itchiku Tsujigahana"; it is this that is largely practiced today. *Shiborizome* forms the basis of the technique, onto which further details are painted, embroidered, or impressed with gold or silver foil. Often various colors were used and the technique is distinguishable by its pictorial quality. Although few in number, archival examples of *tsujigahana kosode* (*kosode* is the earlier term for what is now kimono) still exist, such as those worn by Toyotomi Hideyoshi, Tokugawa Ieyasu, and Oda Nobunaga, as well as their relatives.

Fukumura Takeshi (32) and his father Hirotoshi (70) are contemporary *tsujigahana* artisans, working under the brand name E-Shibori-An. They work from their house in northeastern Kyoto, where they receive customers and take their orders. Their customers are mainly women in their 50s and 60s who have the time and money to spend on kimono, and who are often practitioners of *ikebana* or *cha no yu* (tea ceremony). Hirotoshi learned *tsujigahana* from his neighbor, artisan Ogura Kensuke, or "Tsujigahana Kensuke" as he became known. Ogura Kensuke was from a *yūzen*-dyeing family dating back to the Meiji era. Kensuke's son, Atsushi, is a well-known *tsujigahana* artisan, reproducing dyed cultural assets such as Tokugawa Ieyasu's *kosode*, as well as creating kimono.

Fukumura Takeshi also learned *tsujigahana* from his father. He claimed that only two or three people can do the classical form of the technique, and about ten people can do the Ogura-family version that he and his father practice. He told me, "there is fake-looking *tsujigahana* done by inkjet or other methods, but there are very few people who can do the real thing" (personal interview November 7, 2012). He translated the term as "*michi no hana*" (street of flowers) and imagined it as like entering an area of natural beauty surrounded by cherry blossom, plum blossom, chrysanthemums, or autumn leaves. These are the main motifs of *tsujigahana*, demonstrated by Fukumura's *sakura* kimono (Figure 2.11). He showed me a photograph taken on his mobile phone of flowers cascading

Figure 2.11 Fukumura Takeshi's *sakura* kimono, 2012. Design © Fukumura Takeshi. Photo: Jenny Hall.

Figure 2.12 Fukumura Takeshi's "born to be wild" kimono using *arashi shibori*, 2012. Design © Fukumura Takeshi. Photo: Jenny Hall.

down a wall near his home that he planned to use for his next design. But nature is not the only influence on his designs—he considers the different techniques available and their effects, as well as the specific characteristics of *shibori*. Fukumura showed me a kimono that he described using English as "born to be wild," utilizing the technique of *arashi shibori* (the fabric is wrapped around a pole bound with string, and compressed) (Figure 2.12). He said *shibori* is soft and fluffy rather than precise and delineated like *yūzen.* But like *yūzen* or other methods, he must consider the "rules" of kimono design. For example, there are particular points on the kimono such as the front bottom right-hand side of the fabric, or the center of the kimono at the wearer's waist, which will not be seen so there is no point putting detailed patterns on those sections.

Unlike *yūzen* or *orimono*, *tsujigahana* is primarily done by one individual—there is no division of labor. Fukumura's workspace is a small area near the entrance to his home (Figure 2.13). The surrounding suburb is quiet and semirural, and the pace of the interview gave an indication of the pace of his work—a contrast to the noise and relative speed of the power weaving or digital *yūzen* industries.

Yūzen

In the late seventeenth century, fan artist Miyazaki Yūzen pioneered what has become known as *yūzen* (The Japan Craft Forum 1996: 74). His technique involved hand painting and using dye-resist paste on silk to create designs and color the background of the fabric (Hall 2018b: 15). The basic method of *yūzen* dyeing involves a technique called *itome-nori*, in which a paste made from glutinous rice is piped onto the fabric using a conical tube (*tsutsu*). The design is traced onto the fabric with the paste, the fine lines containing any dye applied to the area within them, while leaving the fine lines themselves undyed. An example of this hand-painted method, Figure 2.14, by young artisan, Saeki Akihiko, who

Figure 2.13 Fukumura Takeshi's workspace, 2012. Photo: Jenny Hall.

Figure 2.14 An example of *yūzen* before the paste resist has been washed off, by Saeki Akihiko, 2012. Design © Saeki Akihiko. Photo: Jenny Hall. First published in *Thresholds 42: Human*, p. 181 (2014).

dyes kimono for geisha and *maiko*, shows the fabric before the paste has been washed off. Nowadays, "*yūzen*" is used to encompass this hand-painted form, known as *tegaki yūzen* (or freehand *yūzen*), as well as *kata yūzen* (or *katazome*), a stencil-based paste-resist method[14] of dyeing that was developed in 1881 (The Japan Craft Forum 1996: 74). *Yūzen* became a leading method of dyeing kimono because it "was a more painterly technique than earlier methods of dyeing, and it provided the technical means to create wonderfully detailed pictorial themes. With *yūzen* came unabridged freedom of expression in kosode design and execution" (Dalby 2001: 43).

There were other factors that led to an increase in the popularity of *yūzen* as a technique. Social shifts from the era of the warrior to that of the merchant-artisan early in the Edo period caused a growth of the consumerist mentality toward clothing as fashion (ibid.: 42). This resulted in a new aesthetic and a new way of thinking about design whereby the kimono was "treated as a canvas for a single bold subject, writ large and asymmetrically placed, sweeping diagonally from shoulder across sleeve and down to hem" (ibid.: 43). As a result, authorities attempted to restrict the degree of luxury allowed among the lower classes, and *yūzen* was deemed by authorities less ostentatious (and therefore legal) than techniques such as labor-consuming embroidery (*shishu*) or *kanoko shibori*. A similar effect to *kanoko shibori* could be obtained by painting the small dots rather than tying each knot. However, *Kyō-yūzen* is labor-intensive, especially by contemporary standards, and it is a method that takes a long time to master. Kameda Kazuaki laments that as his craftsmen approach retirement age, there are few that have the skills to replace them.

There are two main styles of *yūzen*—*Kyō-yūzen* and *Kaga-yūzen*. *Kyō-yūzen* is *yūzen* in the Kyoto style—patterns are symbolic and idealized rather than realistic, and generally bright colors are used. *Kaga-yūzen,* from Kanazawa city in Ishikawa Prefecture, is more naturalistic, to the point where decay and insect damage is depicted on flowers and leaves (The Japan Craft Forum 1996: 72). *Kaga-yūzen* typically uses dark red, indigo, and purple as base colors (ibid.). Although Miyazaki Yūzen invented the *yūzen* process in Kyoto and then introduced it to Kanazawa where he spent his final years, the styles diverged. This divergence is likely to have occurred because of the influence of a contemporary of Miyazaki, the Kyoto painter, Ogata Kōrin (1658–1716). Ogata Kōrin was a painter of the famous Rinpa school (named after him—*rin* from Kōrin and *ha* from "school") who broke from tradition by developing his own distinctive style; he used simple highly idealized forms and disregarded realism (Caruso 2012: 3). Even designers today, such as digital *yūzen* artisan Kawabe Yūnosuke mentioned above, cite Ogata Kōrin as an influence on their work and consider Rinpa patterns the standard classics in Japanese design.

Tegaki Yūzen

As explained by *tegaki yūzen* master Kobayashi Shumei, most kimono-makers do not complete the whole process of *tegaki yūzen* alone—as with traditional woodblock printing (*ukiyo-e*), it is very labor-intensive and takes several days, so specialists in the various techniques of design, paste-application, and steaming execute their part of the process. The process begins with a design, usually inspired by a figure or an idea in nature that is drawn by a specialist sketch artist (*shitae-shi*). It is then applied freehand by a specialist in creating the outline (*sobyōkishi*) onto the fabric with a thin brush using the nonpermanent dye, *aobana* (mentioned above), that will later be washed out of the material (see Figure 2.15a–d).

Meanwhile, the fabric is refined using an agent such as soda ash to prepare it for the dyeing process. Soda ash changes the pH to activate the fiber molecules, making the dye connect permanently to the fiber. For silk, it is first soaked in warm water to soften the sericin, a protein in the silk. Then the silk is boiled in the

Figure 2.15a A pattern drawn onto silk with *aobana* that will be washed out after dyeing. Artisan: Kobayashi Shumei (2011). Photo: Jenny Hall.

Figure 2.15b Silk stretched taut using narrow bamboo dowels (*shinshi*). Photo: Jenny Hall.

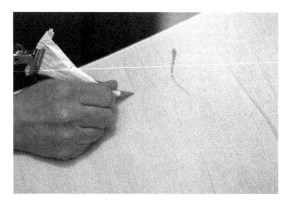

Figure 2.15c A *tsutsu*, used to pipe on the paste resist. Photo: Jenny Hall. First published in *Fashion Theory*, Vol. 22:3, pp. 283–307 (2018), https://doi.org/10.1080/13627 04X.2017.1319175.

Figure 2.15d Dye blending techniques. Artisan: Kobayashi Shumei (2011). Photo: Jenny Hall.

soda ash solution for two to three hours, after which it is washed and rinsed a few times before drying. For wool, hemp, or cotton, the temperature is adjusted accordingly. Once the silk has been dried and ironed, it is stretched taut using narrow bamboo dowels (*shinshi*) and tensioned on a freestanding frame, ready for the designer to sketch on the pattern. The sketch will serve as a guide for applying the rice-paste resist.

The paste (*tsutsunori*) is made of glutinous rice powder mixed with rice bran, salt, and water. The amount of each depends on the fabric type, but also on season and climate. The salt is increased for higher humidity so the quantities depend on the time of year and the geographical area. Once combined, the mixture is kneaded until it is the "consistency similar to that of an earlobe" (Kobayashi 2011: 3); notably, I have also heard this expression used during a *soba*-noodle making class in Japan, demonstrating the crossover sensuality between cooking and dyeing. The dough is then steamed for one to five hours, depending on the type and temperature of the heat source, and kneaded again. Slaked lime and sappanwood extract is added so that the paste will be more visible on the silk. The paste is also strained to remove any lumps and rough particles, to ensure smooth application.

A specialist in the application of rice paste (*noriokishi*) traces over the designer's *aobana* sketch on the fabric, applying fine lines using the cone-shaped *tsutsu*, which is similar to a piping bag used for decorating cakes. Today, paste is usually only applied to one side of the fabric, but for thicker fabric such as hemp, it might be necessary to apply it to both sides. The paste resist prevents different dye colors from running into each other.

Traditionally, the use of natural pigments meant that they needed to be applied twenty to thirty times on both sides of the fabric (called *hikizome*) so the paste would also need to be applied on both sides. Nowadays the use of more resistant chemical dyes eliminates this necessity. Depending on the size of the fabric, the type of material, and the intricacy of the design, this might take several hours or days. Sawdust is sprinkled on the paste to encourage drying. Once the paste is completely dry, a soybean juice (*gōjiru*) mixture (also referred to as soybean milk) is applied to stabilize and smooth the paste prior to coloring. This process is called *ji-ire*. It is applied using a wide brush, to both sides of the fabric.

When the fabric is again dry, the dyeing (*irosashi*) begins. Quantities of each chemical dye and pigment are mixed, ensuring there is enough in quantity for the whole of the fabric. Some of the colors can be watered down for lighter shades. Color is applied by a specialist in dye application (*hikizome-shi*) within the confines of the rice-paste pattern using a variety of brushes, from very fine to wide, and colors can be graduated (*bokashi*) using careful brushstrokes and blending.

Once the color has been applied, it must be set using a mordant before steaming (*nakamushi*) to fix the dye. Depending on the design, the fabric may need to be steamed once, or a few times. If the whole fabric is colored in one application, then it only needs to be steamed once (*honmushi*). After steaming, the dyed sections can be covered with paste to protect them (*fusenori oki*) when applying more colors or the background color. If this is necessary, then when the paste is dry, *ji-ire* must be repeated before applying more color dye. Soybean juice, or *funori* paste (made from seaweed) can be used for *ji-ire*.

The background is dyed using a wide brush and swift movements (*jizome*). Natural dyes may need to be applied over thirty times to achieve the desired depth of color, but chemical dyes usually only need one or two applications. At last, the fabric is given a final steam (*honmushi*), to fix the dye. Steaming is one of the most important parts of the process, not only for fixing the colors, but for their durability. The amount of time the fabric should be in the steamer varies and depends on the type of fabric, the dye used, and the quality of the steamer. The paste is then washed off the fabric using a neutral detergent and water. To further prevent the dye from fading, a fixing agent is used before washing the fabric again.

Kata Yūzen

Kata yūzen, an abbreviation of katagami (paper pattern) and yūzen zome (dye) (also known as katazome), another paste-resist method, is a subgenre of yūzen and was developed by Kyoto artisan Hirose Jisuke (1822–1890) in the late nineteenth century (Milhaupt 2014: 80). Kata yūzen employs the use of a stencil rather than a tsutsu to apply the paste, thereby facilitating multiple copies of the pattern at a faster pace. The ability to replicate patterns rejuvenated kimono design, and reduced production costs also meant that middle-class women could afford higher quality kimono (Hall 2018a: 294).

Katagami stencils must be strong and durable because the rice-paste resist will be pushed through them over and over again. They are made with a kind of washi composed of layered kōfōzo (mulberry paper) that has been treated using persimmon tannin and then smoked. This makes the paper strong, waterproof, and preserves it, the persimmon tannin acting as a laminate that allows the stencil to withstand the wet rice paste and to be washed and reused. The design is transferred onto the paper and cut out using knives and punches. Thinner papers are used for more delicate designs, and thicker for bold designs applied to coarse fabrics. For printing runs of fabric the stencils are stabilized by attaching them to a fine silk net, which is stretched onto a frame. There must be a separate stencil for each color applied. Synthetic dyes can be mixed with the rice paste to dye colors and to resist other dyes.

The color combinations for each of the patterns are selected from contemporary dye pigments—this can involve up to twenty different colors and is crucial for the success of the design. The design team then pass their color schema, along with the amount of material required, to the dye artisan who must plan the dyeing sequence and calculate the amount of dye to make. If it is a complex pattern, all of the dyes must be mixed before starting the dyeing process because it will be almost impossible to recreate the same shade again. The pigment's true color (i.e., its resulting color at the end of the process) must be ascertained and mixed with glue before it can be applied according to the color scheme chart. Mixing the dyes takes considerable specialist skill, and each powdered pigment is carefully weighed out and mixed in a beaker—even a small disparity of a few grams can alter the resulting color and potentially waste tens of meters of fabric. Each bucket of dye is coded because there may be several dozen buckets of dye in the dye-mixing room, and, even to a trained eye, the exact color is not always distinguishable in its liquid form (see Figure 2.16).

Before the artisans can begin applying the dye, they check the stencil for anomalies using a special backlight (Figure 2.17). The stencil screen is made of

Figure 2.16 Coded buckets of dye at the Kamedatomi factory. Photo: Jenny Hall. First published in *Fashion Theory*, Vol. 22:3, pp. 283–307 (2018), https://doi.org/10.1080/136 2704X.2017.1319175.

Figure 2.17 A Kamedatomi artisan checking a stencil for anomalies prior to dyeing. Photo: Jenny Hall.

a piece of porous, finely woven fabric called "mesh," stretched over a frame of aluminum. If no repairs are needed, the artisan begins the process of dyeing, laying the stencil on the first section of the fabric (which is laid out on a long wooden board called a *nassendai*), and applying the first color according to the chart. Because the dye mixture is thick, a squeegee rather than a brush is used to move the dye across the stencil, forcing the dye into the mesh of the fabric (Figure 2.18). After one dye is applied to one section, the artisan moves the

Figure 2.18 An artisan applying the dye with a squeegee at the Kamedatomi factory. Photo: Jenny Hall.

stencil along and slots it into place to apply the same color to the next section, traversing the factory while moving down the length of the fabric. Once the first color has been applied, the process starts again for the next color in the schema. When the fabric has been completely dyed it is then steamed to set the dye, and washed, ready for sewing.

The *kata yūzen* process was automated in the Meiji period with the introduction of Adam Parkinson's textile printing machine (invented in 1785), which enabled up to six colors to be applied onto the fabric at the same time through the use of rollers (Mori 2012: 124). With roller printing, the design is engraved onto a copper plate roll and reactive dye (*nassen nori*) is applied along the plate. The fabric is passed across the plate mechanically and six plates could be connected for different colors. Roller printing suits repeat patterns and automates some of the dyeing steps but it still has its limitations; namely, machine printing (*kikai nassen*) can print no more than twelve colors, and it cannot print connected designs over seams, which is a design feature often utilized in making kimono.

Kyō-yūzen production peaked in 1976, followed by a rapid decline (Mori 2012: 124). Although the *kata yūzen* process enables production of kimono fabric on a faster scale than previously existing techniques, it remains a labor-intensive method. It is physically demanding and the working conditions are hard, which are two reasons the younger generations are reluctant to learn the craft. Another reason is the advent of an alternative that is physically far easier and utilizes modern and familiar technology—digital *yūzen.*

Digital *Yūzen*

Since 2000, digital *yūzen* has provided designers with ease of design and delivery. There are three key components in digital textile printing systems: the printer, the software, and the ink. Within these are subcomponents such as the garment mounting system, color management, and workflow management. The artisan can create their design on a computer, and using fabric that has a special backing to maintain its shape and stiffness, print it immediately. As mentioned above, I interviewed three individuals utilizing digital *yūzen* during fieldwork: Mori Makoto, Kawabe Yūnosuke, and Takahashi Seisuke. While these designers still refer to their craft as "*yūzen*"—Kawabe called it "digital *yūzen*" while Mori called it "inkjet *yūzen*"—this method eliminates many of the processes of traditional *yūzen* as can be seen in Mori Makoto's diagram below (Diagram 2.3); they merely design, print, steam, and iron the fabric.

Mori's diagram gives a comparison of the processes of *tegaki yūzen*, *kata yūzen*, *kikai nassen* (machine printing), and inkjet *yūzen*. After the design stage, the first three methods must create a way to output the design onto the fabric (the pre-processing section), either by tracing it using *nori* paste or using stencils. Then each color has to be laid down separately with the ground color last, before

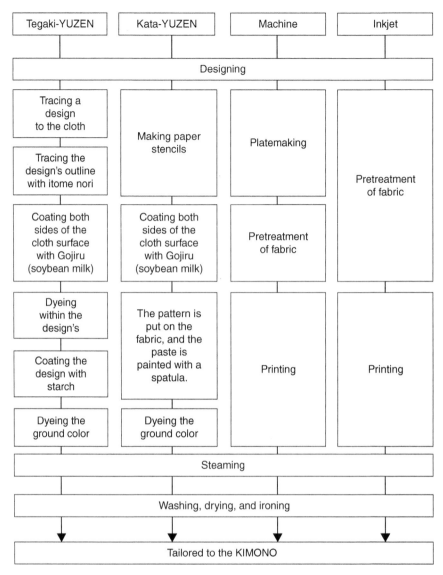

Diagram 2.3 Production process comparing traditional *yūzen* and digital *yūzen*.
Source: First published in Mori (2012: 117–34, 126) (reproduced with the kind permission of Mori Makoto).

steaming, washing, and ironing (the post-processing section). These steps are done by separate specialists, whereas for digital *yūzen* one designer can complete all processes up to the steaming stage. Digital *yūzen* designers can view fabric samples at the click of a mouse, or make alterations to it before producing a single meter or hundreds of meters whenever they want (Hall 2018a: 296). Inkjet sampling gives the designer direct control over the appearance of the design on fabric, without reinterpretation by other artisans. Currently inkjet printing has a relatively slow production speed, approximately 12 meters per hour (George et al. 2006).

As an example of digital *yūzen* design, I interviewed Mori Makoto, a young (he was 26 years old in 2012) kimono designer based in Kami-Katsura, to the west of Kyoto. He mainly designs *furisode*, long-sleeved formal kimono worn for the coming-of-age ceremony, for a wholesale company called D&A Yamabishi. Mori's workplace was on the second floor of a two-storey house, the ground floor of which accommodated another kimono-making company that was using airbrushes and stencils to create their designs. Mori views his work as having three core aspects: creating CG (computer graphics) kimono design, processing the designs on fabric using inkjet printing, and the creation of doll-sized kimono for advertising purposes. Mori said there are a number of advantages to using CG and inkjet printing (some of which have been mentioned above): sizing of elements or color schemes can be easily and quickly changed to suit customer tastes, the same patterns can be replicated exactly, and samples can be printed at the click of a button (Figure 2.19). Mori also pointed out that "*bokashi* (graduated color) is very difficult to do using *kata yūzen* or silkscreen—you can't repeat the same thing, but with the inkjet you can, the same way, it's not a problem" (an example of this can be seen with the purple flowers in Figure 2.19). But for this and other aspects of kimono design, the designer needs to have a thorough understanding of traditional kimono design, in particular what elements can be combined, the sections of a kimono that will be most visible when the garment is worn, and how to create balance between the elements. Mori is very

Figure 2.19 Mori Makoto's computer showing a section of one of his kimono designs. Design © Mori Makoto. Video still: Jenny Hall.

conscious of this and studies books and archival kimono catalogs to help him more fully understand traditional design concepts. He told me that because he is young he is more in tune with contemporary color trends but aims for a balance between traditional and contemporary sensitivities.

Mori told me he decided to use inkjet printing over traditional techniques because the use of traditional techniques is declining. One reason he gave for this decline is that the university students studying the arts are mostly women (men study architecture, but graphic design and art students are mostly women).[15] It takes ten years to acquire the traditional craft skills but women in their 20s get married and have children so it is hard for them to get enough experience to master the traditional techniques, then they do not continue practicing them, leaving a shortage of young people in these industries.

Although there appear to be many advantages to digital *yūzen*, Mori also recognized a difference between it and traditional methods. He told me, "Of course I can print a really complicated design but even if I can do the same design and colors as those done using *kata yūzen* or *tegaki yūzen*, I can't replicate a deep feeling" (Hall 2014: 180). This "deep feeling" is linked to the sensory aspects of creating an object discussed in Chapter One whereby the spirit or heart of the artisan is passed into the object through their mastering of *kata*, and "the objects take on a certain density, an emotional value—what might be called a 'presence'" (Baudrillard 1996: 16).[16] Unlike traditional *yūzen*, a digital-*yūzen* artisan can claim sole attribution for their designs but ironically this does not lead to claims that the final product is an embodiment of their spirit. Whereas artisans using traditional techniques see each of their final products as having *kosei* (unique characteristics) because they cannot be exactly reproduced, Mori told me he sees exact replication as a positive feature of his process; if a customer sees one of his designs, he can replicate it exactly for them (Hall 2014: 180). However, there are negative aspects to replication, as he pointed out. For example, to create a pattern like *kanoko shibori* he must scan in sections of handmade *kanoko shibori* because to replicate the dots using the computer would give too uniform an effect (the piece of handmade *shibori* he showed me was made in China) (Figure 2.20). In addition, inkjet printing sprays evenly onto fabric so tends to be "impersonal and plain, which can produce a bland kimono" (Mori 2012: 129). In comparison, *tegaki yūzen* artisans can produce detailed gradations and their brushwork sometimes pools dye on the perimeter of a design near the paste resist, causing bleeding in a way that is unique to that item. In order to recreate such characteristics through inkjet printing, the designer needs to include it in the design intentionally (Mori 2012: 129).

As he noted, Mori's workspace is very similar to a contemporary office, with computers and the constant hum of the inkjet printer (Hall 2015: 70) (visit https://www.youtube.com/watch?v=xolgTYEEuPc to view his workspace). The printer operates independently with little contact from Mori (Figure 2.21), and perhaps it

Figure 2.20 Mori Makoto scans in hand-created *kanoko shibori* (the black section with white circles on the right) rather than using computer graphics to repeat the pattern of dots. Design © Mori Makoto. Photo: Jenny Hall.

Figure 2.21 Mori Makoto's inkjet printer, printing one of his designs, 2012. Design © Mori Makoto. Photo: Jenny Hall. First published in *TAASA Review*, Vol. 27:3, p. 16 (2018).

is this separation, creating a special as well as psychological gap between human and machine that results in a lack of deep feeling between them (Hall 2014: 180). He was keen to point out that digital *yūzen* does not require the division of labor that traditional *yūzen* does (see Diagram 2.4), but he acknowledges that the whole responsibility also falls on him if something does not go well. However, the similarity of his workplace and work skills to that of a graphic designer are more likely to be an enticement for young designers than traditional *yūzen* working conditions (Hall 2015: 70).

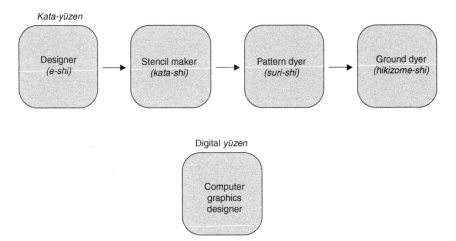

Diagram 2.4 Comparison of artisans required for traditional *kata yūzen* and digital *yūzen*. Adapted from a diagram by Mori Makoto (reproduced with the kind permission of Mori Makoto). This diagram is an extremely simplified version of the process, as it does not include other principle artisans such as the specialist in dye mixing.

Kawabe Yūnosuke formed his company, Japan Style System, in the late 1990s. His father, Zenji, is recognized as an Exceptional Artisan of *tegaki yūzen* by the governor of Kyoto Prefecture (Dickens 2012: 109) and was working at the Nishijin Textile Center in 2012. Inspired by posters for the 1976 Montreal Olympics, initially Yūnosuke decided not to follow his father. Instead he studied graphic design and worked in advertising. However, in 1988 he returned home to help in his father's studio and started learning *tegaki yūzen.* Dissatisfied with the medium of traditional *yūzen*, Yūnosuke experimented with alternatives, combining his knowledge of graphic arts with his knowledge of kimono. Since then, he has designed kimono but also a variety of more contemporary items such as clocks, cushions, chairs, and the official swimsuits of the Japanese synchronized swim team for the Athens Olympics (Figure 2.22). An area of distinction for *yūzen* studios is color, with combinations and intensities of color rendering artisans or studios identifiable, as mentioned above. Yūnosuke feels that his inheritance of design techniques from his father is crucial to his success as a digital *yūzen* artisan. He told me, "For a child growing up in a musician's house, sound is important. Inside the womb, they can hear sounds. Then naturally they get lots of information about music. In my case, from childhood, I was surrounded by kimono, so I learnt what colors to use … the family business is my backbone" (personal interview October 9, 2012). This narrative of transmission of techniques from generation to generation is important for providing legitimacy to the concept of tradition as well as providing

Figure 2.22 The official swimsuits of the Japanese synchronized swim team for the Athens Olympics, designed by Kawabe Yūnosuke. Fabric design © Kawabe Yūnosuke. Photo: Jenny Hall.

Figure 2.23 Some of the original designs on which Seisuke88 have based their patterns. Video still: Jenny Hall.

legitimacy for innovative techniques such as digital *yūzen*. This is discussed further in Chapter Five.

The Seisuke88 brand also creates digital *yūzen* products. Seisuke88 was created by Takahashi Seisuke, current president of Takahashi Rensen Co. Ltd., which is one of the largest fabric finishing companies in Kyoto. After discovering a warehouse of about two thousand Meiji-era kimono designs (Figure 2.23), Takahashi was inspired to establish his own brand of bags and accessories based on these designs (Figure 2.24), and he makes them in a section of the finishing factory. In-house designers copy the original patterns, resize the elements, and select colors using computer technology, and then print them out onto cotton fabric. Takahashi was keen to point out that his company could do all of the production in-house—"*kikaku seizō hanbai no subete*" (planning, manufacture, selling—everything), even the fabric finishing which involves washing, waterproofing, drying, and setting the cloth (personal interview November 2, 2012). The way in which all fabric is finished means that, from a tactile perspective, there is no discernible difference between fabric that has been digitally printed or that has had *yūzen* applied by hand. Takahashi told me that inkjet kimono started about ten years ago and in 2012 constituted 70 percent of the kimono-making market, a figure I have not been able to verify. However, Mori has also stated that inkjet printing "now dominates the contemporary kimono market" (2012: 124).

Figure 2.24 An example of Seisuke88's products. Design © Seisuke88. Photo: Jenny Hall.

Conclusion

This chapter has described the textile production site, in particular the area of Nishijin and the location of the companies I researched in order to provide a sensory picture of how they function in a postindustrial setting. Detailed descriptions of the fabric and fibers, dyes and technologies used in the textile heritage industries illustrate that although some of them, such as indigo-dyeing or the treadle loom, may be from the preindustrial era, they are still used in Kyoto alongside high-tech dyeing, printing, and weaving options. The three case studies in Chapter Three demonstrate how these materials and technologies are used in the production of contemporary apparel. The relationship between historical background, traditional skills, and culture are vital to understanding the sociology of consumption, in this case how artisanal practices inform a product's particular color, design, and, ultimately, meaning. For example, not only do Sou Sou designers see those links as important to appreciating their product, but also that they are crucial for a feeling of satisfaction in both the creator and consumer. Pagong owner, Kameda, also saw this link between creator and consumer as important, commenting on the company's Taishō-era production of kimono fabric for kimono makers, "We dyed fabric every day in our factory but we never really knew what it became after we delivered it. When someone puts their heart into making a product that people are going to use in their everyday life, they want to see the end user interacting with it" (Pagong Kamedatomi Co. 2014). This reference to "heart" or "deep feeling" is a notion mentioned by all three of the companies in the case studies and is a basis for their brand concepts. It plays a part in the authentication of their products and in the cultural construction of Japanese identity through use of "traditional" techniques.

It seems contradictory that more traditional methods of *yūzen* create this deep feeling, even though labor is divided between many individuals. And, conversely, that the production of digital *yūzen* involves a sole creator who is therefore more empowered and has more control over the final product but that this results in a product that somehow lacks this "deep feeling." Kyoto, as the "authentic" source of the Japanese heritage industries, provides not only a valuable example of the complexities of textile production but also an insight into the future of these industries.

3
CASE STUDIES

This book arises from research conducted with more than twenty companies, but in this chapter I provide an in-depth look at how three contemporary apparel companies are utilizing some of the traditional technologies and techniques discussed in Chapter Two in their manufacturing processes. I chose to look at these brands—Pagong, Kyoto Denim, and Sou Sou—in particular because they illustrate a range of methods for dealing with the decline in heritage industries and innovative attempts at keeping these industries alive. They also all suggest in their explanations, both implicitly and explicitly, that they are trying to retain the "essence" or "feeling" of kimono in their products, although what this essence entails differs slightly for each of them. For Kyoto Denim and Pagong, the essence of the kimono represents Japanese techniques, colors, and patterns rather than the shape of a kimono. For Sou Sou, it is about making kimono ride a bicycle; that is, making clothes that are suitable for contemporary life but that exhibit forms and shapes of kimono and other *wafuku*.

Like any other organization, there was a public face (*omote*) and a private face (*ura*) of the companies I researched. This meant that one of the main difficulties I encountered during fieldwork was gaining access to the behind-the-scenes staff members such as those working on the factory floor. Pagong is the only company of the three that carries out the majority of its manufacturing in-house; while owner Kameda Kazuaki permitted me to ask the factory workers questions while they worked, this access never yielded any interviews as they were too busy during my visits. Both Kyoto Denim and Sou Sou outsource production locally.[1] Kyoto Denim manager Miyamoto Kazutomo was reluctant to introduce me to their Kyoto artisans because of his own challenging relationship with them: Kyoto Denim designs require the artisans' know-how and skills but they don't always see the value in the company's innovations. But Kyoto Denim was keen to display its artisans' technical skills to consumers via videos on its website and on the shop walls using digital displays. Sou Sou outsources *shibori* to a Kyoto artisan, Tabata Kazuki (mentioned in the previous chapter), to whom Wakabayashi was happy to introduce me and I interviewed. Sou Sou also uses manufacturing companies that are based in Shiga, Okayama, and Hyogo Prefectures, but I was not able to observe operations in these companies. However, Sou Sou also features images of its factories on its websites and on the walls of its retail shops, although of course it is difficult to ascertain the reality of working conditions from these or from Kyoto Denim's PR images.

The reluctance to introduce me to more senior artisans or any other auxiliary artisans could also be a reflection of consequences of the system of employment. Hareven gives a detailed description of the *chinbata* and *debata* systems that have been prominent in the weaving industry since the Taishō era (2002: 55–68). These systems, whereby the weaver rented the looms from the manufacturer (*chinbata*) or worked from home using their own looms for outside orders (*debata*), differed from the earlier paternalistic *totei* system of live-in apprenticeship. It meant that weavers had "a more precarious relationship with the manufacturer, more prone to fluctuation depending on the amount and frequency of orders they received" (ibid.: 57). Pay was per piece and was negotiated between the weaver and the manufacturer. This resulted in a high level of competition between manufacturers for skilled weavers, and competition among weavers for reliable manufacturers. Thus, there was a high degree of secrecy within the industry about who was working for whom and how much weavers were paid. Although Hareven was talking about the weaving industry in particular, I believe this kind of secretive working culture was pervasive in the textile industry more generally and remains a contributing factor in the reluctance to introduce outsiders to artisans. My interviews with the designers, however, provided enough information to address the question of how their companies are reinventing *wafuku*.

Pagong (Kamedatomi Co. Ltd.)

Background

Pagong is the retail face of the Kamedatomi Company Ltd., first established in 1919 during the Taishō era (1912–25). At that time, the company dyed kimono fabric (woven elsewhere) for external kimono makers, and became well known for their large range of original patterns. Kamedatomi commissioned *nihonga* artists (Japanese-style painting artists) to design the patterns and Kamedatomi artisans would then cut stencils (*katagami*) based on the artists' designs (Hall 2015: 76). In 1949 Kamedatomi became a public company and employed 120 people including office staff, and artisans who did dyeing, hand printing, and machine printing (*kikai nassen,* explained in Chapter Two). However, with postwar decline in demand for kimono, especially from the late 1980s, the company had to reduce the size of the business and in 1989 it had sixty staff members. In order to adapt to the new economic situation of the 1990s, it started to produce *yōfuku* (Western-style clothing) and the number of employees was again reduced. Now there are only ten members including artisans and office staff.

The company's third-generation owner, Kameda Kazuaki, took over in 1984 but it was not until 2001 that he created the brand Pagong.[2] Kameda was born in 1953 and told me that since childhood he has enjoyed drawing. After high school, he worked for another kimono dyeing company, doing *tegaki yūzen* for five or six years. This is a common practice in Japanese families where the potential successor will work outside the company to gain more skills and then bring them back to enrich the family business. When Kameda was 30 years old, his father died and he became the director of the Kamedatomi Company.[3] In his new position and facing the contraction of the kimono industry, Kameda searched for an alternative way to make use of and preserve the family company's knowledge of traditional dyeing techniques. The website describes kimono as "being in our company's DNA" and Kameda looked to the kimono for inspiration (Pagong Kamedatomi Co. 2014). He learned about the little-known origins of the Hawaiian or "aloha" shirt: apparently in the 1930s, Japanese immigrants to Hawaii refashioned their old kimono into short sleeved, loose fitting shirts that were more suited to the tropical climate (this is one version of many stories regarding the shirt's origins). He then started printing men's shirts using kimono patterns. He ceased production of fabric explicitly for kimono shortly after in 2002. Kamedatomi now produces a range of aloha shirts and women's apparel under the label Pagong, using the original kimono stencils and *kata yūzen* techniques that his family's artisans have used for almost a hundred years. Originally the focus was on aloha shirts, so Pagong sold mainly to men, but in recent years the women's apparel has become popular and now women make up the majority of its customers. Its customer base is very broad, ranging from approximately 30 to 80 years of age. The Pagong website displays an anecdote about one family, who told them the grandmother, mother and daughter went to a party, all wearing Pagong clothing (Pagong Kamedatomi Co. 2014).

In 2012 Kameda had three retail shops in Kyoto: the main shop was beside the Kamedatomi *yūzen* workshop on Gojō-dōri, the Sanjō store was on Sanjō-dōri, and the Gion store was in Gion, Shimbashi. The main shop is on a wide boulevard away from major shopping areas, whereas the latter two stores are in high tourist traffic areas. He told me in 2007 that he was not interested in expanding his business, stating, "We have only three shops in Kyoto. I don't want to add more branches in Osaka or Tokyo or such places. I firmly believe in protecting our existing business [in Kyoto]" (Hall 2008: 97). However, in October 2015, Kameda opened a new Pagong shop in Jiyugaoka in Tokyo. Pagong now supplies goods to other shops (such as one at Narita International Airport) and has also opened two overseas stores located within the Japanese department store Isetan in Singapore and Bangkok, so it is likely that increased success and recognition of the brand over the years changed his mind.

Process

While the final product manufactured by Pagong is quite different, some of the processes used are the same as its Taishō predecessors. When the Pagong design team decide on the products for a new collection, designs are selected from the vast storehouse of six thousand Taishō-era patterns (Figure 3.1). The design team consists of four women and Kameda: Kameda is the overall creative director, Narazaki (the only team member that has been with Kamedatomi since the Pagong brand's inception), oversees the planning of new products and projects; Inamoto is in charge of quality control, especially the sewing of garments; Morishita is in charge of production scheduling, including dyeing in the workshop and the manufacture of garments; and Inagaki is in charge of color selection and the *yūzen* dye workshop production schedule. Kameda describes his current products as "contemporary everyday fashion handcrafted with Kyoto's centuries old *yūzen* dyeing tradition" (Pagong Kamedatomi Co. 2014). The primary fabrics used are silk and a special 100 percent cotton knit fabric that is light and strong. Kameda worked directly with spinning and knitting companies to create the cotton knit fabric so that it has the ability to stretch. Because of this tactile characteristic, customers often mistakenly think the fabric includes elastic.

Figure 3.1 Kameda Kazuaki showing one of the *katagami* stencils in his warehouse. Photo: Jenny Hall.

In the Kamedatomi *yūzen* workshop, located in Ukyō ward, only five artisans carry out the dyeing process, with two specializing in mixing dye on the ground floor of the factory, and three working in the dyeing room on the second floor. I first saw the workshop in 2007, at which time both of the dye mixers were older men. The Pagong website boasted that the team of five craftsmen together had more than 170 years of experience with *yūzen* (Pagong Kamedatomi Co. 2014). Kameda was lamenting the fact that young people did not want to do such work because it was messy and difficult. However, in 2012 there was a new employee working in the mixing room, a young woman, demonstrating some change in the demographic on the floor. On my visit, I asked Kameda how artisans learn their craft and he replied, "I was taught to a degree but in the case of the artisans, mostly they see and memorize. How do I say? Teaching doesn't involve minute details. We call the memorizing way 'look and remember' [*mite oboeru*]. That's the best way" (personal interview September 24, 2012). This quote illustrates the *kata* method of learning discussed in Chapter One, whereby skills are passed on through copying and repetition.

The Kamedatomi dye room had long double banks of slanting tables (*nassendai*) where the material was spread out smoothly (Figure 3.2). The artisan placed the metal frame of the stencil onto one section, applied the dye, and then moved the stencil frame along to the next section of the 30-meter cloth (visit https://www.youtube.com/watch?v=meBDlVYbbBA to see the artisan printing

Figure 3.2 The *nassendai* (slanting benches used for dyeing) in the Kamedatomi factory. Photo: Jenny Hall.

Pagong fabric). When he got to the end of the row, he started the process again with the next stencil, sometimes repeating this up to twenty times. The banks were heated to set the dye faster but this also made the room unbearably hot in summer, sometimes pushing temperatures to 40 degrees Celsius (Hall 2018a: 300). After the fabric is dyed, it is steamed (to set the dye), washed, and dried. The fabric is sent out to other workshops, because Kamedatomi outsources its steaming, cutting, and sewing to other companies before the finished product is ready for sale in Pagong shops.

Products

Pagong's aloha shirts are cut from a custom-made figured silk that incorporates a jacquard pattern of *nami* (waves) and pagong (sea turtles) woven into it (Figure 3.3). Kamedatomi then dyes over the figured fabric using its stencils, to create "a doubly rich and deep visual effect" (Pagong Kamedatomi Co. 2014). Pagong's women's apparel includes dresses, tunics, skirts, blouses, scarves, camisoles, and accessories such as handbags and Japanese-style *gamaguchi* coin purses (literally "toad mouth"; these are small purses with a metal "kiss lock" clasp) (Figure 3.4).

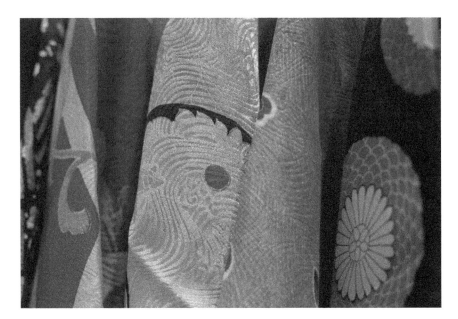

Figure 3.3 Pagong's custom-made figured silk that incorporates a jacquard pattern of "nami" waves and "pagong" sea turtles woven into it. Fabric design © Kamedatomi Co. Ltd. Photo: Jenny Hall.

Figure 3.4 A *gamaguchi* (toad mouth) coin purse by Pagong. Fabric design © Kamedatomi Co. Ltd. Photo: Jenny Hall.

Pagong's clothing is very much international in shape: short sleeve tank tops and camisoles, shift dresses, sheer blouses in looser-fit drop-waist styles, polo-necks, zippered fleece tops, and of course the original aloha shirts (Figure 3.5). However, the positioning of the Taishō stencil pattern motif on each item is not randomly placed, but based on kimono design "know-how"—the design team consider the placement of designs such as flowers or waves within the overall composition as per their experience dyeing kimono. The patterns use between fifteen and twenty-five stencils for each design—a single flower in a pattern might have four or five colors, and each color is dyed separately so the dyeing process is very labor intensive. Through these contemporary fashions, Kameda said he hopes to inspire young Japanese to learn about kimono and Japanese history by using these kimono patterns. He feels that many Japanese have become unfamiliar with their "traditional" culture and his aim is to create contemporary apparel that expresses Kyoto's kimono culture. The patterns range from delicate florals to children's toys from the Taishō era and each one has a story behind it. Kameda sees these stories as one of the most important aspects of his products,

Figure 3.5 Part of Pagong's autumn collection 2012. Fabric designs © Kamedatomi Co. Ltd. Photo: Jenny Hall.

and wants his products to convey the meanings behind the stories to customers (I give a more detailed description of Pagong's marketing approaches in Chapter Five). He told me, "First of all, the important tradition is the kimono design and the dyeing technique. Then each pattern has been given an original name. Each fabric has a story, and it's important to understand and protect that tradition" (personal interview September 24, 2012).

For example, one of Pagong's designs, "hatodokei to kodomo" (cuckoo clock and children) is an example of a print that has a definite late Taishō–early Shōwa flavor (Figure 3.6). According to Kameda, the boom in children's picture book publishing at the time was the inspiration for this design. The cuckoo clock, cockatoo and parrot were added as "foreign" motifs that contribute to the exotic, fairy-tale atmosphere that twenty-first century Japanese consumers imagine that period to entail. Kameda explained,

> In those days, for example, poor people couldn't afford to keep a dog in their house. Even stray dogs couldn't come to the house. The people would get angry if they did. Birdcages and cuckoo clocks were also only objects for rich households. These were things that people longed for in the Shōwa era. But today people don't know that. My company conveys those meanings. Nowadays children say "cute." "Ah, cute. I want to try this shirt. How much

Figure 3.6 Pagong's "Hatodokei to kodomo" (cuckoo clock and children) pattern. Fabric designs © Kamedatomi Co. Ltd. Photo: Jenny Hall.

is it?" But in the olden days, things had more complex meanings. (Personal interview September 24, 2012)

This echoes the point made by academic Kawakami Shigeki, mentioned in Chapter One, about Edo period designs not merely being decorative but rather serving as clever patterns that allowed for imaginative interpretations; this statement could be also seen as a motto for Kameda's work. However, as Kameda pointed out above, many of these associations or interpretations have been lost over time so the Pagong website features the origins of their patterns. Another example is the *omocha* (toy) pattern (Figure 3.7); this was designed for a young girl's kimono and includes various old-fashioned toys such as a Chinese-style chrysanthemum fan. The fan references the legend of *Kikujidō*, who, according to the Pagong website, was born in a mountain ravine and drank the valley water made up of drops of dew from the chrysanthemum leaves and thereby remained a child for many centuries.[4] There is also a drum, flute, and bell in the pattern which are traditional musical instruments (*narimono*) used in

Figure 3.7 Pagong's *omocha* (toy) pattern. Fabric designs © Kamedatomi Co. Ltd. Photo: Jenny Hall.

kagura (Shinto music) to call the gods and ask favors. A cap with plum blossom is Chinese in origin and denotes success for literary talent. Sato points out that Chinese motifs and patterns in the 1920s, or lack of them, in kimono can show the level of nationalistic sentiment of different historical periods (2010: 31). The butterfly is worn on the dancers' clothing in Japanese court music when they are conducting a memorial service for children. There is also a *hanetsuki* (a battledore, or an early form of badminton racket) that was a popular game at New Year. All of these items were to ensure a healthy and prosperous life for the child who wore the kimono (Pagong Kamedatomi Co. 2014). The patterns' meanings are made clear to customers through the Pagong Facebook page as well as a desk calendar sent to subscribed customers every year that includes explanations of various Pagong designs. Some Japanese designs are very common among other companies' products and have specific names in the Japanese design lexicon, such as *karakusa* (a plant motif), *asanoha* (hemp leaf), and *seigaiha* (a wave design made of arched concentric circles) (Figure 3.8a–c). These designs also have specific meanings—for example, *asanoha* is considered good for babies because hemp grows quickly and is strong, and therefore the hope is that a baby wearing such a pattern will also grow quickly and be strong (Sato 2010: 31). Of the companies I researched, Pagong's designs were the most decipherable in terms of the historical meanings behind the patterns they used on fabric. Of course, the aim of each of the companies was different, and Kameda's was to showcase these unique designs that were part of his company's heritage.

Figure 3.8a Example of the pattern *karakusa* (an arabesque-like plant motif). Photo: Jenny Hall.

Figure 3.8b Example of the pattern *asanoha* (hemp leaf). Photo: Jenny Hall.

Figure 3.8c Example of the pattern *seigaiha* (a wave design made of arched concentric circles). Photo: Jenny Hall.

Kyoto Denim

Background

Designer Kuwayama Toyoaki and business manager Miyamoto Kazutomo started their company, Homay, in 2007 and launched their brand of jeans, Kyoto Denim, in 2008.[5] Kuwayama comes from a Kyoto family who specialized in kimono dyeing since the Edo period, but Homay is a new company that creates and sells jeans and other denim apparel. Kuwayama applies kimono-dyeing techniques to denim, and designs denim apparel inspired by Japanese traditional clothing and objects. He draws on the talents of Kyoto artisans, skilled in traditional techniques such as *Kyō-yūzen* and *kumihimo* (braiding). A silk braid of *kumihimo* called an *obijime* was originally used to secure the *obi*, and although *obi* are now elaborately tied, *obijime* are still used for decorative purposes. Kuwayama incorporates these techniques into his designs, thereby continuing to employ the traditional skills these artisans have embodied.

Kuwayama and his partner Miyamoto met at the Osaka University of the Arts, with Kuwayama a *senpai* (senior) to Miyamoto. The seeds of the company were sown in 2000–1 when they were both university students and worked part-time for a company making and selling kimono. Miyamoto told me that at that time they could see that even though kimono was part of traditional Japanese culture it was rarely worn in contemporary life, only for special occasions like weddings, and the coming-of-age ceremony. Miyamoto said that those in their generation (born in the late 1970s) wanted to wear kimono but it was too expensive, so he and Kuwayama thought about how they could create everyday wear such as t-shirts, bags, or shoes with the "essence" of kimono. They wanted to create a "kimono that could be worn everyday" and for them, the essence of kimono was in the colors, patterns, and techniques. They could see that denim fabric had been widely used and worn in the Japanese fashion industry since the 1950s. Denim jeans are a global fashion phenomenon and are widely worn in Japan, varying in price from expensive brands such as Louis Vuitton to cheaper ones such as Uniqlo. They decided one way to achieve their goal of creating contemporary products with a "kimono essence" was to combine denim and the "designs and colors of Japan" (personal interview November 2, 2012).[6] Miyamoto described their product as "*denimu no kimono*" (literally, denim kimono).

Kuwayama studied textile design, specifically dyeing, for five years at university. Miyamoto initially studied broadcasting and music production, but changed to advertising and marketing. While Kuwayama is the creative arm of the business and designs the products, Miyamoto is the business arm of the partnership. Miyamoto told me that he wanted some form of creative expression and tried to be an artist, but he was not good at drawing or painting. He realized that his strengths were in promotion. He manages Kyoto Denim's small retail outlet in Shimogyo Ward, gives advice to customers about what suits them, designs advertisements, takes photographs, collects sales data, and manages newspaper advertising and the company website. He said that because he knows the background of each product he is best suited to this position.[7] He told me, "In Kyoto those who express themselves through making things are shy [embarrassed; *hazukashii*] and hesitate to say 'my product is really good.' If I say that those things are excellent, when he [Kuwayama] hears that he can have confidence in what he is creating. That's why I represent the artisan's work to the public" (personal interview November 2, 2012).

More than half of Kyoto Denim's customers are from the Kantō region of Japan, from cities such as Tokyo, Saitama, Chiba, and Kanagawa. The rest of its customers are from Aichi, Nagoya, Osaka, Kobe—Kansai's larger cities— as well as Hiroshima and Fukuoka. The shop is near Kyoto station, but not on a main shopping street so customers must learn about it from advertising or the website and social media. Kuwayama and his brand have been featured in various newspapers such as the *Asahi Shimbun*, on television channels such as KBS Kyoto, Nippon Television, and Yomiuri Television, and in print media such as men's magazine *Oceans* and women's magazine *InRed*. Kyoto Denim has a Facebook page and blog, and is also featured in a primary school textbook in the context of the succession of traditional industries. Miyamoto told me many customers come from further distances such as Kyushu and also from Hokkaido, depending on the season.[8] Customers also come from abroad, but not so many from Asia; Miyamoto speculated that this was because China and Korea have similar textile cultures to Japan, so Kyoto Denim products are not so appealing to them. He also said he believes that "now Japan's relationship with China and Korea has deteriorated because of the history of aggression with those countries" (personal interview November 2, 2012). He told me those Asian visitors buy other things rather than kimono, such as Japanese food, but he hopes they will become more interested in Japanese traditional techniques in the future.

Miyamoto believes that customers buy Kyoto Denim products because they are "*Kyoto-rashī*" (typical of Kyoto in that they have the feeling of Kyoto). He gave several reasons for the popularity of the brand. He told me,

> Japanese people's *minzoku* [ethnic or folk] roots give them a tendency to prefer handmade things. As years go by, and people get older, some of them want to have such handmade things, for example, pottery. Pottery for flower arrangement is very expensive and not many people can buy it but a tea cup, something that is everyday pottery, some people prefer to buy those that are handmade. It's the same for kimono, some people may prefer to wear everyday casual kimono when they are get older. So that's one reason why people might buy Kyoto Denim. Denim is everyday wear. Kyoto is the handmade city! We are making handmade things in the handmade city. Some people are searching for things made by fastidious artisans in a *minzoku* style

that goes back to Japanese aesthetic roots and uses traditional techniques. (Personal interview November 2, 2012)

However, Miyamoto is aware that the price of Kyoto Denim jeans is beyond many consumers' budgets as they retail for between 30,000 yen and 50,000 yen. As he told me, it is possible to buy ten pairs of jeans in Japan for 30,000 yen, or purchase three pairs of better quality jeans for 10,000 yen each, making his product significantly more expensive in comparison. But the cost arises from the handcrafted nature of the jeans, in particular, the *yūzen* detailing added by artisans. Not only are Kyoto Denim's jeans handmade, Miyamoto believes another reason customers are attracted to them is because they are what he calls a "mismatch."

> Jeans are from America, so they are a foreign product for Japanese. To give them the essence of kimono is a real mismatch (*misumachi)* but humans are attracted to mismatches. Mismatches in fashion are interesting. There are mismatches that are bad taste, but jeans and kimono are completely different, the culture of each of them is different and we are creating our jeans through the fusion of these cultures. Jeans that sell for 3,000 yen are just ordinary. We don't need very ordinary things. Kyoto Denim jeans are a mismatch that has resulted in a really special product. (Personal interview November 2, 2012)

Laura Miller has also noted the popularity of mismatching appropriated styles in apparel, especially among young Japanese men, stating, "Among young men, a practice called *mikkusu shivoo* (intended mismatch) combines different apparel, such as a rock-style print T-shirt with baggy surfer shorts, deliberately upsetting coordination with a particular form" (2003: 85). As Miller points out, the results of mixing styles can encompass sincerity, mockery, and kitsch, and it is often impossible to tell the wearer's real intention (ibid.), but this kind of mismatch is important because it includes the element of surprise. Surprise is seen as one of the most powerful marketing tools, and scientists have shown it to be addictive, suggesting humans are designed to crave the unexpected (Redick 2013). At the same time, Kyoto Denim products incorporate the everyday. Miyamoto reiterates a common theme among Japanese artisans, that the essence of Japanese design is the small discoveries in ordinary or insignificant things.

Process

First, Kuwayama develops a design concept including the silhouette of the jeans and the patterning that will be used on them. Kyoto Denim sources its raw cotton (*menka*) from Okayama Prefecture, the "birthplace of Japanese jeans" (Masangkay 2013). Before the item is cut and stitched, Kyoto artisans dye sections of the denim with a fine pattern using traditional methods such as *kata yūzen* following

Figure 3.9 A detail of *yūzen* designs on Kyoto Denim jeans. Design © Kyoto Denim. Photo: Jenny Hall.

Kuwayama's design—these will be used for details such as pockets (Figure 3.9). The fabric is steamed to set the dye pattern (often at this stage the stencil pattern is bleached so that it appears white), washed, and dried. Then it is sent to Okayama for sewing into the jeans. When the jeans are returned to Kyoto they are then dyed with one background color such as green or red. After that any further details are added such as hand-painted designs by *tegaki yūzen* artisans or *kumihimo* braid. The added decorations depend on the fabric, pattern, method, and season— each is unique. Originally Kuwayama completed many of the production stages himself, but now he outsources to specialists in Kyoto.

Sourcing the specialists was not easy. Miyamoto told me, "It took time to find the people who understood the real meaning of what we wanted to do and could do the techniques" (personal interview November 2, 2012). There were other issues as well: not only are many artisans with the necessary skills elderly, but they thought what Kuwayama was requesting was not possible. Miyamoto explained, "When we wanted them to dye our denim, out of twelve, half said it was impossible. With the exception of that half, the others thought it might not be possible but they also thought it was interesting. And even though some of them said it was impossible they also said '*gambatte*' [do your best] to us" (ibid.). Kyoto Denim finally found five accomplished but elderly artisans who would work with them. The *kumihimo* artisan they currently outsource braiding to is a woman in her 80s—Miyamoto thought she was 85 or 86, or even a bit older. The *tegaki yūzen* artisan is about 60 years old, and he also continues to do his own original kimono designs. He has been doing *tegaki yūzen* from the age of 18 or 20 so has more than forty years' experience doing only that technique. The artisans are not only employed with Kyoto Denim work; they are also doing more traditional work for other companies at the same time. Despite their initial reluctance to do Kyoto Denim work, these particular artisans did not have a large quantity of kimono work so were happy to be engaged by Kyoto Denim. Miyamoto told me that one of the problems he has with innovation in textile making is the clash between young designers and experienced artisans. He thinks that as people age they become stubborn, suggesting some difficulties in dealing with the artisans, but he also said, "We need stubborn people because they are the ones that continue to use classic techniques" (ibid.). He also believes that new types of work can bring new energy to people. He said, "For humans, if you are only doing the same things all the time it's hard, with no stimulus … by making new things using traditional techniques the artisans can gain new strength" (ibid.).

Products

There are five basic cuts of Kyoto Denim jeans for women (which mirror popular styles in the West): straight, slim straight with high waist, slim straight with low waist, skinny, and skinny with high waist. Within that there are variations regarding the details; pocket styles, waistbands, stitching color, and decorative details. For women, there are nine different styles: *Kyō kumihimo* (braiding), *sakura rokku* (cherry blossom rock), *miyabi* (elegance), *tsukiyo* (moonlit night), *yozakura* (cherry blossoms at night), *orizuru* (crane), *tsutsumi* (cloak), *nami* (waves), and *kozakura* (small cherry blossom), and these categories reflect the fact that Kuwayama's designs incorporate traditional motifs and design elements. For example, the back pocket of his "tsutsumi" jeans is based on the folding of a *furoshiki* (*tsutsumu* means to wrap or fold) (Figures 3.10 and 3.11). His "kumihimo" jeans integrate braiding into the back pocket (Figure 3.12). *Kumihimo* was once used by samurai as a functional and decorative way to lace their armor and is now used primarily to fasten *obi* and for the ties on *haori* (a lightweight jacket that is worn over a kimono). *Tegaki yūzen* and *kata yūzen* are used to decorate the denim with cherry blossoms, and other traditional motifs from the Muromachi or Edo periods.

Another aspect that Kyoto Denim has reproduced from traditional apparel is the decoration on the inside of its women's jeans, from the ankle to the knee (Figure 3.13). This hidden decoration is inspired by the concept of *iki*, whereby Edo-period kimono or *haori* were lined with colorful patterned silks in order to circumvent the sumptuary laws mentioned in Chapter One. In fact, the Kyoto Denim blog explanation for these products explicitly mentions *iki* as a design inspiration, and the website suggests that the pant legs can be worn rolled up to show off the pattern (Kyoto Denim 2007–2014b).

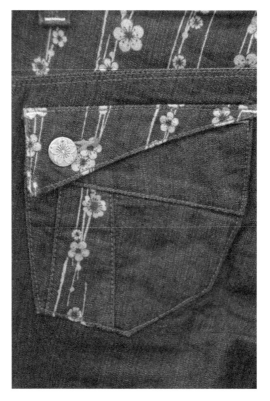

Figure 3.10 Kyoto Denim's "tsutsumi" jeans. Design © Kyoto Denim. Photo: Jenny Hall.

Figure 3.11 Sketch for the "tsutsumi" jeans which was featured on the company website. Image © Kyoto Denim. Reproduced with kind permission.

Figure 3.12 Kyoto Denim's "kumihimo" jeans. Design © Kyoto Denim. Photo: Jenny Hall.

Figure 3.13 Decoration on the inside of Kyoto Denim jean legs. Design © Kyoto Denim. Photo: Jenny Hall.

For men, there are two types of cut: straight and tapered leg. The men's range draws influence from Japanese military apparel and there are five styles: *zan* (decapitation), *yoroi* (armor), *ikazuchi* (thunder), *jin* (battle formation), and *shinobi* (endurance). The website gives a brief summary of their notion of the birth of "*wafuku*": it emerged from the influence of the Tang Dynasty, underwent simplification during the Sengoku period, acquired certain (unspecific) trends during the Edo period, and was finally overtaken by the dominance of Western apparel during the Meiji and Taishō periods when people chose mass-produced and machine-made Western clothes over Japanese crafted clothing. The website then poses the question, "What if this transition never happened? What if we continued to let our *wafuku* and spirits evolve? The answer is Kyoto Denim Men's line, 'The Brave General'" (Kyoto Denim 2015). The company is keen to tie the men's wear to what it considers an era of chivalry, the Warring States period. This emphasis on romanticism and nostalgia are key marketing concepts for its products.

Kyoto Denim claims to be fanatical about product details to the point that each design and cut has original stitches handpicked by Kuwayama from hundreds of colors. The website states that "not only do we take in account of the harmony between the thread and fabric color, but we try to recreate the astounding scenery of Kyoto in our jeans" (Kyoto Denim 2014b). It also has different tags on its jeans for men or women—the men's feature a crescent moon and dot stitched onto leather or *kanji* (Chinese characters) of the product name stitched onto leather, while the women's have a cherry blossom stitched onto leather (Figure 3.14). The metal buttons on the jeans are also custom-made in the form of cherry blossom (Figure 3.15). This obsession with details, expressed by the word *kodawari* (mentioned in Chapter One), is something Kyoto artisans often express as a positive in their work. Such "attention to detail is not for its own sake: it is part of a densely constructed relationship based on trust and responsibility among all levels of provision, production, and consumption" (White 2012: 68). In addition, on a practical level, it is a "value-adding practice" because "you can charge more for an item with *kodawari*" (White 2012: 68).

Figure 3.14 Kyoto Denim's tag, cherry blossom stitched onto leather. Design © Kyoto Denim. Photo: Jenny Hall.

Figure 3.15 Kyoto Denim's metal buttons, custom-made in the form of cherry blossom. Design © Kyoto Denim. Photo: Jenny Hall.

Sou Sou

Background

Textile designer Wakisaka Katsuji, architect Tsujimura Hisanobu, and apparel designer Wakabayashi Takeshi founded Sou Sou in 2002. The name "Sou Sou" originates from a common expression used in Japanese speech to signal agreement or confirmation, a vital component of Japanese communication, mutual understanding, and social relations. All three of the main designers at Sou Sou were born in Kyoto. Wakisaka Katsuji is well known in design circles for being the first Japanese designer to work for Marimekko, the Finnish textile company, which had global success in the 1970s. He trained at the Kyoto School of Art and Design before traveling to Finland at the age of 24 and landing a job with Marimekko in 1968 where he stayed for eight years. After that he worked for Jack Lenor Larsen in New York and Wacoal Interior Fabrics in Japan. His style is naive and has a child-like quality, with cartoonish characteristics such as bright colors and simple geometric patterns, illustrating the influence of his time working at Marimekko (Figure 3.16). Many of his drafts for Sou Sou designs are initially done on postcards that he mails to his wife—he has made more than ten thousand postcards according to the recent book published about his work (Wakisaka 2012). Tsujimura Hisanobu worked for a company called Livart for over ten years before starting his own company in 1995. He still heads an architectural and furniture design company in Kyoto, called Moonbalance Inc., as well as working at the Kyoto University of Art and Design. Wakabayashi Takeshi studied custom-made men's clothes at the Japan Men's Apparel Academy before working as a pattern maker for a clothing company. From 1994 to 2004 he lived in America and had his own brand of women's Western-style clothing. In 2004 he returned to Japan and ceased designing Western-style clothes. He now

Figure 3.16 Some examples of Wakisaka's designs for Sou Sou. Fabric designs © Sou Sou. Photo: Jenny Hall.

designs various garments for Sou Sou as well as being an associate professor of Kyoto University of Art and Design.

The first Sou Sou shop opened in Tokyo in 2003, selling fans (*sensu*) and *furoshiki*, but this shop was not successful. In October 2003 Sou Sou held exhibitions in New York, Tokyo, and Kyoto, after which it decided to open a shop selling *jikatabi*, or split-toed work shoes, in Kyoto. In 2005 Sou Sou opened its Ise-momen shop selling cotton *tenugui* and also opened Samue, a clothes shop. Shops dedicated to women's and men's clothing opened in January 2009 ("Kikoromo" and "Kei-i" respectively) with Warabegi (children's clothes) following soon after in April 2010. Sou Sou now has nine shops in Kyoto all located just north of Shijo-dōri in the high-end retail area between Shinkyogoku-dōri and Kawaramachi-dōri. Each is carefully designed and specializes in different products: *tabi* (split-toed socks), women's wear, men's wear, children's wear, *tenugui* (hand cloths), *furoshiki*, dyed fabric, a tea house serving *wagashi* inspired by Sou Sou fabric patterns, and Sou Sou Le Coq Sportif collaboration sportswear. The company also has one shop in Tokyo and one shop in San Francisco, both selling a variety of Sou Sou products.

Process

Sou Sou makes a number of textile-based items including *jikatabi*, *tabi*, *noren* (fabric room dividers), *tenugui*, clothes, and fabric furniture coverings. Sou Sou outsources production of its items to various factories in Japan. The *jikatabi* are produced by two companies: Takasago Sangyo Corporation, in Hyogo Prefecture and Marugo in Kurashiki, Okayama Prefecture. According to Takasago Sangyō Corporation's website, most of the commercially sold *jikatabi* in Japan are mass-produced in China nowadays (Takasago Sangyō Corp. 2015). Wakaybashi told me that Japanese producers outsourced the work to China, which caused the price of *jikatabi* to fall during the mid-Shōwa era (*c.* 1955) and they came to be considered a disposable item as a result. The two companies mentioned above are some of the last still producing Japanese-made *tabi* shoes. The Sou Sou US website states that "currently, Sou Sou is the only company solely dedicated to making *tabi* shoes in Japan and each pair is hand made by trained Japanese artisans" (Sou Sou US 2014).

Wakisaka's contemporary, and often colorful patterns are used for the *jikatabi*, and this contrasts with traditional shoes which were primarily dyed dark colors such as indigo because of their use as work shoes (Figure 3.17). The Sou Sou website states the company philosophy that *jikatabi* is a traditional Japanese handicraft and being such should be made in Japan, by factories that have a history of producing authentic versions of the products, in order to fully satisfy suppliers and customers. The designers conclude that "this philosophy holds true of all other Japanese handicraft. Because each place of production has its own cultural background, traditional skills and sense which have been inherited" (Sou Sou US 2013).

Wakabayashi said he realizes that compared to other traditional techniques such as *shibori*, the current techniques (outlined below) used to make *jikatabi* are not so old (one hundred years compared to several hundred years) and therefore are "shallow" in this regard, but he said that nonetheless they are traditional Japanese shoes so he thinks it is important that they are made in Japan. This is not to say *jikatabi* themselves as footwear are not old in design terms—the actual

Figure 3.17 Sou Sou's *jikatabi*. Fabric designs © Sou Sou. Photo: Jenny Hall. First published in *New Voices in Japanese Studies*, Vol. 7, 2015 (The Japan Foundation, Sydney).

Figure 3.18 *Kohaze* clasps used to fasten *jikatabi*. Fabric designs © Sou Sou. Photo: Jenny Hall.

jikatabi form has a long history, and the Sou Sou US website states, "the basic design can be traced to roughly around the 10th century and are thus a symbol of traditional Japanese culture" (Sou Sou US 2014).

The process of making *jikatabi* starts with screen-printing the fabric with Wakisaka's designs. The fabric is then cut to the *jikatabi* pattern and the *kohaze* clasps are sewn on using a specialized sewing machine (Figure 3.18). The fabric is sewn to the inner lining and glue is applied to the fabric edge where the base of the shoe will be attached. A unique roller is used to fix the inner sole securely and more glue is applied to the base in order to attach the rubber sole. The shoes are put in a particular dryer to dry the glue completely before attaching the rubber tape around the outside edge of the sole. The tape is especially difficult to attach between the split toes because of the narrow space. Once the final rubber sole is attached to the bottom of the shoe, it is heated in a kiln to 135 degrees Celsius to bind the glue molecules and make the rubber stronger. Every step of the process is done by hand.

As mentioned above, Sou Sou uses *momen* (cotton and fiber) from Ise Prefecture, a locale well known for quality cotton since the Muromachi period, for its *tenugui* and some of its clothing. For its clothing, the company uses another kind of cotton fiber, *chizimi* (Japanese crepe cotton), from the Takahashi Textile Company, Takashima city, Shiga Prefecture. Many of Sou Sou's trousers are made of Takashima *chizimi* cotton because the uneven texture apparently absorbs sweat better and is therefore suitable for more humid climates. The sensory experience of the consumer is obviously an important aspect of Sou Sou's design and production, and an important part of its marketing strategy. The Takahashi Textile Company, the oldest Takashima company to produce *chizimi* cotton (established in 1851) refers to tradition, stating it uses a "sturdy German-made 60 year old bobbin and 20 year old loom" and produces 40,000 meters of fabric a year, according to Sou Sou's company website (Sou Sou US 2015).

Sou Sou collaborates with the French company, Le Coq Sportif, to create sportswear, a topic that will be discussed in regard to innovation in Chapter Five. Wakabayashi also works at Zōkei Geijutsu Daigaku (Kyoto University of Art and Design) where he teaches a fashion course and a textile course. He said that generally students there are not interested in traditional techniques (they prefer Western fashion) but he does teach a dye course involving hand printing and *shibori*. "The fashion course students love European clothing so they are not interested in Japanese culture," he told me (personal interview October 5, 2012). In his courses, he does not teach about kimono but teaches about *kantōi*, or Yayoi period clothing (300 BCE–300 CE). *Kantōi* is a simple garment made from a rectangle of cloth with a hole for the head. He asks students to make *kantōi* from muslin and they apply decorative patterns with the aim of exhibiting and selling their garments. Many of Sou Sou's tops and dresses are based on this design.

Wakabayashi believes that a good designer creates and sells products that people want to use. He told me,

> I'm not doing difficult things, simply doing everyday design. There's good and not so good design in the world but it could be garbage if it isn't wanted by customers. For example, if I created something I don't like but someone does, it will be important for them. A designer is someone who makes things someone else wants to have. It's better to create something which will be meaningful to someone. Good design is that which becomes better in the future. The concept of Sou Sou is to make Japan better. (ibid.)

Products

As mentioned above, Sou Sou sells a range of fabric products as well as the rubber-soled *jikatabi*. The *tenugui* comes in the standard 35 cm x 90 cm size (Figure 3.19) but Sou Sou also makes other fabric accessories such as a longer *kubimaki* (neck scarf) 35 cm x 190 cm; a *himejō* (wall hanging), 35 cm x 50 cm; and *furoshiki* (a square wrapping cloth) in three sizes 54 cm², 106 cm², 113 cm². These are all regular sizes according to accepted Japanese historical customs

Figure 3.19 *Tenugui* by Sou Sou. Fabric designs © Sou Sou. Photo: Jenny Hall.

Figure 3.20 *Asabura zōri* (straw sandals) with modern print straps by Sou Sou. Fabric designs © Sou Sou. Photo: Jenny Hall.

for those products. It also makes *asabura zōri* (straw sandals) (Figure 3.20), *sensu* (Figure 3.21), *hanten* (Figure 3.22), and *yukata*. Wakabayashi aims to invoke the essence of kimono forms in Sou Sou's practical contemporary clothing range. Rather than restrain bodies as the kimono does, he creates clothes that allow bodies more freedom of movement, to fit with contemporary lifestyles (Figure 3.23). Sou Sou apparel retains some design elements of the

Figure 3.21 *Sensu* by Sou Sou. Fabric designs © Sou Sou. Photo: Jenny Hall.

Figure 3.22 *Hanten* by Sou Sou. Fabric designs © Sou Sou. Photo: Jenny Hall.

Figure 3.23 An example of Sou Sou's clothing that shows inspiration from kimono's flowing lines. Fabric designs © Sou Sou. Photo: Jenny Hall.

Figure 3.24 A Sou Sou top with kimono-shaped sleeves and front overlap collar. Fabric designs © Sou Sou. Photo: Jenny Hall.

kimono—for example, square-shaped sleeves, front overlap collars (left over right), ties as fastenings, and long flowing lines (Hall 2015: 71) (Figure 3.24). It is this distillation of traditional designs into contemporary forms and the reinvestment of traditional design iconography with new meanings that is informing change in the industry.

At first the *jikatabi* were Sou Sou's bestselling items according to Wakabayashi, but more recently its *wafuku* designs have also become popular. The company's customers are ordinary people, from children to grandparents, or "really just typical people." Wakabayashi said they do not market to a special target group and approximately 20 percent of customers are non-Japanese. He believes customers buy the products because "they won't already have something similar. They are excited to see something they've never seen before. Sou Sou is a space they've never felt before [*hatsu taiken zōn*; literally, a new experience zone]. If we sold normal jeans and t-shirts, we wouldn't sell much. People buy to get a new feeling" (personal interview October 5, 2012).

Wakabayashi's inspiration for clothing designs comes from Japanese history: library books, museums, and the annual Kyoto *Jidai Matsuri* (the Festival of the Ages, discussed in more detail in Chapter Four). He told me that during the Edo period there weren't so many varieties of products in people's lives.

> A person might only have two or three kimono, which they wore their whole life. The lifespan at that time was about 30 years so one kimono for every 10 years. Now people can buy a lot so they enjoy fashion. If someone has a high income they can buy experiences. Even those with less money can enjoy fashion. Originally humans could live without fashion. So it depends on the era, but I think gradually people will not spend a lot on fashion. Instead they will buy meaningful and good quality items, not waste money. Fashion makes someone's feeling deeper. (ibid.)

Other companies that I looked at in Kyoto reflect some of the same kinds of work as that done in my three main case studies. For example, Seisuke88 produces bags and accessories using digital *yūzen*, and Kyoto Montsuki uses black dye techniques, traditionally for kimono, to create black jeans. However, these activities are not their major line of business so I have not included them here as main examples. I mention it here to show that traditional Japanese artisans are flourishing in pockets of activity embedded in the wider market, but their work is not so visible as a community of practice. Although the companies' product lines do not overlap directly, I did get the sense that there is competition between them. My research showed that while they are keen to collaborate with other companies and designers, they do not collaborate with each other. This is shown in my discussions about collaborations, as well as in their marketing activities, in Chapter Five.

Conclusion

As mentioned in the introduction to this chapter, all of these companies are trying to capture what they believe to be the "essence" or "feeling" of Japanese heritage industries and crafts in their products. Miyamoto's explanation of that essence was

> a small discovery in ordinary things. For example, looking at the moon and thinking, "ah, today's moon is beautiful." This kind of moment is difficult to capture in design—you draw a picture, the moon is there, a cloud is there. It's difficult but people try to translate the feeling onto a *fusuma* [an architectural element or sliding screen] or clothes. (Personal interview November 2, 2012)

This idea about the essence of tradition as encapsulated in contemporary products is the focus for Kyoto Denim's women's range of jeans. The men's range is more focused on conveying Kuwayama's notions about the Sengoku period of Japanese history as that of masculine bravery and chivalry (Hall 2015: 75).

We don't know if jeans really have the power to make the wearer feel "brave," but the suggestion that a design attribute could inject such feelings into the experience of wearing garments says something about the relationship between people and things, the process of production and consumption. If we refer back to the concept of wrapping in order to refine the object within that I discussed in Chapter One, it would seem that Japanese cultural views incorporate such possibilities and even prioritize them. Goldstein-Gidoni has already discussed this in reference to the kimono; the act of donning a kimono for *seijin shiki* (coming-of-age ceremony) can be used to shape a Japanese woman's character, to train her in Japanese qualities of femininity such as endurance and patience, and this physical way of being is believed to have a moral and psychological influence (1999). Goldstein-Gidoni states, "For the kimono expert, kimono is much more than a constraint on the body. It has a mental influence and its ultimate role is to cultivate the perfect Japanese 'good wife, wise mother' (*ryōsai kenbo*)" (ibid.: 363). The consumption of these designers' essence of tradition, then, is viewed as something that cannot only help promote our desired impression to the world at large, an incorporated image of self, but something that affects the wearer and can therefore change how they view themselves. However, it is evident from my discussions of kimono history in Chapter One, as well as perceptions of kimono presented in that chapter, that a "good wife, wise mother" is not the only result of donning a kimono. Kimono, like all clothing, can be worn as a form of subversion or to show political discontent, and can be "read" in a variety of different ways. This will be discussed further in the following chapter with regard to changing contexts and ways of wearing and donning kimono.

For Kameda, the essence of tradition lies in his family's original patterns and the dye method used, as well as the stories each pattern conveys. Kameda is well aware that the patterns have a defined place in Japanese history, which gives them a particular mood. The website offers this explanation:

> The Taisho era in which our company was founded was a very unique time in the creative culture of Japan. Japan was a modern country, fully aware of the outside world, yet, culturally, we were still purely Japanese. The art of this time looks completely Japanese but often has a modern feel to it. The "feel" of things created in this era is sometimes called "Taisho chic." (Pagong Kamedatomi 2014)

In contrast, Sou Sou's idea of Japanese design "essence" is the opposite in that, while Pagong has preserved the patterns but put them on contemporary Western-style clothing, Sou Sou has put contemporary patterns by Wakisaka on apparel designed with *wafuku* characteristics. Wakabayashi believes these *wafuku* characteristics can be obtained by studying Japanese historical dress and using some of the garments' features to create clothes suitable for contemporary life. It is the innovation and adaptation of these companies (discussed in more detail in

Chapter Five) that helps deliver their concepts of a Japanese "essence" or "feeling" to customers, and is resulting in a revitalization of the Kyoto textile industry.

All of these designers view the decreasing opportunities to wear kimono in contemporary life a loss of culture, history, and tradition, and therefore aim to bring kimono back into everyday life rather than considering them reserved for events such as weddings, *seijin shiki*, and funerals. And, as we can see from the desire to educate customers about the techniques and stories behind the patterns, this is not just about the functional nature of clothing, or about whether it can ride a bicycle or not. It is also about the relationship between history, clothing, tradition, and culture. Of course, they are able to use this perceived loss of culture to their advantage in marketing and promoting their products to increase sales, but their passion for Japanese craft and heritage is no less genuine because of this fact. Wakabayashi's statement that he wants to create something meaningful for people lies at the heart of the motivations behind these designers. Kameda wants to pass on his kimono patterns' stories from a particular period of Japanese history. Kuwayama wants to remind Japanese people to notice the ordinary miracles of life such as cherry blossom scattering in the wind and to cultivate a greater consciousness of history and heritage. Wakabayashi wants to create apparel that gives consumers a new feeling and to recontextualize occasions, such as tea ceremony, so that more casual clothing can be worn for them (I discuss this further in the following chapter). This recontextualizing of the space in which the clothes can be worn is important. It is not just a reinvention of *wafuku*, but the designers aim to change consumers' perceptions about where kimono and *wafuku* might be worn. It is interesting to note that both Kameda and Kuwayama, having grown up in Kyoto textile dyeing families, now apply traditional patterns to contemporary clothing, whereas Wakabayashi spent time in the US designing Western clothing, but now prefers to design clothes based on historical Japanese garments.

All of the designers are, through their clothing, expressing sorrow at the loss of techniques while at the same time striving to keep those techniques alive. This demonstrates the importance of fashion in Japan, as argued in Chapter One. It is evident that Veblen's notion of "elegant dress" as "wasteful consumption" (2008: 263) does not sit well with contemporary Japanese textile design, because it denies any kind of deep understanding of what dress is and the role it fulfils, for producers and consumers. These three companies demonstrate the role of fashion in various ways that are both meaningful in the context of fashion's role in Japanese society, and in its role in terms of cultural heritage. Pagong is concerned with preserving its unique patterns that capture a set historical period, Sou Sou is playful in its creation of a new *wafuku* that can be donned and worn in contemporary life, and Kyoto Denim is aiming for a fusion of Japanese and Western that retains Japanese ideals of cultural identity. All are doing this, in part, to preserve what they feel is a key component of Japan's cultural heritage.

4

KIMONO AS SARTORIAL EXPRESSION – CLOTHING, PLAY, AND IDENTITY

"Kore wa kimono kedo kimono ja nai … kosupure-ppoi kimono desu" (It is a kimono but it is not a kimono … it is a cosplay-like kimono). A Kyoto kimono wholesaler made this comment when showing me a kimono design by his young business partner, Mori Makoto. Mori, discussed in Chapter Two, is one of a handful of young designers successfully creating kimono designs using new techniques. Mori designs the figures on a computer and prints them directly onto fabric using an inkjet printer, thus cutting out several laborious stages in the kimono-making process. He mainly designs *furisode* (long-sleeved kimono) for events such as *seijin shiki* (the coming-of-age ceremony). The kimono he displayed for me was a complicated pattern involving flowers and butterflies in a multitude of fuchsia, peach, and green hues overlaid with silver and gold (see Figure 4.1).

I was intrigued by the wholesaler's comment—what was the difference between a kimono design and a cosplay-like kimono design? The term cosplay, an amalgamation of "costume" and "play" (*kosupure* in Japanese), usually refers to individuals who dress in the clothing of a *manga*, *anime*, video game or movie character and role-play that character, mimicking the character's behavior (see Dailot-Bul 2009a; Gagne 2007; Gn 2011; Hall 2015: 78; Norris & Bainbridge 2009; Sharp 2011). An important aspect of cosplay is display: cosplayers dress up and act out roles for spectators. It is through this public enactment or "performativity" that members become part of an imagined community (Mackie 2009).

"Cosplay" is distinguished from other staged forms of dress and display such as the Gothic Lolita (abbreviated in colloquial Japanese as *gosurori*) subculture, where participants act out a more generalized social role (Gagne 2007; Daliot-Bul 2009a). Although Gothic Lolita adherents also enjoy the display aspect of their public demonstrations of the gothic aesthetic, they claim they are not pretending to be someone specific such as the titular character from Nabokov's book, or Mana, the cross-dressing guitarist from rock band Malice Mizer who first inspired

Figure 4.1 Mori Makoto's kimono design that was considered "cosplay-*ppoi*" by his partner, 2012. Fabric design © Mori Makoto. Photo: Jenny Hall. First published in *Fashion Theory*, Vol. 22:3, pp. 283–307 (2018), https://doi.org/10.1080/1362704X.2017.1319175.

the Gothic Lolita style (Gagne 2007).[1] Researchers have already noted that in recent years the meaning of cosplay "has expanded to include almost any type of dressing up outside traditional boundaries" (Rahman et al. 2012: 318). And this expansion appears to be played out by cosplay participants themselves, as evidenced by individuals dressed not as anime or manga characters but in more general costumes such as the Second World War French general at Comiket 2015 (*The Secret World of Comiket* 2015). The important characteristics of cosplay appear to be that the transformation is temporary; the players display their attire to an audience (this can include the general public as audience); and that it is deemed a kind of *asobi*, or "play" (as opposed to wearing a uniform for work) (Hall 2015: 78).

Cosplay has until recently been the domain of fringe communities but today cosplay has crossed over into more mainstream leisure practices. In a variety of social spaces, we see participants performing cosplay—it is no longer limited to certain areas such as Harajuku in Tokyo but has become visible internationally, with research already existing on cosplay subcultures in other countries such as Hong Kong (Rahman et al. 2012) and Australia (Norris & Bainbridge 2009). Those who wish to try cosplay in Japan without purchasing or creating all of the paraphernalia themselves can go to a rental studio such as Jewel in Shinjuku, Tokyo, and hire a manga- or anime-themed costume—this can be viewed as a kind of *kankō taiken* (personal experience tourism). Various kinds of *kankō taiken* have become available in Japan and it is in this context that I argue that being dressed for a day in a rental kimono or other *wafuku* in order to experience the city of Kyoto can also be viewed as a kind of cosplay. Kimono *taiken* (kimono experience) is aligned with the cosplay characteristics of temporary transformation, performativity, and *asobi*. Individuals dress up in kimono in order to experience a different identity that takes them outside the bounds of normal everyday experience, and this experience is as much about "doing" as it is about "being."

I will focus on three Kyoto-based *taiken* that involve dressing in certain kimono-like costumes or *wafuku* that can be viewed as a kind of "cosplay": kimono *taiken* (being dressed in a kimono), *maiko henshin* (transformation into an apprentice geisha), and *tezukuri yoroi* (making wearable Japanese amour). While not an explicit form of *kankō taiken*, I will also look at local participation in festivals as a form of "cosplay" because it also involves many similar attributes: the temporary donning of a garment which is outside one's daily routine, worn in a social context of public display, and an altered sense of self-presentation and behavior ("play"). I will then analyze how these forms of *kankō taiken* fit with the concept of "cosplay" and discuss why this is a useful approach to my research.

Wearing Kimono in Contemporary Japan

Today, wearing a kimono plays a minor role in the life of most Japanese people but perhaps more than any other Japanese city, Kyoto's residents can be seen wearing kimono as well as other *wafuku* such as *yukata*, *haori*, and *mompe* (Hall 2015: 63). Many locals working in the tourism industry, in shops selling souvenirs or traditional crafts, and in restaurants, wear kimono. Kimono is also worn on special occasions, such as weddings, funerals, coming-of-age ceremonies, and tea ceremonies, although the use of Japanese clothing at these events tends to be gendered, with women wearing a kimono and men wearing a suit (the bride and groom are the exception to this as both usually wear traditional clothing if it is a Shinto ceremony, which might be held at either a shrine or in special "chapels" in hotels catering for wedding receptions). There is a certain irony to this gender divide, as dressing in kimono is a much more simplified process for men than for women—there are less steps and pieces involved. In fact, women who wish to wear kimono often attend training schools to learn *kitsuke*, to be taught how to select and wear kimono but also the etiquette (*reihō*) involved in wearing kimono. Even with less formal versions of kimono, such as the *yukata* (a summer robe made of cotton), the manner of dressing is gendered, as Assmann points out, "Kimono wearing for women involves complex rules and a need to observe the proper etiquette. Whereas for men wearing a *yukata* in a more relaxed form is socially acceptable, women need to adhere to a more formal way of tying the sash, even when they are wearing a *yukata*" (2008: 371).

As discussed in Chapter One, today's tendency for kimono to be more associated with women's rather than men's wear is primarily due to the legacy of the Meiji era when Japanese politicians in the 1890s constructed the image of men as Westernizing (or, in other terms, modernizing) Japan by wearing Western clothes, in opposition to women as upholding traditional values by wearing the kimono (Dalby 2001: 71). Thus, the kimono "became a symbol of 'distinctive Japaneseness,' which was expressed in contrast to the foreign while seeking to establish continuity with the historic past at the same time" (Assmann 2008: 361). At the time imported Western clothing was quite expensive and the privilege of wearing it was given first to men; it was only when Western clothing was more cheaply available in the postwar period that women began to forgo kimono for daily wear. Today, with regard to the cost of clothing, the converse is true: kimono requires knowledge in the selection of the kimono and accessories, and of the appropriate way to don it; it also requires a significant financial outlay. Liza Dalby estimates that a silk kimono and *obi* can easily amount to one million yen and a kimono suitable for casual gatherings costs about 380,000 yen (2001: 152). It is interesting to note that this does not appear to have changed much in the past 15 years as other scholars also state that to commission or purchase a kimono that is made by hand costs a minimum of one million yen (Dickens 2012: 107; Moon 2013: 82). Mori also quoted 900,000 yen for a traditionally made kimono in October 2012. He has stated that "with kimono demand falling, the kimono business has been trying to survive by cutting manufacturing costs. As a result, while artisans are expected to produce kimonos of ever higher quality, their wages have declined" (2012: 128), a trend common to many industries.

Statistical data on kimono consumption is difficult to obtain because of the minor role the industry plays in retail, and because kimono and their accessories are often inherited. According to the Yano Research Institute's[2] statistics, the kimono market has been in continued decline since the 1980s, with production revenue dropping from a peak of 1,766 billion yen in 1981 to 342 billion in 2009 (Mori 2012: 127). It is clear that the market continues to shrink (Assmann 2008), even taking into account the increase in different consumer groups interest mentioned in Chapter One, which I will discuss later in this chapter. Even though the cost of good quality, new kimono is prohibitive for most, the market for second-hand kimono and casual kimono remains small and does not have a positive image among women (ibid.).[3] Its image today is a garment that is expensive, impractical, difficult to put on, and daunting to wear (in terms of adherence to the rules of etiquette). Yet the kimono in Japanese culture still persists, partly because of the idea that wearing a kimono is linked to constructions of national identity, as discussed in Chapter One, and also because "mastering the art of the kimono can be interpreted as a form of cultural capital whereby the kimono fulfils a role in social distinction" (Assmann 2008: 360). Similar to reasons that women train in tea ceremony or *ikebana*, an education in how to wear a kimono can be used to gain an advantage in the marriage market because it implies that the woman comes from a certain socioeconomic background; in other words, she is a member of the upper class, wealthy and well educated in terms of cultural training. Kimono is associated with an upper-class identity, or at least aspirations to such lifestyles which value practices such as tea ceremony and *ikebana*, and permit the leisure time to pursue these activities. Just as a young man may try to get a job promotion as a form of *konkatsu* (activities leading to marriage), a license in how to wear kimono is an item that can be added to a woman's *omiai* (formal marriage interview) profile. This is the predominant view of contemporary kimono, what Dalby describes as the "samurai-turned-bourgeois" style (2001: 126) mentioned in Chapter One, because of the connection between these contemporary values and the historical sartorial etiquette and leisure pursuits of samurai women in the 1800s.

Of course, there are alternative uses and views of kimono, such as those seen in the *mizushōbai* (literally the "water trade"; a euphemism for the night entertainment industry): tropes that represent this are the kimono of the *oiran* (courtesan) or the *mamasan* (bar, brothel, or geisha house owner). This kind of kimono wearing is seen as more erotic (especially in the former case), and more associated with a sector of the working class than the upper class. In this context, the working class borrow the samurai bourgeois dress code to lend them respectability. This alternative use of kimono is also expressed by contemporary consumers, as seen in the various ways to wear kimono promulgated by rental shops such as Kimono Hearts, discussed below. Anime and manga cosplayers engage with kimono in an alternative realm, and the design, shape, and mode of wearing might go against normal kimono wearing rules, because their aim is to imitate the anime or manga characters as they appear in the media, rather than conform to sartorial custom. In general, however, kimono wearers who are not part of the pop culture practice of cosplaying, nor are part of the *mizushōbai*, are seen as having cultural capital, or are associated with the upper class in contemporary Japanese society. I surmise that in the majority of kimono *taiken* as seen in Kyoto, wearers aspire to this refined experience, striving to adhere to the strict rules of etiquette. This is evident from the success of this form of *taiken* and the rarity of alternative experiences on offer.

What Makes a Kimono?

A few years ago, I attended a friend's wedding in Kyoto. It is common for guests, as well as the bridal party, to wear kimono to such an occasion, and so one of the foreign female guests had bought a new kimono and *obi* for the occasion and wore it on the day. The dressers at the shrine helped the guest don her attire: the kimono was wrapped left over right, the *obi* was tied in a perfect *taiko* (drum knot) style, and the shrine dressers lent her an *obi-jime* (the thin braided cord tied over the *obi*), an *obi makura* (*obi* pillow to create the *taiko obi* style), and an *obi-age* (to tie over the *makura*) to complete the outfit. Even though the robe appeared to be the required length and proportions of a kimono, I remember thinking, "that's not a proper kimono"; at the time I was not sure why I thought that. Surprisingly, even though the woman had not lived in Japan (it was her second or third visit), she also expressed a certain embarrassment concerning her kimono, saying that she had bought it in a hurry and that it was only a cheap one.

While it is difficult to pinpoint exactly what was "wrong" about the kimono, a few factors contributed to my impression: the fabric was thin, shiny polyester, rather than the natural fibers such as wool, linen, cotton, or silk that most of the designers I worked with required. It had no body and therefore did not hang in the usual *zundō* (cylindrical container) style. Typically, *furisode* have brighter colors and bolder patterns than kimono worn by married women, but the pattern was garish even by *furisode* standards (the woman was unmarried so a *furisode* would have been the acceptable kimono for attending a wedding). The sleeves were not the typical *furisode* length, the collar was too narrow and did not sit neatly around the neck—perhaps Japanese would describe it as "kimono-*ppoi*," just as the wholesaler quoted at the start of this chapter described the kimono design as "cosplay-*ppoi*." There is an important linguistic nuance in this description: kimono-*ppoi* implies that it is like a kimono, *but is not a kimono* (Hall 2018b: 15). Other examples of this linguistic nuance would be to describe an adult as *kodomo-ppoi* (child-like or childish) such as Japanese singer Kyary Pamyu Pamyu, or describing a cup of tea as *mizu-ppoi* (watery) when it should be stronger (this is opposed to another grammatical suffix—*rashii* that indicates that something is as it appears, e.g., kimono-*rashii*—it appears to be a kimono, *kodomo-rashii*—it appears that she is a child).

Therefore, the kimono wholesaler, by saying Mori's kimono design was "cosplay-*ppoi*" (implying it is similar to but not in fact cosplay), demonstrates that he saw the garments on a graded continuum in which the design was closer to being an "authentic" kimono than to being a "fake" kimono for the purpose of cosplay (ibid.). There are garments on the other end of the continuum between these two clear values: cosplay costumes that are kimono-*ppoi*—they are like kimono but are designed specifically for the cosplay market. There appear to be three main features that affect a kimono's "authenticity": garment structure, the decorative composition, and the mode of dress, which will be discussed below.

Garment Structure

As has already been discussed in Chapter One, decorative compositions for kimono changed over time and depended on contemporary trends, but the overall shape of the kimono has remained static for centuries. In answer to "what defines kimono?" Liza Dalby states that "all garments of kimonoid [sic] genealogy have in common four elements of costume construction: geometric use of standard fabric widths sewn with minimal cutting; an open, overlapping front; an attached neckband sewn around the front opening; and sleeves consisting of a width of fabric attached to the selvages" (2001: 18). Kimono material is produced in *tan*, which are bolts of cloth of a standard width, approximately 34–40 centimeters and a bolt contains approximately 11–12 meters, enough to make one adult-sized kimono (Milhaupt 2014: 21). The back consists of two lengths of fabric joined in the center, each front panel is two half-widths providing the overlap, and the sleeves are each made of a width of fabric joined to the sides of the body (as previously mentioned the length of the sleeves varies primarily in accordance with marital status). The sleeves are open from the bottom of the rectangle up to the wrist and underneath the arm,[4] as opposed to a cosplay kimono where the sleeves are closed up to the wrist. Presumably the cosplay kimono sleeves are designed in a way to increase the dramatic impact of the sleeve length—a characteristic that distinguishes it from the "traditional" shape and thus possibly makes it appear more modern and playful.

Decorative Composition

When questioned, Mori's business partner elaborated on the rules concerning kimono design—he said that it is not just about how the kimono is worn, or the right selection and combination of accessories that makes it a "real" kimono (although this is important and will be discussed below). There are certain stylistic elements that can be acceptably combined within the decorative composition of the fabric—for example, some flowers can be used together and some should not, the size of the elements in a pattern is a key factor, and certain color palettes are conventionally matched to seasons and occasions—these features contribute to creating a design that can be recognized as a "proper" kimono design (Hall 2018b: 16). Mori also showed me some of his early designs, describing them as "lacking balance" and therefore resulting in unsuccessful kimono designs that were rejected by buyers. He said he had to learn how to create the right balance between the elements in the decorative composition (ibid.). Elsewhere Mori has stated that "unfortunately many inkjet designers possess little knowledge about kimonos and this lack of knowledge is often apparent in the design—and can generally be discerned by consumers" (Mori 2012: 129).

For Mori, the learning process involves consultation with those in the trade. During my interview with him, his business partner brought a man and woman to the office (Hall 2018b: 16). The man was the business partner's superior at the kimono wholesale company where they both worked. The woman was another kimono designer, albeit with more experience. She had previously worked at a kimono-making company but had become freelance. Mori asked their advice about colors for specific samples he had printed and the woman sat on the floor with the samples and a thick book of color swatches, suggesting color combinations (ibid.). Because this interactive business relationship requires flexibility, Mori sees using a computer for kimono design gives his business an advantage (ibid.). After they left, he showed me a design on his computer, saying, "for example, if, in this yellow area the wholesaler thinks this pattern seems a little strange I can change it in a moment. If I also want to make a sample I can instantly print one out" (personal interview September 21, 2012). He says that his work is the same as a graphic designer, using software such as Photoshop and Illustrator, but software skills are not enough, he "has to be able to understand traditional kimono patterns and old kimono designs in order to do it" (Hall 2018b: 16). This exchange demonstrated the notion that the pattern on the fabric of a kimono plays a part in the classification of a "kimono" as well as the more discernible features of the robe's shape.

The factors determining what is "acceptable" in kimono design accord with tradition. Throughout Japanese history there have been texts documenting dress that designers still refer to today when they are learning about design or for inspiration during the design process. One early example is the record entitled *Masasuke shōzokushō* (Masasuke's notes on court costume) that documents Heian period Empress Fujiwara Tashi's robes, especially the *kasane* lists of colors, describing color combinations for her robes (Dalby 2001: 253). One of these color conventions is that of *ura koki suo* (deep maroon linings) that combine maroon with a blue-green, a color combination "that even now continues to rule the assemblage of kimono and obi" (Dalby 2001: 262). From the seventeenth century through to the Meiji era a large number of catalogs were published by artists such as Hishikawa Moronobu (Dalby 2001: 289), and also by dye houses located in Kyoto. These catalogs were the equivalent of fashion magazines and had a variety of purposes and audiences. The *Ohiinagata*, published in 1667, is oft quoted (I discussed one of the kimono designs in Chapter One) but there are many other existing catalogs, such as the *Yūzen hiinagata* (Yūzen Catalog) published in 1688 by the House of Yūzen (the most famous *yūzen* dye workshop in Japan according to Dalby, 2001: 329), *Wakoku hiinagata taisen* (A Collection of Japanese Catalogs, 1698), the *Shōtoku hiinagata* (Catalog of the Shōtoku Period, 1713), and the *Hiinagata Gion Bayashi* (Catalog of the Gion Quarter, 1714) (Kawakami 1997). All of these catalogs have detailed drawings of kimono designs, and some of them also include either anonymous models or kabuki

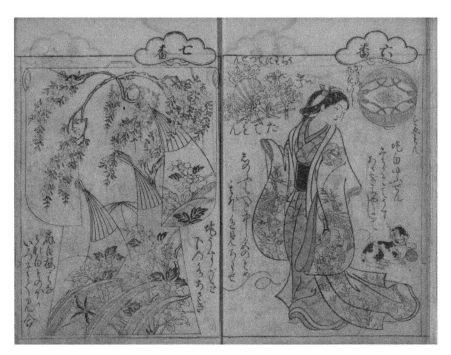

Figure 4.2 Image of a model (right) by artist Nishikawa Sukenobu, published in the *Hiinagata Miyako Fūzoku* (1716).
Source: National Diet Library Digital Collections.

actors wearing some of the kimono (see Figure 4.2). There is also a practical element that comes in to play in pattern design—how the kimono is worn determines where the pattern is placed. There is little point putting most of the design elements on the right front panel if, when the garment is donned, that section is not going to be visible.

Decorative designs are one factor that determines a kimono's level of formality, especially where the pattern occurs on the garment. Dalby states, "A kimono grammatical rule seems to be in operation here. The more pervasive the pattern, the less formal the garment" (2001: 196). Therefore, *komon*, a repeat pattern that covers the kimono signifies the lowest level of formality; *tsukesage*, a diagonal pattern on the left shoulder and hem is the next step up (*tsukesage* can be made more formal if crests are added); then *hōmongi*, asymmetrical patterning that continues without break across the kimono; and finally, the black three-crested *iro muji* (Dalby 2001: 197–8). The level of formality is also determined by material—even each of the natural fibers has a hierarchy that has been determined by the sumptuary laws through the ages, and by colors.[5]

However, it is evident from Mori's designs, that there is the potential for designers to experiment with kimono design. Kawabe Yūnosuke, a designer who,

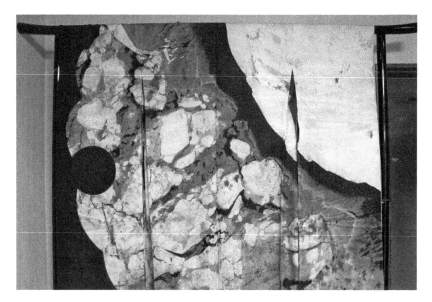

Figure 4.3 Kawabe Yūnosuke's kimono design using images of the earth from space. Fabric design © Kawabe Yūnosuke. Photo: Jenny Hall.

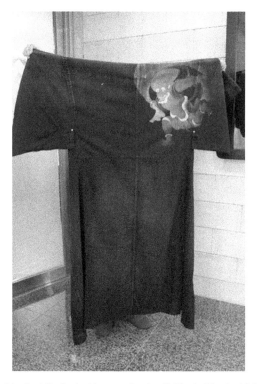

Figure 4.4 Kyoto Montsuki's denim kimono. Design © Kyoto Montsuki. Photo: Jenny Hall.

like Mori, uses contemporary technology such as the computer and inkjet printer combination to create kimono designs, designed a kimono based on images of the earth taken by the Japan Aerospace Exploration Agency (JAXA) (Figure 4.3) (Hall 2018b: 16). And kimono-making company Kyoto Montsuki, known for their traditional *kuro montsuki* (black-crested kimono), has experimented with denim kimono (see Figure 4.4). These designers are clearly challenging the definitions of what constitutes kimono through pattern design, materials, and technology (ibid.).

Mode of Dress

While it is clear that the world of cosplay blurs the lines between traditional yet this-worldly and fanciful, playful garments, recently some designers and stylists in the world of kimono have also been blurring the lines with their innovative suggestions as to how kimono are worn. Individuals and shops are challenging conventional ways of wearing kimono. *Kimono Hime*, a Japanese magazine published since 2003, illustrates ways to combine antique kimono and *obi* with modern Western accessories (2003). Stylist for the magazine, Aizawa Miki, juxtaposes kimono with tights and high heels, earmuffs, gloves, and lace (*Kimono Hime* 2009: 3–9), in ways that recall trends of the early Meiji period when, as Dalby notes, "high button shoes, red flannel shirts, hats and capes—all worn with kimono—were thrown together into eclectic and exuberant outfits" (2001: 71). Aizawa even includes a front-tied *obi*, a feature bound to provoke many kimono wearers due to the practice's sexual connotations; this mode of wearing was common among courtesans in the Edo period (Hall 2015: 78).[6] "Kimono activist" Mamechiyo, "whose mission is to take kimono to the masses—and never mind what the highly conservative world of traditional Japanese costume might think" (Webb 2005) is also creating styles such as the front-tied *obi* to challenge the strict rules espoused by the *kitsuke* schools. Traditionally this was about communicating sexual availability but I surmise that today new ways of tying *obi* might be less about communicating the wearer's *mizushōbai* profession and more about making kimono accessible to younger wearers by changing the image of kimono, as well as introducing easier ways of wearing and adjusting them (Hall 2015: 78)). Rather than an outright rebellion against the kimono's traditional form, I would say that the aim of these designers is more about widening the kimono genre by providing a more accessible way of wearing it.

Young Japanese as well as kimono retailers are embracing these sartorial deviations (ibid.). Kimono Hearts, a chain of stores in western Japan, rents kimono for various events and the *furisode* displayed on their website are categorized as: glamorous, gothic, romantic girlie, neo classic, Japan "trad," floral feminine, *Kyō-maiko* (Kyoto *maiko*), *oiran* (courtesan), and retro trip (Kimono Hearts Corporation 2014). This is convincing evidence that such companies are bringing cosplay noticeably closer to the realm of kimono (Hall 2015: 79). For example, the neo classic style is described as being for women coveting "antique taste" with accessories such as pearls and lace. The gothic style is a "mix of Japanese kimono and Western medieval styles" and includes gold and black ribbons, mesh and velvet. The "Edo rock style" of the *oiran* features women wearing off-the-shoulder kimono and front-tied *obi* with accessories such as a tobacco pipe, *takageta* (tall wooden clogs), and *wagasa* (Japanese umbrella) (Hall 2015: 79). It is interesting that the *oiran* style promoted here illustrates the alternative image of kimono mentioned above, rather than the general view of kimono as upper-class attire. Retro trip is a combination of "Taishō romance and Shōwa modern" that features kimono with either large flowers or hypnotic stripes in black and white, red, royal purple, or cobalt blue, matched with equally bright *obi* in contrasting colors (ibid.). The models' hairstyles are contemporary; long cuts worn loose or in a chignon and decorated with floral clips or bob cuts with bows (ibid.). The models are seen to don elements grouped in a particular category, and thereby act out a role from a historical era or fantasy world, making these photographs extremely suggestive of cosplay. The marketing materials of Kyoto rental and retail shop Guiches also provide a good example of this mix of traditional and contemporary styles, again demonstrating how companies are encouraging consumers to challenge the pervading norms of kimono-wearing (Guiches 2015). While the cosplay world has always involved kimono-wearing participants, these sartorial deviations are inviting cosplay into the kimono world. They also expand the perception of cosplay and indicate that cosplaying is now a pastime observed outside the manga/anime world (Hall 2015: 79). There is an increasing sense of playfulness (as below) and a nonserious view of kimono enabled by the growing affordability of digital *yūzen*, second-hand and rental kimono (ibid.).

Osaka University of Arts students are adopting some of these new styles, as images of them from their University magazine dressed for a 2011 graduation illustrate. The students wear a mix of clothes from those that could be labeled "cosplay" to more traditional kimono but it is clear that none of the kimono wearers adheres to the conventions of kimono wearing completely: some are wearing boots or shoes as opposed to traditional footwear, others have adopted Western style headwear, and so on (ibid.). There are informal institutions that also encourage individuals to "play" with wearing kimono. Kimono Jack (also known as Kimono de Jack, or Kimono Jakku in Japanese) was established in 2009 by Akagi Mihiro. The name of the association refers to the Japanese use of "hijack" when referring to flash mobs (Jackman 2014). The Kimono Jack website says, "Let's hijack Kyoto's sightseeing spots wearing kimono and astonish those who are wearing Western clothes" (Kimono Jack 2015, my translation). Akagi owns a kimono rental shop, Kyoshoan, near Shijo-dōri in central Kyoto so there is little doubt that he also has a marketing objective but participation in Kimono Jack is free and casual. Participants range in age from 8 to 80 and are encouraged to attend events whenever they like (Okazaki 2015: 187). The first Kimono Jack event was held at Kyoto's Shinto shrine, Yasaka Jinja, attracting forty participants (Jackman 2014). According to Akagi, events in the larger Japanese cities now consistently attract about 100 to 180 participants (ibid.). The Kimono Jack website shows that the Kyoto group organize an event once every six months in Kyoto (Kimono Jack 2015), but the idea has spread via social media and gatherings have taken place in nineteen cities in Japan and twenty cities overseas, in particular in the Netherlands (Okazaki 2015: 187). The leader of Kimono Jack Tokyo, Morikawa Hiroyuki, has found that foreign participants are beneficial for the association because they tend to "judge a kimono on its own merits rather than grading the wearer on how they've stuck to the rules" and that "rather than weighing them [kimono] down with heavy words like 'culture' and 'tradition' we should explore how fun they are to wear" (Jackman 2014). Author of *Kimono Now*, Okazaki Manami, was struck by the cosplay-like aspect of Kimono Jack wearers, stating they wear "all manner of kimonos, from formal to vintage and ensembles bordering on cosplay" (Okazaki 2015: 187).[7] The elements of temporary transformation, play and performativity all apply to these situations, but, "unlike other 'simulation games' during which a player temporarily plays a character of her/his choice, by adopting eccentric fashion styles a person plays himself or herself while constructing his or her personal and social identity" (Daliot-Bul 2009a: 369). This aspect of the consumption of kimono and *wafuku* demonstrates that, as Stevens (paraphrasing Giddens) notes in her broader discussion of popular culture consumption in Japan, "this is not just 'play' but serious identity work that has consequences in other public arenas such as political and economic spheres" (2010: 204).

Kankō Taiken

Kankō taiken (personal experience tourism) has become a way for traditional industries in Kyoto to revive interest in their products and to showcase their skills. There are several types of *taiken* on offer in Kyoto such as those that involve making something using a traditional technique. In terms of textiles alone, it is possible to learn simple weaving techniques at the Nishijin Ori Kaikan (Nishijin Textile Center), *shibori* (tie-dyeing) at the Kyoto Shibori Kōgeikan or *yūzen-zome* (stencil dyeing) at the Kodai Yūzen-en (see Chapter Two for descriptions of these techniques). Private companies have also seen the value of offering *taiken*: the *yūzen* company Kamedatomi offers a *katazome taiken* (stencil-dyeing workshop) in their factory, the *kurozome* (black dye) company Banba Senkōgyō Co. Ltd. holds a *kamon* (family crest) dyeing workshop, and at Yamamoto Roketsuzome, visitors can learn *roketsuzome* (wax-resist dyeing), to name only three. There are also *taiken* in *washi* (paper-making), *urushi* (lacquer), *wahon* (bookbinding), and *Kyō-sensu uwaetsuke* (fan-painting). As mentioned above, I am focusing on three *taiken* that involve dressing in certain costumes and can be viewed as a kind of "cosplay": kimono *taiken*, *maiko henshin*, and *tezukuri yoroi*, as well as looking at dressing in costumes for festivals.

Kimono *Taiken*

Since 2009 I have observed both an increase in the number of kimono rental businesses such as Okakimi on Hanamikoji in Gion and an increase in the prevalence of individuals, especially couples and groups, wearing kimono and *hakama* around the Gion area. Even before that, it was not so common to see people wearing kimono outside of the special occasions such as weddings and coming-of-age ceremonies mentioned above. It appears to have become increasingly popular among domestic and international tourists to rent and wear a kimono as part of the Kyoto tourism experience—*kankō taiken*.[8]

I first noticed kimono *taiken* in March 2010 when I saw a group of eight young teenagers standing on the steps of Ninenzaka, the laneway leading down from Kiyomizudera (Kiyomizu temple) in Kyoto. The surprising thing about the group was the number of males dressed in *hakama* (see Figure 4.5)—it was unusual to see any young man, let alone that number (four), wearing *hakama*. However,

Figure 4.5 Group of young people dressed in kimono and *hakama* on the steps of Ninenzaka, 2010. Photo: Jenny Hall.

Figure 4.6 Five women wearing kimono at Yasaka Jinja, 2012. Photo: Jenny Hall.

during trips to Kyoto in 2010 and 2012 I witnessed several men wearing kimono or *hakama*, usually accompanied by a girlfriend in kimono. During my fieldwork period, I also witnessed more than thirty groups of women or couples wearing kimono at popular Kyoto tourist destinations such as Yasaka Jinja, Kiyomizudera, Ninenzaka, Gion, and on Shijo-dōri. I cannot attribute this increase to one particular season, occasion, or event, because I first noticed it throughout my visit from February to May 2010, and then during my subsequent fieldwork trip from September to November 2012, although it is clear that tourists do visit Kyoto for particular events and decide to rent a kimono to enhance their experience. For example, two female high school students from Tokyo told me they had rented their kimono to wear while watching Jidai Matsuri in October 2012, thinking that this would make their experience of the festival more enjoyable.[9] However, kimono *taiken* can also be spontaneous; a group of women told me they were visiting a friend who lived in Kyoto and decided to rent kimono for a day out in the city (Figure 4.6).

Renting a kimono has become a part of the Kyoto tourism experience, and is advertised as such. Tourism magazines such as *Kyoto Toraberakko* ("Little Kyoto Traveller," published by JTB) (Hirahara 2012) run articles recommending tourists dress in kimono for an "elegant" walk around the Kiyomizu area (Hall 2018a: 303). One particular article states that "kimono suits these undulating streets" (*kimono ga niau Kyō no sakadō*) (Hirahara 2012: 16). Another small paperback book from the Rakutabi Bunko series, titled *Kyō no kimono hajime*, gives suggestions for the best places to wear a kimono in Kyoto such as temples, cafes, museums, and souvenir shops (Takahashi 2008). It serves as a pocket-sized instructional for Japanese on wearing kimono in Kyoto, which also lists all of the basic accessories necessary to wear a kimono, recommends shops selling antique and new kimono, includes some details on how a kimono is made and even step-by-step instructions on how to move in a kimono. An association called the Kyoto Foundation for Promotion of Japanese Dress (comprised of various Kyoto government bodies and textile industry associations) established the *Kyoto Kimono Passport* in 2001 to encourage tourists to wear kimono, presumably to increase business for kimono producers and other related industries. The *Kyoto Kimono Passport* is a small booklet that offers special privileges and discounts for those wearing a kimono, and includes information about Kyoto city.[10] This encouragement of tourists to don kimono in order to see the sights enhances what Urry and Larsen have dubbed the "tourist gaze" (2011). They assert that people learn how, when, and where to "gaze" through guidebooks, photographs, and other tourists (ibid.). This codification of the tourist gaze forms a part of sociocultural ways of seeing that are learned: "Tourists are choreographed by guides and visible signs but also by absent or invisible cultural codes, norms and etiquettes for how to perceive and value tourist objects" (ibid.: 192). This socialization of tourists aids in the construction of the imagined national community (discussed later in the "Clothing, Play, and Identity" section of this chapter) and the scopophilic aspect works both ways, promoting a love of seeing and a love of being seen.[11]

I was able to experience this scopophilic aspect in 2012 when I was invited to a tea ceremony event at a gallery/event space near Kinkakuji (Temple of the Golden Pavilion) in the north of Kyoto. The gallery holds a range of events in its traditional *machiya* and also has a kimono rental business for those wanting to sightsee in the area while dressed in kimono. I decided to rent a kimono to attend the tea ceremony. As soon as I arrived at the *machiya*, I was ushered to a room with a row of kimono to select one, along with an *obi*. Then I was led through the *machiya*, around a small garden and upstairs to the dressing room. The kimono dresser said she had been dressing people for about two or three years but she got her *kitsuke* license many years before that and had not used it until then. As kimono rental is becoming popular, she (and her husband) decided to establish the business in the *machiya* she had inherited (the *machiya* was used exclusively for the purposes of renting kimono, tea ceremony and other events rather than as a residence). She quickly dressed me—it took only a matter of a few minutes for her to wrap and adjust the kimono to the right length, and tie my *obi* before I was ready to go back down the stairs in my rented attire.

One of my friends, a businessman, was also attending the tea ceremony. When I entered the room where he was drinking tea, there were three other businessmen with him wearing suits. I was the only one wearing kimono and everyone commented on my kimono. I was also very conscious of my actions. The kimono was polyester, a fact that I could not help being aware of—it was scratchy on my skin and made rasping sounds as I moved. I surmise that most kimono *taiken* rental companies rent polyester kimono rather than higher quality silk kimono because they will stand more wear, can be easily washed, and they are cheaper to purchase. In my experience, these companies do not stock kimono for more formal occasions such as weddings—companies specialize in their chosen field of kimono rental.

The actual tea ceremony had yet to begin so we chatted. As we did so, I noted that wearing a kimono makes you sit straighter because the *obi* is wide and stiff. Perhaps because I have seen many people wearing them, it made me mimic the way they walk, using small steps to avoid the flap at the front from flaring open too much. The kimono dresser's husband told me that nowadays life is fast but kimono is slow. His comments made me think of the "slow food" movement—kimono is "slow clothing" because you cannot dress in a hurry nor do things quickly while wearing it. It makes you slow down and the husband, who wears kimono while practicing tea ceremony, finds this aspect particularly appealing in his otherwise fast-paced life (he is also an *obi* manufacturer). I return to this concept of slow clothing in Chapter Six.

Maiko Henshin

Maiko henshin (*maiko* metamorphosis) is a more specific form of kimono *taiken* because the participant is dressed in the kimono and accoutrements of a *maiko*, or an apprentice geisha. This activity is not referred to as *taiken* because the participant does not experience being a *maiko*—they do not perform or entertain customers—they are merely dressed as a *maiko.* Years before I began this research I was aware of and had experienced *maiko henshin*. I dressed as a *maiko* on two occasions at Studio Shiki in Ninenzaka (in 2003 and 2005). Studio Shiki has been operating since 1987 and now has two studios—the main shop in Ninenzaka and another not far from Kiyomizu temple. I had also seen tourists dressed as *maiko*, such as the two Chinese women spotted on Shirakawa-dōri in Figure 4.7 and the group of women in Figure 4.8, on several occasions. *Maiko henshin* has been gaining popularity with overseas tourists; when I first went to Studio Shiki, none of the staff spoke English but their website now states that English, Chinese, Italian, and Spanish speaking staff members are available for customers.

Most *maiko henshin* studios offer makeup, hair styling, and kimono dressing for a set of studio photographs. At Studio Shiki, the first step is to select from several plans that vary in price between 13,000 and 40,000 yen, depending on the elaborateness of the outfit (the mature *geiko* costume is more expensive than the *maiko*) and photographs (in the studio or outdoors, for example), and

Figure 4.7 Chinese tourists dressed as *maiko*, Shinbashi-dōri, 2010. Photo: Jenny Hall.

Figure 4.8 A group of women dressed as *maiko*, Ishibeiko-michi, Shimokawara-chō 2010. Photo: Jenny Hall.

Figure 4.9 The author in the makeup room at Studio Shiki undergoing *maiko henshin*, 2003. Photo: Tracy Houston (reproduced with kind permission).

whether or not customers want to stroll the streets of Ninenzaka wearing their costume for one hour (this is not available on rainy days).

After placing their belongings into a locker, customers don *hadajuban*—the simple white cotton underlayer that crosses the chest (named because *hada* means skin in Japanese), and white *tabi* socks. Hair is flattened onto the head with a hairnet. Next, the makeup is applied in the makeup room—first, the skin is covered in a special kind of protective wax as a primer that enables the white foundation to be applied more easily. Then, the whole face is covered with a white foundation, including the upper chest and back of the neck, two V-shaped areas of skin left clean, reaching up to the nape (see Figure 4.9). The eyes are rimmed in black, the outer corners edged in red. Lips are also red. The makeup takes about ten minutes before customers go downstairs to select kimono. This may seem quick, especially considering the pampering that usually accompanies salon sessions in the Australian beauty industry; this felt like being on a production line. Goldstein-Gidoni also noticed this "production" aspect of dressing couples in the wedding industry in Japan, stating, "My use of the term 'production' is not unintentional. Not only does it refer to the 'performative' aspect ... of a wedding, in the same way that a film or a play is a 'production,' but it also suggests the process of production in the sense of manufacturing, especially of mass-production" (2000: 34). This "production" feeling has no doubt become more pronounced as the *maiko henshin* experience has become more popular. *Maiko henshin* may be viewed as more akin to the *esute* (aesthetic beauty) industry in Japan, whereby "the main purpose of the *esute* salon is not to pamper the client but to correct her body 'defects'" (Miller 2006: 43). While transformation into a *maiko* is not about correcting bodily defects as such, having to adapt corporeally to wearing a kimono, "the female body is not just constrained; more significantly, it is moulded into a ready-made pattern, which is the model Japanese woman"

(Goldstein-Gidoni 2008: 8). The metamorphosis into a more beautiful, better executed version of themselves is similar to those in the *esute* industry's target audience who model themselves on more contemporary ideals such as Crown Princess Masako, or J-Pop stars Hamasaki Ayumi, or Aikawa Nanase (Miller 2006: 46), even if it is a short-term transformation.

There are about a hundred kimonos to choose from at each of the studios (Maiko-Henshin Studio Shiki 2015). Two kimono fitters work quickly and efficiently, slipping on another under garment and attaching more layers around the body. They add padding around the torso to create the desired flat and straight cylindrical effect, strapping it all tightly. There are more than twelve different pieces, which must be put on in prescribed ways. The sash, or *obi*, is a very important part of the outfit, and it must be selected carefully with consideration of the season, the occasion, and the kimono pattern. *Obi* often cost more than the kimono because they involve complicated weaving procedures (as detailed in Chapter Two). There are also multiple ways to tie an *obi*, but again, the actual donning of the kimono and *obi* only takes ten or fifteen minutes.

The final step in the transformation process is hair. Real *maiko* have their long hair oiled and pinned, sleeping on a special raised wooden pillow in order to preserve their *ware shinobu* (*maiko* hairstyle) for several days. At Studio Shiki, if the customer's hair is long enough they might select a *han-katsura* (half wig) that can be worked in with the front of their own hair for a more natural look. It takes about twenty minutes to fit the *han-katsura*. Otherwise, in just five minutes they can have a *zen-katsura* (full wig) fitted. The *zen-katsura* is already twisted into the typical *maiko ware shinobu* style, complete with flower decorations and ornamental pins (see Figure 4.10). A staff member will try several wigs on the customer before finding a good match. Even so, she then wedges small cushions under the *katsura* to ensure a tight fit. High wooden *okobo* (clogs that have tapered wooden platforms) complete the ensemble.

Dressing as a *maiko* is not a comfortable experience for the uninitiated. Within ten minutes of having my weighty full wig fitted, I had a piercing headache. The padding and tight *obi* made it difficult to breathe and I was unable to take a deep breath. The ensemble was heavy and cumbersome, and the *okobo* made walking on Ninenzaka's cobbled streets extremely precarious. My friend and I could only take small steps because of the restrictive kimono that reached our ankles. We were compelled to walk slowly because we were unused to the *okobo* and because we were worried about damaging the expensive kimono. The staff had also given us strict instructions: no drinking, no eating, and no shopping (we were not sure why the last rule applied but perhaps it was just a practical rule as the long hanging sleeves and the protruding *obi* could have caused havoc in a shop). Every movement had to be done with care and attention, and we were conscious of our swinging silk sleeves and the large protuberance of the long hanging *darari-no-obi* (a style originating in the Edo period that is popular with

Figure 4.10 *Zen-katsura* (full wigs) at Studio Shiki, 2003. Photo: Jenny Hall.

Kyoto *maiko* now—*darari* means loosely, or languidly, referring to how the long *obi* hangs down) on our backs.

Nevertheless, we gained a lot of attention from other tourists, both domestic and foreign, which made us feel like celebrities (and also gave us an idea of the extent to which real *maiko* are often hounded). We were constantly stopped so that people could pose with us for photographs, even if they were at first a little surprised to find what they thought were *maiko* were actually two *gaijin* (foreigners)—from recent observation this no longer appears to be the case— Japanese tourists are more aware of "fake" *maiko*, easy to spot because they are often photographing each other (see Figure 4.11) and pay less attention to them. On a Japanese culture blog, in a posting titled "How to distinguish between real and fake maiko (geisha)," the author writes, "The most certain way to distinguish them is to see their actions. Maiko are well mannered and they are trained to do every action beautifully; for example, they walk with their toes turned inward" (Japan Style 2011). Although the limits of the costume altered our behavior to a degree, we could not really emulate *maiko* unless we had some knowledge of how they moved and correct movement is part of a *maiko's* training. In fact, it is very difficult to photograph real *maiko* as they are usually hurrying to appointments, demonstrating how they become adept at wearing the kimono ensemble and the *okobo* (see Figure 4.12).

Figure 4.11 Women dressed as *maiko*, photographing each other at Yasaka Jinja, 2006. Photo: Jenny Hall.

Figure 4.12 A real *maiko* hurrying to an appointment on Shijo-dōri, 2006. Photo: Jenny Hall.

The act of dressing as *maiko* or geisha for leisure is not a new practice, but originally it occurred only in the Gion quarter of Kyoto and was done by wealthy patrons with a lot of time on their hands. Studio Shiki sought to offer the service to a wider clientele and their foresight has paid off. The studio celebrated its thirty-sixth anniversary in 2018 in what is becoming a booming industry in *maiko henshin* (Maiko-Henshin Studio Shiki 2018). According to the studio's website, now more than twenty thousand people visit this studio each year, compared with about a thousand customers ten years ago.[12] There are now a plethora of studios, packages, and prices around Kyoto from which to choose. Along with *maiko* and *geiko* plans, Yume Koubou offers an *oiran* plan, whereby women can dress in "the splendour of a woman from the red light district" (Yume Koubou 2011). At this studio men can dress either in "*dansei wafuku* style" (which literally means male Japanese clothes, but here they mean kimono) or *shinsengumi* (shogunate police), which are offered possibly as the counterpart to the *oiran*.

There is also a Samurai Plan available for men at Studio Shiki—*haori, hakama* and long and short swords—in which the aim is to transform the man into Sakamoto Ryōma[13], thus bringing it even closer to cosplay because of the specific character to role-play. It is the only plan available for men at this studio and the website explicitly states that "the Maiko/Geiko transformation service is not provided for men [*sic*] customers," an oblique reference to the fact that they will not serve cross-dressing customers (Maiko-Henshin Studio Shiki 2015).[14] However, the plans for women can also be deemed cosplay: the transformation is for only a couple of hours at most, customers have the chance (and are forced by the clothing) to modify their behavior and act as *maiko* (to a limited extent), fulfilling the performative aspect, and in this context the clothing is not a uniform (as it is for real *maiko*) but is for play. It is clear that young Japanese women enjoy the display aspect of *maiko henshin*, and enjoy being photographed and photographing each other, as Figure 4.11 shows. This scopophilic aspect of *maiko henshin* is location-specific—it is less likely that tourists would want to dress as *maiko* in other areas of Japan such as Shinjuku in Tokyo (although it is possible in Ginza) or Dōtombori in Osaka. This is also the case with other forms of cosplay, highlighted in the film *Kamikaze Girls* when one of the main characters, Ryūgasaki Momoko, appears to be completely displaced in rural Ibaraki wearing her Lolita outfit. The gaze is location specific—reinforcing Kyoto's position in the kimono capital stakes.

Tezukuri Yoroi

Another *taiken* activity that involves "cosplay" and traditional garments in Japan is the making and wearing of *yoroi* armor, worn by men of the samurai class in battle and in ceremonial settings.[15] *Yoroi* dates back to the Heian period and was traditionally made of rectangles of leather (*kozane*), lacquered (*urushi*) twenty

Figure 4.13 Tiered scales laced together to form *yoroi* armor. Photo: Jenny Hall.

times to give it strength, and laced together in tiered scales using braided cord (*kumihimo*). Originally it took one person three years to make a set of armor that weighed about 30 kilograms. The color of the cords signified rank and clan.

In Kuromon Street in Nishijin, there is a studio called "Yoroi Noya Usagi Juku" where people can learn the art of making *yoroi* armor and *kabuto* (helmets). Uzuki Nagatoshi and his wife, Ako, hold the classes in their traditional house. Their customers range from grandmothers making armor for their grandsons, to foreigners with an interest in Japanese military history. Students are from primary school age up to 80 years old. At the school students learn the traditional craft of braided cords (*kumihimo*), fringed thread (*fusashimo*), and metal fittings (*kanamono*) as well as learning how to create *kozane-ita* (the lacquered tiered scales) that make up Heian period court costumes (see Figure 4.13). Making a complete set of armor takes about a year, but is ten times cheaper than simply buying a modern replica of an ancient piece, which would cost about five million yen. Parents can make something with their children, which both find rewarding, and they learn about Japanese history at the same time. Through making the armor, Uzuki Nagatoshi says that individuals can get a better sense of the values and aesthetics of the Heian period such as the importance of *shina no sadame* (literally "the determination of rank or value"), *miyabi* (courtliness and refinement), *makoto* (sincerity), and *mono no aware* (a sensitivity to things) (Tsunoda, de Bary & Keene 1958). Making armor may seem a far cry from these concepts but if we examine *yoroi* it is possible to see the beauty in the braiding, colors, and designs, especially on areas such as the *kyūbi no ita* (literally, pigeontail plate—the small front-left breastplate whose shape is that of a dove tail, a symbol of divinity) and *tsurubashiri-kawa* (the main breastplate made of deer skin that usually had flowers, motifs, or pictures on it) (see Figure 4.14). The concepts of *miyabi* and *mono no aware* related to these design elements. *Shina no sadame* is seen in the color, design, and material of the lacing on the *kozane* that served to identify

Figure 4.14 The main breastplate of *yoroi* often had flowers or decorative motifs. The color of the braid signified rank and clan. This example was photographed at Yoroi Noya Usagi Juku. Photo: Jenny Hall.

the clan of the warrior as well as their rank. The act of making the armor, and the extra learning involved regarding the history of the garments, distinguishes this *taiken* from the others I have discussed above. These aspects align this form of *taiken* more closely to cosplay, which often involves the cosplayers creating their own costumes and learning about the characters. In this respect, the personal investment of *tezukuri yoroi* is more cosplay-like than other kinds of dress-up *taiken*.

Many customers may learn *yoroi* merely for the experience and so that they can own a set, but for those who successfully complete their armor there is a special event held in Kyoto once a year in which they can don and parade in their armor. The event is called *Yoroi Kizome Shiki* (armor-wearing ceremony) and is held at Kamigamo Shrine every November. It is a highly ritualized event and participants look solemn and serious during the ceremony. On entering the shrine they must purify themselves by rinsing their hands and mouth as is the usual practice. Then they must bow to the shrine and clap to call the gods. A priest performs special rites after which their material hats are replaced with *kabuto*. A spokesperson for the students (sometimes this is a child) makes a short speech thanking those who helped in the making of the armor. The ceremony is only held in Kyoto. Uzuki Nagatoshi said that the goal of the ceremony, for him, is to express that this art form still exists. However, for those who wear their armor for the ceremony, it is much more than this as they experience wearing the garment and performing rituals in it. These actions give them a deeper understanding of the armor and its sensorial imprint on their bodies. This deeper understanding comes when "tourist performance is embodied practice" (Urry & Larsen 2011: 193).[16] Even though their sets of armor will weigh 20 kilograms rather than 30 kilograms as the originals once did,[17] in most other aspects they are replicas of the Heian period *yoroi*. Wearing their armor, students must be able to gain a sense of what a samurai warrior experienced in terms of restrictiveness of movement and weight. Higher ranking samurai would have worn this form of armor on horseback, so technically it does not give the students a complete corporal experience, but it certainly brings them closer than looking at *yoroi* in a museum or book. Making *yoroi* and participating in the *Yoroi Kizome Shiki* are open to either gender, but this is an event where Japanese and foreign men can enjoy dressing in costume, unlike the *maiko henshin* from which they are excluded. It also promotes the imagined community—both on a "local" and national scale as students can recognize those who have taken part in the acquisition of skills to make *yoroi* as well as wear an outfit symbolic of Japanese spirit and history.

Matsuri

Although not a form of *kankō taiken* (and participation is sometimes not open to the public) dressing up and taking part in Japan's festivals can also be considered an activity that involves sartorial display much like cosplay. Kyoto has three main festivals per year: Aoi Matsuri (held in May), Gion Matsuri (held in July), and Jidai Matsuri (held in October).[18] The newest festival is Jidai Matsuri, established in 1894 as part of Kyoto's 1100th anniversary. It is the "festival of the ages," as participants dress in costumes representing various periods of Kyoto's history from the Meiji Restoration (1868) back to the Enryaku era (782), including the major famous historical figures of each period. Participants parade through the streets from Kyoto Gosho (the Imperial Palace) to Heian Jingu shrine. The route is over two kilometers and the procession takes over an hour to pass a spectator standing in any given position on the route. There are about two thousand participants. Uzuki Nagatoshi and his wife, Ako, from Yoroi Noya Usagi Juku (discussed above) supply *yoroi* armor and help with dressing participants. All of the costumes are historically accurate and recreated by artisans such as the Uzukis using traditional techniques.

It is unclear how participants for Jidai Matsuri are chosen and individual's responses to this question were evasive but presumably place of residence is a factor and it does involve paying a monthly fee as security of a place. Younger participants are recruited from schools and universities (and therefore the *asobi* aspect of participation could be questioned in this respect as some of them may be less than willing participants). In 2012 I was able to speak to some university students about to take part in the parade, a *shibori* artisan who had taken part in Jidai Matsuri throughout his school years, and a rice shop owner who had been taking part since 2001.

Before the parade begins, participants must don their costumes and be briefed in their role during the morning. All participants martial in the Imperial Palace grounds and wait for their slot to join the parade. Some of them wait

Figure 4.15 Students dressed as Meiji era troops play flutes in the Jidai Matsuri parade, 2012. Photo: Jenny Hall.

for several hours so while waiting, many participants were picnicking with their families, dozing, or chatting. At this time, I approached six male university students waiting in the shade. They were dressed in the costumes of young noblemen. During this interview, they were not very forthcoming about the details of their participation, but this was perhaps because it was their first time taking part in Jidai Matsuri. I asked them what wearing the clothes made them think about, and one man said it made him consider the lives of people from the olden days. Another said wearing the costume made him feel more dignified, but others commented on how uncomfortable the costumes were. They said it was difficult to do practical things like go to the toilet, and the straw sandals hurt their feet because the bindings were stiff. They had a long walk ahead so these issues were an important consideration.

Tabata Kazuki, a *shibori* artisan, participated in Jidai Matsuri from age 8 until he was 20. He played the *fue* (the Japanese bamboo flute), and that appears to be one reason for his participation as he was part of a marching band representing the *shinsengumi*, the police in Kyoto who were dedicated to suppressing anti-shogunate sentiment at the end of the Edo period. Members of this band all play the flute during the parade (see Figure 4.15). The costumes were rented from Heian Jingu and comprised of a white headband, a black *haori* jacket over blue kimono and purple *hakama*, leggings, *tabi* socks, and straw sandals. The costume also included an imitation matchlock rifle and toy

Figure 4.16 An example of my informant's costume, Heian period *yoroi*, Jidai Matsuri, 2012. Photo: Jenny Hall.

Figure 4.17 An example of an Imperial Court aristocrat costume (*kugyō*), Jidai Matsuri, 2012. Photo: Jenny Hall.

katana (sword). Tabata said when he was a school student he felt happy wearing the costume, "I thought it was cool because the clothes weren't usual clothes. I became a samurai" (personal interview October 7, 2012).

Another informant, a rice shop owner, told me he had been participating in Jidai Matsuri since 2001. He is vice chair of the organizing committee for his *chō* (neighborhood) and is an enthusiastic supporter and participant of the festival. He does not always wear the same costume for the parade. In 2010 and 2011 he was a Heian period cavalry archer and wore *yoroi* for Jidai Matsuri. Because he was a cavalry member, he rode a horse. He said he did not particularly like wearing Heian period costume as he did not think it suited him. He also said wearing *yoroi* was heavy, and his costume weighed 40 kilograms (see Figure 4.16). In 2012 he wore a costume of the *kugyō*, an Imperial Court aristocrat, which he enjoyed more (see Figure 4.17). This informant obviously relishes the scopophilic aspects of being involved in Jidai Matsuri and is very proud of his participation, despite his comments about the difficulties involved in wearing some of the costumes. He supplied photographs of himself in the parade without prompting, showed me his own *katana*, and was keen for me to attend Jidai Matsuri while I was there.

Taking part in Jidai Matsuri requires a large amount of personal effort. Participants practice dressing and moving around in their costumes for weeks before the parade, but they can only be worn in public on the day of the festival (Powell and Cabello 2014). Some participants must arrive at the Imperial Palace grounds at 6:00 a.m. for lengthy preparations, including logistics. The dressing and makeup can take time, the costumes are uncomfortable, and there is a lot of waiting around before anything happens. The parade is over 2 kilometers long and in 2012 the day was extremely hot. Participants might not reach Heian Jingu until 4:00 p.m. or 5:00 p.m. and then must go back to where they started and change back into their ordinary clothing. However, having observed it in 2009 and 2012, I recognized many of the same faces, some of whom were wearing the same costumes, so it is clear from the repeat participation that many enjoy the transformative, performative, and *asobi* aspects of participation. The satisfaction they achieve in their involvement in the Jidai Matsuri also produces a camaraderie and collective spirit, reinforcing what it is to be a *Kyotojin* (a Kyoto person) with a long and rich historical heritage. As an analogy with other cultural displays in Japan, Smith's discussion of *bōsōzoku* (motorcycle subculture), is relevant here: "Collective participation … produces the intense comradery [*sic*] of 'communitas' (Turner 1974). And perhaps most importantly, *bosozoku* membership provides a dramaturgically rich role, abundant in exciting scripts, colorful props, and demanding performances" (Smith 2010: 31).

Like motorcycle gang members, my informants engage in a form of communal nostalgia for past eras that bring them together. This feeling of nostalgia is an important factor because, judging by my informants' comments, the costumes worn for Jidai Matsuri are not always physically comfortable—feelings of camaraderie, "communitas" and the scopophilic aspects are part of what makes participants return year after year and participate in the festival. This is also perhaps part of the reason that young Japanese domestic tourists, such as the two women from Tokyo with whom I spoke, rent and wear kimono while watching the Jidai Matsuri parade—it enables them to be part of this "collective participation"—they become "honorary villagers" (Robertson 1997: 106) or, in this case, honorary *Kyotojin*. They can be part of the performance and engage in the feeling of nostalgia it evokes.

Clothing, Play, and Identity

The relationship between cosplay, fashion *taiken* and *matsuri* participation arises from the key concepts of "imagined community" and "performativity." Benedict Anderson's concept of "imagined communities" (2006 [1983]) is thus important in regard to the fashion world, where people recognize affinity and preference for aesthetic and other values through the signals projected by the wearing of particular styles. For example, cosplayers and Gothic Lolitas create transnational imagined communities who recognize in each other a passion to create and wear those costumes—the costumes "presuppose the audience's familiarity with the costume and the meanings for which they stand" (Ragalye 2012: 22). In the Kyoto context, kimono *taiken*, *maiko henshin*, and wearing *yoroi* and other Jidai Matsuri costumes invoke an imagined (if not historically authentic) national community. Kimono, *maiko* (apprentice geisha), and *yoroi* (samurai armor) are all considered symbols of Japan and Japanese identity, both in Japan and overseas. If we consider local/national as a binary opposition that sits on a sliding scale of imagined communities in Japan, there are many ways that dress demonstrates identity; for example, local (*tezukuri yoroi*) to national (*maiko henshin*, kimono *taiken*). *Tezukuri yoroi* sits closer to the "local" because of the communal experience participants had over time creating their costumes together. Kimono *taiken* and *maiko henshin* can be placed near the "national" limit as the imagined community is on a national level, recognized by Japanese and foreigners as symbolic of Japanese identity. Within fashion *taiken*, those who participate in certain festivals such as Jidai Matsuri (the Festival of the Ages) would straddle the local/national axis because, as noted above, participation is determined on the basis of residence, but they are also recognized as representing the nation's history.

If general (self-expression)/specific (role-play characters) was another binary opposition on a sliding scale of performativity, then *tezukuri yoroi*, *maiko henshin*, and kimono *taiken* would be general rather than specific in terms of roles. Those who participate in *maiko henshin* and *tezukuri yoroi* are dressed as particular professions so would sit slightly closer to the specific terminus, even though the extent to which these participants actually perform the duties of a *maiko* or samurai

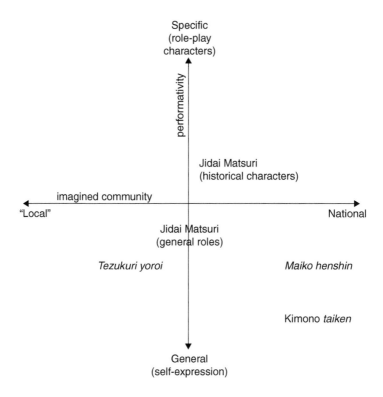

Diagram labels:
Specific (role-play characters)
performativity
Jidai Matsuri (historical characters)
imagined community
"Local"
National
Jidai Matsuri (general roles)
Tezukuri yoroi
Maiko henshin
Kimono taiken
General (self-expression)

Diagram 4.1 Sartorial identity in the context of Kyoto *taiken*.
Source: Jenny Hall.

is arguable (it is also possible that a participant in *tezukuri yoroi* could recreate the armor of a historical figure, making it more specific, but it is rare). In terms of sensory experience, *maiko henshin* is arguably more dramatic a change, both visually and physically, in comparison to kimono *taiken*, and this may also affect interpretations of performativity. Kimono *taiken* participants are not role-playing a historical figure or profession so would sit closest to the general terminus. Jidai Matsuri participants might find themselves dressing as a specific historical figure, but that does not mean they can enact the mannerisms or character of the person (although they might imagine these) so they can be placed nearer the general terminus. Diagram 4.1, based on concepts from Benedict Anderson's "imagined community" (2006 [1983]), illustrates this relationship.[19]

Of course, these placements are contestable, but I aimed to demonstrate how imagined communities are constructed through the performance of various Kyoto fashion *taiken* involving kimono and other *wafuku*. This provides an idea of consumer engagement within these relatively new contexts for wearing traditional apparel.

Two other Japanese linguistic terms may help to clarify the contextual complexity of wearing kimono. The concepts of *hare* and *ke* are often translated into "sacred" and "profane," and the links between *hare* and *haregi* (special formal wear, the suffix *-gi* denotes a form of clothing) are obvious—*hare* refers to the situation in which *haregi* is worn. *Hare* is used to specify occasions and activities that are public or formal, such as rituals, festivals, annual observances, and rites of passage (Stavros 2014: 93). It is also used to refer to occasions where the "spirit" is embodied in a participant—either the spirit of an enshrined ancestor or *kami* (god) or *hotoke* (spirit of the dead)—*hare* refers to the presence of a spirit in this world, and the space, and the interactions of people in this space are altered to accommodate its presence. In contrast to *hare*, the notion of *ke* signifies the private or mundane, the profane, or even the defiled (ibid.: 93). The situation in which an individual participates determines how they perceive and act in the clothing, rather than the actual clothing itself. For example, if an individual is participating in a festival (an event where the enshrined spirit is released from its confines and moves among the public), and wearing clothing such as a *happi* (short coat typically worn at festivals), the *happi* marks the participants as being in close proximity to the spirit, and this gives them permission to act a certain way that would not normally be permitted in situations that are *ke*. It is possible to wear a kimono on an occasion seen as either *hare* or *ke.* The kimono worn on an occasion deemed *hare* is driving the behavior; it allows or facilitates *hare* behavior that is different to everyday life (*ke*).

Some scholars, such as Ragalye, have already suggested that in Japan kimono has become a "costume" rather than "clothing" because kimono wearing is governed by rules that make it an "iconic representation" of an already known image (Ragalye 2012: 21–2). This is true of kimono in the postwar period but this theory fails to take into account the contextual complexity of kimono wearing as well as the changes in current kimono fashion. Linguistically "kimono" means "object of wear" (Dalby 2001: 65) but since the Meiji period it has become associated primarily with *haregi* (special occasion clothing, or "fancy wear" as Dalby puts it [ibid.: 69]) as opposed to *fudangi* (everyday wear). However, not all kimono is considered *haregi*. For example, a *maiko's* kimono is her uniform and therefore she might consider it *fudangi* even if others do not. This is also the case for certain restaurant employees and retail staff in Kyoto. Japanese academic colleagues surmised that both a cosplay kimono and kimono *taiken* would be considered *fudangi* because they are not worn for a special occasion, but that renting a kimono for a wedding, coming-of-age ceremony, or graduation would be *haregi*. However, for the participant of kimono *taiken*, it might be considered *haregi* because it is definitely not their everyday wear. There are calendar events that everyone recognizes would entail *haregi* such as *hatsumōde* (the first shrine visit of the New Year), and there are personal events that individuals experience and regard as special, such as weddings. These personal events are ranked in terms of social distance to the core participants, and it is possible to gauge that distance by what people wear. For example, an individual might make the effort to wear kimono for a wedding of a family member but not for people they are not related to or do not know well. In this regard, clothing is an expression of social relationships. The wearing or not of kimono can also demonstrate personal opinion—for example, an informant told me that her mother-in-law wore a kimono for her wedding but not for her son's wedding to show that she approved of the former match but not of the latter.

Therefore, the word "costume," which according to Craik "is characterized in opposition to fashion, as traditional, unchanging, fixed by social status, and group-oriented" (1993: 4), does not adequately explain the special occasion/ everyday wear distinction in regard to kimono, or the *hare* and *ke* distinction that determines context and therefore behavior. In addition, it does not take into account that, as the opening comment about kimono above suggests, according to conventional kimono producers, the distinction between what is kimono and what is not kimono is becoming blurred as young designers and kimono-wearers play with the concept of kimono. This discussion is relevant to my research because how kimono and other *wafuku* are defined determines opinions about their decline and influences the preservation and evolution of their production and consumption.

Conclusion

I have argued that despite cosplay's association with anime and manga consumption, other forms of dressing in costume can also be viewed as a similar sartorial display practice, including the occasions of wearing kimono described in this chapter. Even at the term's most literal transcription—a combination of "costume" and "play"—we can see that kimono *taiken*, *maiko henshin*, *tezukuri yoroi*, as well as participation in such festivals as Jidai Matsuri are all playful uses of the kimono. In addition, these forms of dressing up fulfill other important characteristics of cosplay, such as temporary transformation and performativity. In terms of the latter three examples, the costumes still adhere to traditional forms—costumes are made by artisans using traditional techniques. However, the boundaries of what constitutes a kimono are becoming blurred as kimono makers and wearers challenge the conservative industry as well as Japanese society through design and modes of dress, even sometimes tipping it well into the "cosplay" camp, as illustrated by the Hearts Kimono categories and the Osaka University of Arts students' graduation apparel.

Despite the contraction in the mainstream industry, kimono *taiken* has become a booming business in recent years, domestic and foreign tourists both enjoying the experience of wearing kimono to see the sights (and to become part of the sights themselves). The kimono *taiken* rental industry is likely to profit young designers such as Mori as his production techniques have reduced the cost of buying a kimono significantly, so it will be easier for kimono *taiken* companies to purchase new designs and less expensive for them to replace old stock (in addition kimono *taiken* is hard on the fabric as the wearers are unused to it and the kimonos are worn more often than they would be if owned by an individual). And new technologies such as inkjet printing are already changing the kimono rental industry in the context of rituals such as *seijin shiki* and weddings. New technologies have lowered production costs. Mori's business partner told me that rental versus buying a kimono is now about 50:50 because inkjet printing is making production much cheaper, so more people are finding that they can afford to buy rather than rent kimono. Buying one of Mori's kimonos with *obi* and accessories costs about 300,000 yen, whereas before utilizing the new technologies, it was about 900,000 yen.

By lowering production costs and making kimonos more affordable, Mori undoubtedly opens up the kimono market to a wider customer base than merely those from the upper classes of Japan. And kimono *taiken* also allows other classes to experience wearing a kimono by creating an occasion outside of the usual formal occasions where a kimono is worn. *Maiko henshin* and *oiran taiken* further challenge the class dimension of wearing kimono by promoting the alternative image of kimono as signifying the entertainment and *mizushōbai* trades. The different modes of wearing kimono, especially wearing a front-tied *obi*, also challenge the conventional image of kimono.

Affordability and wearability are key aspects facing producers of kimono but this chapter has demonstrated the effect of consumers' desires on the production of kimono. In both production and consumption (in this case, the act of donning and wearing) there is what can be perceived as a "speeding up" of kimono to make it more affordable and wearable. If I return to my metaphor of how the kimono is being made to ride a bicycle, this speeding up of kimono appears to be another way in which individuals and retailers are challenging conventional ways of wearing kimono—through renting kimono for a day or through altering how the kimono is donned and worn. In addition, the increasing focus on *asobi* (play) and self-expression serves as a further connection to contemporary lifestyles by bringing the world of cosplay into the world of the kimono.

5
INNOVATION AND CHANGE

This chapter looks at the mechanics of innovation and change in the Japanese textile industry, arguing that these forces are enabling cultural revitalization. Innovation—the application of a new original method, process, or product—is sometimes viewed as the antithesis of "tradition." Yet, as we saw in Chapter Two, the Japanese textile industry has incorporated innovations from around the world throughout its history. More recently, innovation has also occurred within all aspects of the Kyoto textile industry supply chain: design, production, distribution, and marketing, as I will illustrate below. Some of these are innovative applications of existing technology, and some of them are new methods or products. First, I illustrate how designers are addressing the industry's decline by making kimono and other *wafuku* more suitable for contemporary lifestyles, or how they are making "kimono ride a bicycle." Then, I focus on two areas of recent local innovation and change in production methods: digital *yūzen* and outsourcing. After that, I examine the role of the internet in changing the distribution relationships of the Kyoto textile manufacturers, thus enabling a reduction in retail prices. Finally, I look at marketing, including multisensory marketing and the unique ways through which Kyoto companies are selling their products while retaining the aura of "tradition."

In all of these areas we can see faster kimono production but also a speeding up of kimono wearability in terms of ease of donning the garment in order to make it more compatible with contemporary life. Companies are attempting to reduce production costs to make *wafuku* more affordable, and they are trying to change perceptions and broaden the image of *wafuku*, in particular the strict rules surrounding wearing kimono, by creating products that link symbolically or aesthetically to traditional apparel but with more practical structures for contemporary lifestyles. Some of these innovations are resulting in processes or products that challenge participants' concepts of tradition and authenticity, revealing not only the concepts' ambiguity but also that there is plenty of scope for interpretation depending on the players, context, and power relations. I demonstrate how in some contexts the authenticity of products is intertwined with the construction of a "national style" in which the various stakeholders— in this case, artisans, textile associations, and METI—decide the legitimacy of products through membership, certification, and official recognition. As stated in Chapter One, METI recognizes various traditional techniques employed throughout Japan, including Kyoto's Nishijin *ori*, *kanoko shibori*, and *Kyō-yūzen*, as "officially designated traditional craft products" (METI 2013), certifying them as such with a specific label, and this state recognition of Kyoto kimono techniques distinguishes them as worthy of preservation.

Innovation in Design

As we saw in the case studies in Chapter Three, one way that designers are attempting to revitalize kimono is by creating apparel suitable for contemporary lifestyles. They are doing this in various ways: for example, designers help to maintain the use of traditional apparel such as *jikatabi* by applying modern print designs (Sou Sou—Figure 5.1); they are retaining the core elements of traditional apparel such as kimono—long flowing lines, long wide sleeves and attached neckbands that cross left over right, and *yoroi* armor—plate-like shoulder guards and waist protectors (Kyoto Denim—Figure 5.2) but creating new clothing more suitable for present-day lifestyles; or they are making contemporary clothing from traditionally printed fabric (Pagong—Figure 5.3).

Figure 5.1 Sou Sou's *jikatabi* made of contemporary fabric patterns. Fabric designs © Sou Sou. Photo: Jenny Hall.

Figure 5.2 Kyoto Denim's *yoroi* jacket, with woven plate-like sections that mimic samurai armor shoulder guards and waist protectors. Design © Kyoto Denim. Photo: Jenny Hall. First published in *New Voices in Japanese Studies*, Vol. 7, 2015 (The Japan Foundation, Sydney).

Figure 5.3 An "aloha" shirt with *kata yūzen* designs by Pagong. Fabric design © Kamedatomi Co. Ltd. Photo: Jenny Hall.

Traditional Apparel with Modern Print Designs

As stated in Chapter One, Japanese designers' views about the suitability or otherwise of kimono for contemporary life vary greatly. Kawabe Yūnosuke told me, in the context of the government's "cool biz" campaign,[1] that neckties did not suit all seasons in Japan because they originated in a colder climate and therefore do not allow the air to flow around the body, but a kimono lets the air flow—something he deemed more appropriate for life in the humid Japanese climate, even though he rarely wears kimono himself. This air flow might be a part of a man's kimono experience, but women may feel differently when they don a wide and restrictive *obi*. Wakabayashi Takeshi noted the difficulty of riding a bicycle or driving a car while wearing a kimono, while *obi* manufacturer Yamada told me, "You can't hurry in a kimono," an attribute that he saw as both negative (contemporary life is fast-paced) and positive (wearing a kimono makes you slow down and appreciate different things). Yamada told me, "When I wear kimono and practice *ocha* [tea ceremony], my thinking slows down, I become calm" (Hall 2015: 71). Therefore, some apparel producers are attempting to address issues of wearability, re-creating kimono or other forms of traditional clothing in a contemporary style.

As discussed in Chapter Three, Sou Sou produces a variety of traditional apparel and accessories made with its distinctive Wakisaka Katsuji print fabric but its most popular traditional product is the *jikatabi*: split-toed shoes that have close contact with the ground. By reviving production of the two-toed *jikatabi* (traditionally a work shoe worn by construction workers, farmers, and *jinriksha* pullers, and available only in black, white, or indigo) but making it in contemporary fabric patterns, Sou Sou is changing the Japanese perception of this style of footwear (Hall 2015: 72). Sou Sou claims the split-toed shoe aids balance—it "helps the wearer 'feel' the ground better" (Sou Sou US 2014), which is why historically construction workers favored it for traversing beams on site. Tomie Hahn, researcher and performer of *nihon buyō* (Japanese dance), concurs with this theory, stating that in regard to *tabi*, "the isolation of the big toe allows it to spread out slightly from the other toes to grip the floor, greatly aiding stability by creating a stronger base" (2007: 63). Sou Sou's versions of *jikatabi* have a thicker sole than the traditional *jikatabi* for durability but the company reassures wearers that "even with more substantial tread, our *tabi* shoes will still have you moving your feet in a whole new way" (Sou Sou US 2014). By producing *jikatabi*, Sou Sou is continuing to promote a certain physical footwear sensation. That is, it would be difficult for *jikatabi* wearers not to sense their footwear, as they feel different from wearing conventional Western shoes. At the same time they are more likely to be worn combined with Western clothing than other forms of traditional footwear such as *geta* or formal *zōri* because they are comfortable, easy to walk in, and look casual—in other words, they suit contemporary lifestyles

(Figure 5.4). Thus, Sou Sou's *jikatabi* are serving to communicate embodied practices from the past to the wearer, as well as to those who observe this type of footwear being worn by individuals on the street. There is some prejudice among older people about *jikatabi*—when asked about Sou Sou's *jikatabi*, one group of women in their 60s and 70s still associated them with the lower working class and could not understand their new-found popularity among young people (Hall 2015: 72). Sou Sou is changing the image of the *jikatabi* by presenting work shoes as suitable for casual wear, much the same as occurred with American jeans. In addition, the shoes act as a constant sensory reminder to the wearer, of both the traditional and renegotiated meanings of *jikatabi* (ibid.). This revival of the *jikatabi* epitomizes the dialectic between the past that "lives on through the clothes and is revived in the details of sartorial styles created anew each season" and fashion's continual search for new meanings, because "without the connotation of antiquity, modernity loses its *raison d'être*" (Lehmann 2000: 8). The Sou Sou designers sustain this connection between traditional and new meanings by reproducing the main features of *wafuku* in their designs (Hall 2015: 72).

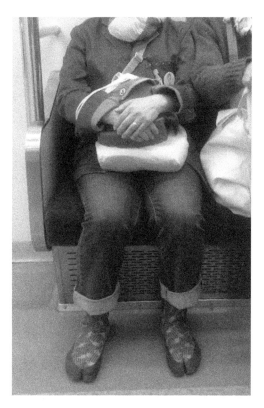

Figure 5.4 Woman on the Kyoto subway wearing *jikatabi* with jeans, 2012. Photo: Jenny Hall.

Other companies are also producing traditional apparel or accessories in new fabrics or patterns. Kyoto Montsuki has created a denim kimono, and a company near Kitano Tenmangu in the north of Kyoto, Denimdosu, is also producing denim kimono. I came upon a group of kimono-clad women who were walking past Denimdosu and I asked them what they thought of the denim kimono in the window. At first they had not realized the kimono was denim, and they were intrigued by the concept, commenting that it was "*omoshiroi*" (interesting) but I surmise that it is doubtful they would have purchased such an item (Figure 5.5a and b). Most people who wear kimono are wearing them for a specific purpose such as for tea ceremony or to a wedding and denim would not suit those events. Because of this, these products are more difficult to sell—they do not suit traditional kimono occasions, although as discussed in the previous chapter, the contexts for wearing kimono are changing.

The other main products that fall into this category of traditional apparel with modern designs are *tenugui* and *furoshiki*. Eirakuya and its subsidiaries RAAK and Enveraak[2] have been very successful at reviving both. Eirakuya, first established in 1615, now has twenty shops, seventeen of which are in Kyoto

Figure 5.5a A denim kimono at Denimdosu. Photo: Jenny Hall.

Figure 5.5b Kimono-clad women looking at a denim kimono at Denimdosu, 2012. Photo: Jenny Hall.

and three in Tokyo. Its main products are *tenugui* and *furoshiki* in a huge variety of contemporary and traditional patterns and fabric weaves. The online shop has over two hundred different *tenugui* alone. In recent years these items have been promoted as environmentally friendly, or "eko" in Japanese (short for ecology) because they can be used as a substitute for plastic bags or wrapping paper.

Retaining the Core Elements of Traditional Apparel

By adapting elements of the kimono to create contemporary garments, it could be said that designers are attempting to "speed up" kimono to suit present-day life styles (Hall 2015: 73). This speeding up occurs in the donning stage as contemporary apparel is much easier and faster to put on than a kimono, as well as in the wearing state because such clothing allows for more freedom (and thus faster) movement of the wearer (ibid.). While it might easily be assumed that new kimono forms are a kimono/Western clothing hybrid, Sou Sou's garments are versions of what Dalby refers to as the "other kimono" (2001: 161)—for example, *jinbei* (a short jacket that crosses left over right with a tie fastening, and loose-fitting shorts or trousers) or *noragi* (regional work clothing) that was also typically comprised of two pieces: a jacket such as *mijika* (single-lined or padded jacket), *hanten* (folk equivalent of a *haori*—a short winter coat), *samue* (short working jacket), or a *sodenashi* (sleeveless straight vest), and *mompe* (loose-fitting trousers that come in at the ankle) or *kyahan* (leggings). Sou Sou refers to its clothing as *wafuku* (Japanese clothing) even though its range includes singlets, t-shirts, dresses, shorts, and shirts (Hall 2015: 73). This marketing of its products as *wafuku* is important because it is encouraging consumers to change their perceptions about what constitutes *wafuku*. For example, Sou Sou draws a direct link between *kabukimono* and their men's clothing range, stating it is "modern-day *kabukimono*" (*gendai no kabukimono*) "for those who dare to be different" (Sou Sou n.d.). The company is directly referencing the group of young men who, during the Tokugawa era, flouted sumptuary laws (mentioned in Chapter One), and it is doing so in order to link its men's apparel with ideas of dressing differently, and in a carefree manner (*jiyūhonpō*) (ibid.).

However, the influence of traditional clothing on its designs is also evident, and the names for items reaffirm this link with *wafuku*: *yukata-mitate* dresses (dresses with features of the *yukata*), *kataginu* (sleeveless ceremonial robe for samurai), *hirogata mompe* (wide-legged *mompe*), *hakamanari* (*hakama*-style trousers), *kyūchūsuso* (imperial court cuffed trousers) (Hall 2015: 73). Sou Sou also produces *tabi*-style cotton knit socks, tops made by stitching rectangles of kimono-width fabric together, and Yayoi period-style (300 BCE–300 CE) *kantōi* (a simple dress made of a large piece of cloth with a hole in the middle for the head). If we compare some of its items, such as the *kyūchūsuso* (imperial court cuffed trousers—Figure 5.6) with clothing worn at Jidai Matsuri (the Festival of Ages) (Figure 5.7), or another participant wearing a court costume at Jidai Matsuri (Figure 5.8) with Sou Sou's *kyūchūsuso ayui* (imperial court cuffed trousers with leg bindings) (Figure 5.9), we can see the influence of traditional clothing forms on Sou Sou's designs. Whether or not all Japanese people would classify Sou Sou's apparel as *wafuku* is debatable but by presenting it as such, Sou Sou is reinventing *wafuku*. In this sense, the company is making tradition.

The changing image of *jikatabi* mentioned above is pertinent to Sou Sou's apparel as a whole. Wearing kimono according to the prescribed social etiquette is expensive, and therefore it is mainly the upper classes that can afford to wear it. It is also the upper classes who are more likely to have the time and money to learn the correct way to put on and wear kimono, have the time to don and wear kimono according to the accepted conventions, and are more likely to attend functions such as tea ceremony where wearing kimono is appropriate. This is one of the reasons for the popularity of kimono *taiken* (discussed in Chapter Four)—it renders this part of Japanese culture accessible to a much wider segment of society, even if it is only for a day. Sou Sou's "*wafuku*" apparel is accessible to a

Figure 5.6 Sou Sou's *kyūchūsuso* (imperial court cuffed trousers). Photo: © Sou Sou. Reprinted with kind permission.

Figure 5.7 A participant in Jidai Matsuri (the Festival of Ages), 2012. Photo: Jenny Hall. First published in *New Voices in Japanese Studies*, Vol. 7, 2015 (The Japan Foundation, Sydney).

wider section of society because it is relatively inexpensive, easy to put on, and can be worn in everyday life. At the same time, it challenges the traditional order of society by mixing imperial court styles with *noragi* (Hall 2015: 73).

Kyoto Denim's *yoroi* jacket and jeans are another example of designs that utilize core characteristics of traditional garments—in this case samurai armor— and render them accessible to wider society (ibid.). Designer Kuwayama's jacket incorporates some of the typical *yoroi* armor features, such as sections that mimic the *kumihimo* braid and plate-like shoulder guards down the shoulders (Figures 5.10 and 5.11), and the ribbed flaring collar that simulates the wide, semicircular neck guard of the helmet (Figure 5.12) (ibid.). Following the conventions of kimono, the fastening overlaps left over right. The *yoroi* jeans

Figure 5.8 Participants in Jidai Matsuri (the Festival of Ages), 2012. Photo: Jenny Hall. First published in *New Voices in Japanese Studies*, Vol. 7, 2015 (The Japan Foundation, Sydney).

Figure 5.9 Sou Sou's *kyūchūsuso ayui* (imperial court cuffed trousers with leg bindings). Photo: © Sou Sou. Reprinted with kind permission.

have seven denim strips on the outside of each leg, similar to the traditional armor's waist protector. The diamond patterns on either side of the hips (called *tasuki-kikubishi*) are a traditional Heian period (794–1185) design (ibid.).

Kuwayama says he wanted to resurrect the chivalrous atmosphere of the Sengoku period (the warring states period, 1467–1598) in his new recreations of "*wafuku*" (ibid.). His interest in the coexistence of "dynamism" and "romanticism," (key terms used in his marketing) is reminiscent of the Taishō era's ideal of modernism and nostalgia (Kyoto Denim 2014a). He is eager to "combine Kyoto cultural virtue with foreign culture, technology and economics" (Kyoto Denim 2014a). His attraction to the progression of Japanese fashion is apparent in his designs, and these designs in turn are evolved further when the customer wears the garments (Hall 2015: 75). The customer's imagining of himself as a

Figure 5.10 Detail of the braiding on the shoulder protector of samurai armor, worn by a Jidai Matsuri participant. Photo: Jenny Hall.

Figure 5.11 Kyoto Denim's *yoroi* jacket sleeve showing the mimicking of braid on the shoulders. Design © Kyoto Denim. Photo: Jenny Hall. First published in *New Voices in Japanese Studies*, Vol. 7, 2015 (The Japan Foundation, Sydney).

Figure 5.12 Kyoto's Denim's *yoroi* jacket—the collar mimics the flaring of a samurai helmet. Design © Kyoto Denim. Photo: Jenny Hall. First published in *New Voices in Japanese Studies*, Vol. 7, 2015 (The Japan Foundation, Sydney).

modern-day samurai, much like Tabata's imagining of himself as samurai during participation in Jidai Matsuri, overlaps with concepts of cosplay discussed in the previous chapter.

Contemporary Products from Traditionally Printed Fabric or Dye Techniques

By far the largest area of production for apparel utilizing traditional crafts is the creation of contemporary products from traditionally printed or woven fabric or dye techniques such as *Kyō-yūzen*, *katazome*, or *shibori*. For Nishijin *ori*, this can be seen in a variety of products such as bookmarks, neckties, purses, cushion covers, wall hangings, and handbags that are made of traditional woven brocade (Figure 5.13). The best example of this I have seen is the Nishijin Ori Kōgei Bijutsukan's recreation of Monet's *Waterlilies* in woven brocade, displayed in a special room complete with a lighting sequence to show the variety of colors and how they change with differing illumination (visit https://www.youtube.com/watch?v=pHuYcbZQdfk for a video tour of the room). However, the Nishijin Textile Industrial Association estimated that in 2011 approximately 90 per cent of Nishijin production was for kimono and *obi*, and only 10 percent was used for these other products (Nishijin Textile Industrial Association 2011: 1). The reason that Nishijin weaving is not used as much for contemporary apparel is

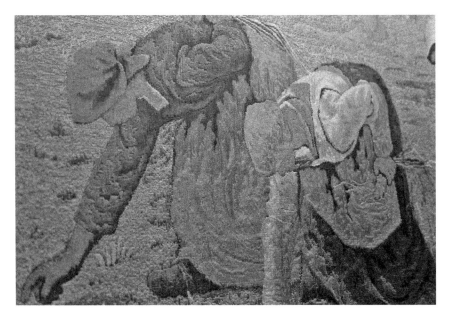

Figure 5.13 Detail of a woven reproduction of *Des glaneuses* (The Gleaners) originally by Jean-François Millet, Nishijin Ori Kōgei Bijutsukan, 2012. Photo: Jenny Hall.

predominantly due to the high cost of production because the work is labor-intensive and is divided minutely according to specialization between family-run businesses. In addition, Nishijin goods are considered high-end goods and branded "officially designated traditional craft products" by METI which pushes the price up more (Moon 2013: 82), even though some goods are now made using digital looms. The irony is that Nishijin *ori* is promoted as being a revered tradition of high-quality craftsmanship in need of preservation but this veneration renders it inaccessible to the majority of people. Dye techniques are much more adaptable to contemporary garments than Nishijin *ori*, in particular *katazome* and *shiborizome*, because more fabric can be produced in less time and at less cost. Pagong provides a good example of contemporary products using traditional dye methods.

Pagong's apparel is unique in its look because the motifs derive mainly from the Taishō era (1912–26). This era was renowned for its modern-looking design, dubbed "Taishō chic," which blended "modern" and traditional elements (Hall 2015: 76). Pagong owner, Kameda, commented on the suitability of Taishō patterns for present-day Japan:

> I sometimes wished that our company had centuries of history like some Kyoto shops and companies, but if we hadn't started in the Taishō era, we wouldn't have our catalog of uniquely traditional and modern designs. Maybe people say that our catalog could not be more perfect for our current time, when people are longing for more connection to tradition and a by-gone world, our patterns in the shape of Western clothing does not look unnatural. (Ibid.: 76)

By employing its Taishō-era stencils, Pagong reproduces a certain "of that time" style in their new designs (ibid.). The 1920s and 1930s are known as being decades of great transition in Japan; Taishō art and design is distinguished by its "balance between modernity and nostalgia" (Carr 2008: 2). It is important to note that here "modern" usually meant "Western," in contrast with "traditional" Japanese designs (Hall 2015: 76). Japanese artists, such as Kobayakawa Kiyoshi (1899–1948), were influenced by the Western art movements of the time such as Art Deco and Impressionism. As Carr notes, "Art Deco and Impressionism were a great inspiration for the Taisho artists who fused the elements of modernity and nostalgia to create a distinctive aesthetic" (2008: 2).

On examining Pagong's patterns, we can see this influence: for example, the company describes their pattern "Asagao" (Morning Glory), a design of red and yellow flowers with white and green leaves on a black ground from the early 1930s, as "high Art Deco," with strong, colorful tints, and a "modern impression" (Hall 2015: 76). If the original context of the Kamedatomi company is taken into consideration, the visual sensory picture becomes more complex; because the

Taishō era was a time when women were starting to adopt Western-style dress, wearing a kimono was a statement in itself (ibid.). "Modern" was associated with "Western" at this time, so wearing a kimono could foster a conservative or nationalistic impression, but I surmise that to wear a kimono that was Western in pattern and color could symbolize a more progressive outlook: "I am both a modern woman and also Japanese" (ibid.: 77).

This could be viewed as a reversal of the present day: during the Taishō era, the garment (kimono) displayed adherence to tradition, whereas the designs printed on the fabric showed a Western influence. Now, Pagong garments are Western in cut, but the printed patterns are perceived as traditional (ibid.). During the Taishō era, young women were adapting to the feel of wearing Western-style clothes, whereas Pagong's customers today are similarly not accustomed to wearing kimono, and are often not able to dress themselves in a kimono without the help of a professional dresser (ibid.). So, Kameda is not attempting to design garments that are kimonoid in shape like Sou Sou; he makes Western-style clothing with kimono patterns. We can view it on a continuum where there are kimono and other *wafuku* such as *jinbei* or *noragi*, and then *wafū* (Japanese-style) garments that give the look of a kimono without actually wearing one—many of Sou Sou's garments would be placed here—and then Western clothing.

Kamedatomi also uses more contemporary color combinations in its present-day designs such as the red, white, blue, and touch of black used for its chrysanthemum shirt (Figure 5.14) or the vivid red background, fresh green leaves, and cream flowers on its poppy top (Figure 5.15). Originally, it would have used colors based on the color charts of traditional kimono, such as those for spring—*momo* (the color combination that represents peach, comprised of a light pink and a light green), *kōbai* (plum, comprised of a deep pink and light pink), *fuji* (wisteria, comprised of green and lilac), or *wakakusa* (young grass, comprised of dark green and light green). Kameda said, "Western styles are different. A kimono is about simplicity, so you use quieter colors. Not with Western styles" (*Moshi Moshi Nippon* 2014). Today, "Pagong uses colors that make the items easier to coordinate with other clothing" (ibid.). Thus, its designs are being updated to suit contemporary fashion color-ways and trends. I observed that, while in the context of kimono, women still select colors according to their age, a woman of any age can be seen wearing Pagong's bright hues—colors that traditionally were reserved for young unmarried women.

So Kamedatomi is combining traditional patterns with apparel suited to the contemporary lifestyle and utilizing traditional dyeing techniques to do it. And Pagong customers, by wearing aloha shirts and other apparel, are, to an extent, embodying the zeitgeist from a particular period in Japanese history, but also renegotiating the original significance of the patterns (Hall 2015: 77). Howes

Figure 5.14 Chrysanthemum shirt by Pagong using contemporary color combinations. Fabric design © Kamedatomi Co. Ltd. Photo: Jenny Hall.

Figure 5.15 Poppy top illustrating contemporary color combinations used by Pagong. Fabric design © Kamedatomi Co. Ltd. Photo: Jenny Hall.

aptly expresses this dynamic process when he says, "What gives objects their sensory meaning—and what may give them new meanings—is not just the memories we associate with them, but how we are experiencing them right now. Sensory signification is a continuing development, not a simple reliving of once-learned associations" (2003: 71).

Another area in which contemporary products are made from traditionally printed fabric is that of recycled vintage kimono. As discussed in Chapter One, trade in second-hand kimono has been in existence for many centuries. There also appears to be a contemporary trend in favor of used clothing. According to an article in the *Japan Times Online*, between 1999 and 2003 the new kimono market shrank from 787.7 billion yen to 590 billion yen, whereas sales of second-hand kimonos rose from 6 billion yen to 34 billion yen (Nakamura 2004). Even Kyoto Denim's designer, Kuwayama, states, "These days the trend is re-using and recycling, and we are always looking for new ways to express ourselves" (Kyoto Denim 2015). This industry is relatively small considering the number of vintage kimono shops and market stalls (in Kyoto there are several shops selling vintage kimono and both of the main temple markets, Tojisan and Tenjinsan, include many second-hand kimono stalls every month). Professor Murayama told me of one graduate from Doshisha University's Innovative Globalization of Heritage Industries program that started a business making handicrafts from antique silk but went out of business because of competition from China, demonstrating that there is a market for such goods, but it is relatively small. However, there are some businesses that have been successful. In Nishijin there is a small atelier that creates women's clothing from recycled kimono. They have been in business for eight years and told me that there are other shops in Kyoto that run the same kind of business.[3] They buy vintage kimono at markets and cut them up to make women's blouses, dresses, skirts, and accessories (Figure 5.16). They also take orders from customers for various items. However, I surmise that one of the reasons this area has not become a larger part of the industry is the reluctance to buy previously owned kimono because of the perceived connectedness of the original wearer and the clothing. Dalby explains, "Even now, 'antique kimono' are cheap for foreigners because there is little market for other people's cast off clothing among Japanese. Something of the original wearer's soul has irrevocably imbued the garment" (2001: 4). Citing the 2006 Yano Research Institute internet survey of women between the ages of 20 and 60, Assmann notes that "there still seemed to be a great reluctance to buy second-hand kimonos: overall 50 per cent of all respondents replied that they felt hesitant about buying a second-hand kimono" (2008: 363). Although Assmann does not give a reason for this reluctance, it appears to be concerned with a negative image surrounding used goods. This notion of the soul of the wearer imbuing the kimono echoes the concept discussed in Chapter Two regarding the "heart" or "deep feeling" passed from the artisan into the object through their mastering of *kata.* Here it is the consumer's "heart" that is passed into the

Figure 5.16 Some examples of vintage kimono recycled into contemporary garments. Photo: Jenny Hall.

object through the experience of donning and wearing, giving the object life and form. However, this idea of a kimono having a "soul" is also sometimes seen as a positive. Kimono de Jack participants frequently wore a new or second-hand kimono with an *obi* they had inherited from their mothers or grandmothers "which shows an aspiration to maintain family traditions" (Assmann 2008: 365). These family traditions often revolve around the concept of *mottainai* mentioned in Chapter Two (and Miyamoto's discussion of a garment's life span in Chapter One), in which cloth fragments are reused. This way of thinking results in people being "generous about fading [of textiles] in Japan" and used cloth that is still valued (Matsui 2015). I have already discussed the tradition of *boro* textiles, in Chapter One, but one example is particularly pertinent here, even though it is characteristic of Aomori Prefecture. *Bodo* or *bodoko* is a patched sheeting cloth sewn from multiple pieces of fabric that had been worn by various ancestors, lasting many generations, in which "generations after generations of history were sewn into each strand" (AMUSE Museum 2015). It was often used during childbirth for the baby to be delivered on, and embodied "the prayers of silent hopes from all the ancestors who would welcome this baby's new arrival" (ibid.). Thus, the recycling of textiles is often viewed in a positive way in regions of Japan.

There is also proof that textiles crossed "the border between the secular and the sacred" with garments recycled into temple and shrine banners (Milhaupt 2002: 132). The act of cutting the garment into smaller pieces symbolically (and most likely literally) reduced its commercial value (ibid.: 124). Therefore, an aversion to second-hand kimono is also connected to cutting the garment. When questioned about cutting kimono cloth, my Nishijin atelier informant told me, "Yes, I'm afraid [to cut the cloth]. It is scary, it is scary. Each kimono has a history. Whenever I hold the scissors, I'm afraid. I've bought several kimono that I haven't been able to bring myself to cut" (personal interview October 18, 2012). My informant does reference the garment's history, suggesting she is concerned about the soul of the kimono, but Harold Koda, costume curator at the Fashion Institute of Technology (FIT) defined this aversion to cutting into cloth as a respect for the integrity of the material and he links "this aesthetic principle to the use of cloth in kimono and regional costume, where virtually the entire bolt is used, with relatively little waste and little cutting" (Kondo 1992: 183). However, it is clear from my previous discussion of the recycling of kimono throughout Japanese history, and from comments such as Miyamoto's regarding *kidaore*, that people do cut up and repurpose their kimono. These aspects are crucial to understanding the evolution and continuing changes in production and consumption of kimono and *wafuku*, as discussed in the previous chapter.

Innovation in Production

Digital *Yūzen*

A recent innovation in the kimono industry is the application of computers and inkjet technology to create digital *yūzen* kimono, as detailed in Chapter Two. While it can be argued that this method of production does not continue the *yūzen* tradition, artisans, even those continuing to use traditional methods, accept it as an innovation in the industry. *Obi* manufacturer Yamada told me, "I'm not against inkjet kimono … they want to produce good products" (Hall 2018b: 17). However, both artisans and consumers assert that digital *yūzen* lacks the *kosei* and "deep feeling" that *yūzen* made using traditional techniques possesses, and so does not convey the artisan's *kokoro* in the same way (ibid.). In fact, it could be argued that digital *yūzen* is not really *yūzen* at all, as the primary method of paste resist is not used; rather the fabrics produced using digital *yūzen* could be viewed as merely designs based on or influenced by original kimono patterns that any skilled graphic designer could perform. As we could see by designer Mori Makoto's diagram in Chapter Two (Diagram 2.1), the only other related part of the process that is shared with traditional *yūzen* appears to be the steaming of the material. So why do the designers call it "digital *yūzen*"? On a practical level, Mori reasons that "if there are no artisans, not only *Kyo-yūzen* but also the kimono culture itself is in danger of extinction. This is why inkjet technology has been widely accepted—as a means to facilitate cheaper production while retaining the culture of the kimono in Japan" (2012: 128). And of course, from a marketing point of view recognizing digital *yūzen* as a new form of *yūzen* adds "uncontested respectability to recently invented cultural products" (Daliot-Bul 2009b: 252–3).

However, this term is also linked to the imagining of artistic tradition, not the process of production (Hall 2018b: 17). Digital *yūzen* represents the traditional craft, consciously invoking "the legacy of the craftsman, seen as creating himself in his products" (Kondo 1990: 245) that legitimizes the neologism. This "legacy of the craftsman" supports the notion that digital *yūzen* is merely a new innovation of *yūzen* production and "it may be that the 'Japaneseness' of Japanese artists is not vanishing once and for all, but rather ever being reinvented" (Mathews 2000: 30). Supporting this argument is the fact that many of the designers who use digital *yūzen*, such as Mori Makoto and Kawabe Yūnosuke, have traditional backgrounds; raised in kimono-making families, they learned the traditional techniques before switching to digital *yūzen*. This enables the designers not only to draw on the traditional craft skills of design but also to claim their artistic legacy as a marketing strategy for their digital products. It also allows Kyoto residents, and Japanese people in general, to legitimize and frame their cultural heritage through reference to the continuation of the past as discussed in Chapter One.

Outsourcing

Although outsourcing is not a new innovation in this industry—outsourcing production processes has been done since the 1970s—it has not been discussed in detail elsewhere. In addition, the internet has had new consequences for the industry in this area, which I discuss below. While the name Nishijin has become synonymous with woven brocade *obi*, Nishijin manufacturers outsource a good deal of the actual weaving, as stated in Chapter Two. Each Nishijin *obi* comes with a mark of authenticity designated by the Nishijin Textile Industrial Association (Nishijin Ori Kōgyō Kumiai) identifying it with the district

Figure 5.17 A Nishijin authentication mark. Photo: Jenny Hall.

(Figure 5.17). Therefore, place is integral to the identity and authenticity of the woven *obi*. How then, do we reconcile the fact that 50 percent of Nishijin *obi* are not woven in Kyoto city and a further 10 percent are not woven in Japan at all (Hareven 2002: 47)? Along with the concept of "tradition," place is one of the ways of establishing authenticity. From local to national, place has been an important element, proving the authenticity of goods; Kyoto designers and artisans readily draw on ideas of "traditional" crafts handmade locally. From a manufacturing perspective, both production techniques and the creation of specialty goods are a source of local pride and identity; Kyoto people in particular foster the idea that their city is the "authentic" source of textile production expertise and knowledge in Japan. The production systems themselves, however, often extend beyond national borders, calling into question the relationship between place and authenticity; silk for Nishijin *obi* was sourced from China during the early Edo era and is now mostly sourced from Brazil, and production techniques have been introduced from Korea, France, and China throughout the centuries. Hareven mentions the irony of the fact that techniques and designs of Nishijin *ori* were first brought to Japan from China, then gradually disappeared in China because of wars and revolutions, and are being revived in China by Nishijin manufacturers with the cooperation of the Chinese government while dying out in Japan (2002: 23).

As noted in Chapter One, Baudrillard's notion of authenticity focused on four key obsessions: the origin, date, author, and signature of a work (1996: 76). These four issues are problematic if they are used to render Nishijin *obi* authentic. Origin could refer to materials or production. As a marker for authenticity, origin is problematic in terms of Nishijin *obi* because the materials (silk) are sourced from elsewhere and part of the production takes place outside of Nishijin as I have already outlined. Even if we look at the origins of production we get a complex picture. The Nishijin Textile Industrial Association's website confirms that weaving technology was introduced to Japan by the Hata clan in the Kofun period (250–538 CE) (Nishijin Textile Industrial Association 2015). As noted in Chapter Two, throughout the centuries Nishijin weavers adopted various foreign loom technologies including the jacquard and the power loom. Both of these types of loom are still used today to weave *obi*, in addition to the treadle loom and the digital loom. Therefore, Nishijin *obi* appear to be made in Kyoto by hand but in fact many are made elsewhere using digital looms, creating a dichotomy between the perception of a local artisan versus the mass-produced assembly-line anonymous worker. However, even if they are "machine-made," the weaver must still utilize great skill to produce such complex work. And, as discussed above, new manufacturing techniques such as digital looms are framed in the light of a further stage of innovation in a continuing tradition. But all of these aspects of origin are rendered irrelevant by the "official" certification from the Nishijin Textile Industrial Association.

In my study of contemporary textiles, the date of creation is not used to render authenticity. However, it is worth noting that in Japan, "authenticity" also includes items that are faithful replicas in certain situations and it is actually replication that creates and legitimizes authenticity of a skill, as mentioned in Chapter One. This is certainly the case with Japanese textiles. Since the Meiji period, there has been a government-run program to induce artisans to reproduce treasures of the Shōsōin repository of medieval artifacts in Nara as well as works designated as National Treasures. The thinking behind this view of authenticity is that if the copies exist, the cultural object is not considered lost even if the original is no longer extant. For example, Kyoto weaver Tatsumura Kōhō creates replicas of textile pieces from the Shōsōin repository, researching the materials and processes of production minutely in order to create an exact copy. Therefore, date can be problematic in terms of rendering authenticity of Japanese cultural items including textiles.

In regard to authorship, as discussed before, the industry in general is characterized by a division of labor, rendering it difficult to designate a single artisan to a work; about a dozen different artisans can be involved in the creation of one piece. According to weaver Tatsumura Kōhō, up to seventy workers are required to complete one of his treadle loom pieces. The *obi* must also pass the quality standards of the Nishijin Textile Industrial Association regardless of who works on it, and how it is made. Therefore, in the case of Nishijin *obi* it is almost inevitable that a certification seal (*shōshi)* is used as a mark of authenticity because of the division of labor, so certification is both origin and author in this respect.

It is highly possible that consumers are not aware that the *obi* are woven elsewhere. This is because the manufacturers create the designs and outsource the weaving, but the *obi* are produced under the Kyoto-based manufacturer's name. For example, Yamada, an *obi* manufacturer, creates designs, sources the materials, and commissions Tango-based weavers to weave them (see Chapter Two). The *obi* produced bear his company's Nishijin certification mark, under his company name. He showed me a thick ledger that has all of the Nishijin *obi* manufacturers listed in it. There are about 2,600 companies listed, but not all of them are still in operation. He pointed to another company—its certification number was 100—and told me that one was very old (that company, called Sanoman, actually ceased operation in 2009 according to the Nishijin Textile Industrial Association). Even my informant's company, at about eighty-five years with a certification number in the 600s, is considered "old" these days (the youngest companies have the highest numbers). The fact that his *obi*, woven not in Nishijin but on the Tango peninsula in Kyoto Prefecture, are sold as Nishijin *obi* may seem like deceit. However, his Nishijin-based company produced them, he is responsible for quality control, and the Nishijin Textile Industrial Association is the gatekeeper for the quality of all Nishijin manufacturers like him. The *obi* pass all of the checks and therefore are "authentic" Nishijin *obi*. When asked about Nishijin *obi* being woven outside of Kyoto, Professor Murayama's response was as follows:

> I do not know how consumers think about it. However, it is a common practice of Nishijin (probably from 1960s) to let Tango people do weaving jobs for Nishijin (we call it *debata* [cottage weavers that own their own looms]). Tango is famous for producing high-quality silk (Tango Chirimen) so I do not see any problems here. It is also that we have to accept the fact that some of the Nishijin *ori* is produced in China in this globalized world. (Personal interview September 18, 2012)

However, these changes in the supply chain are allowing for new production outcomes. Another informant in the kimono trade told me that Nishijin *obi* can now be found for sale on the internet at drastically reduced prices because the Chinese weavers who weave them sell some *obi* directly online. In terms of quality, they are the same as what is sold in Nishijin; they are Nishijin *obi*. The same informant's explanation of outsourcing in the industry was as follows:

> In the Kyoto textile industry there was a bad group who outsourced weaving to China and a good group who continued to make *obi* themselves in Kyoto. Years ago the bad people taught the Chinese weavers the techniques for how to make Nishijin *obi*. But then there was a big difference between prices for the items made by Chinese weavers and those made by the Japanese group. The real [*honmono*] goods were expensive so they did not sell but the Chinese-made ones were cheaper so sales of them increased. Because of the disparity in price no one was buying the Japanese-made work, and everyone was buying the Chinese ones. In time the Chinese weavers' skills improved and the quality improved. (Personal interview October 19, 2012)

According to this informant, the perpetrators were caught, although he did not specify by whom. He said the group justified their actions by arguing that Kyoto people had taught the skills to the Chinese in the first place. He went on to say,

> Now, the Chinese are starting to sell *obi* by themselves on the Internet — that sort of activity is common in China. There's not much difference in the standard of product between them [the Chinese-made and the Japanese-made *obi*]. It's not a lie because the Kyoto people taught the Chinese the techniques. If the fake [*nisemono*] *obi* have the Nishijin certification seal, then Japanese customers can't tell. The honest Kyoto manufacturers are really angry. There's been a decline in local manufacturing of *obi* because of the abundance of Chinese-made products. At first there were a few defiant Kyoto *obi* makers but they are on the verge of giving up because they can't compete

with the Chinese-made goods. There are still Kyoto artisans who can do the highest level of technique but it has already been taught to the Chinese. It's one thing to outsource to Tango but it's another thing to outsource to China. Before they knew it the Chinese goods had flooded the market and the local goods had become redundant, so there are no jobs. Genuine kimono from Kyoto are hard to find these days. To maintain the tradition, the Japanese artisans need to carry on regardless of whether they are making a profit or not. (Ibid.)

There are a number of issues involved here. According to the informant, Japanese customers are unable to tell whether or not the *obi* are "*nisemono*" (meaning "fake," but here synonymous with made in China), and according to my informant the standard and techniques are the same. However, this informant obviously feels that there is a difference between Tango weavers (i.e., Japanese) making *obi* and Chinese weavers making *obi*—indigenous versus foreign artisans— and this makes a difference to the informant's perception of authenticity, and to whether or not they are "*honmono*" or "*nisemono*."

The Nishijin certification seal acts as a kind of collective signature. All Nishijin *obi* are certified with a seal and the *obi* manufacturer must pass the quality standards of the Nishijin Textile Industrial Association in order to be granted a certification license. This appears to be regardless of who works on it, and how it is made. Weaving is not the only "traditional" textile industry technique that is being outsourced: *shibori* is also outsourced to Korea and China. One of my contacts asked me about other companies included in my research. I mentioned a *shibori* company and he replied, "You should ask him about why his items are made in China. It will be like a stake through his heart," and he made a gesture of piercing his own heart with a stake and laughing. This individual was clearly disparaging of using foreign producers, yet some of the products from his own company were made in China, apparent from the labels of their goods and from their website where certain items are labeled with the phrase *seizōkoku chūgoku* (country of manufacture China). This stated prejudice regarding foreign-made goods was also expressed by an *aizome* dyer who told me "Japanese goods are better because Japanese people care more" (personal interview October 3, 2012). Another businessman reiterated this belief, telling me that if he orders one hundred products from a Chinese company, 10 percent will be faulty, but if he orders the same from a Japanese company, none will be faulty. As mentioned in Chapter Three, Sou Sou's Wakabayashi told me that in the 1950s Japanese producers used Chinese factories to produce *jikatabi*, and as a result, the price of *jikatabi* decreased and they came to be viewed as "disposable" (and considering these were work boots they would have been well worn). He said, "*Jikatabi* are traditional Japanese shoes so I think it is important that they are made in Japan" (personal interview October 5, 2012). These comments reflect the pervasive image of Japanese goods as high quality. The industry participants and the consumers seem to agree that indigenous makers render authenticity and are a guarantee of quality in this case. Innovation is often viewed as a way to improve quality, thereby appearing to contradict this relationship between authenticity and quality, but the effect of innovation is not always an improvement in quality as we have seen with the mass production of goods. In addition, even digital *yūzen* designers argue that inkjet innovations have not resulted in better quality kimono, merely a reduction in production costs that have rendered them more affordable. Designer Mori, in comparing digital *yūzen* with traditional *yūzen*, has stated that "these new techniques cannot express the richness and complexity of designs to the same standard as *yūzen*; simply put, the *yūzen* technique produces a product of superior quality" (2012: 126).

Innovation in Supply Lines and Distribution

The decline in the Kyoto textile industry has been, in part, due to the distribution system of goods and this is also driving innovation and change in unexpected ways. Professor Murayama told me that the big wholesalers wielded a lot of power in the organization of Nishijin textile productions. Muromachi (a district of Kyoto) wholesalers controlled the communication between Nishijin manufacturers and consumers, and the manufacturers were not able to break the power of these wholesalers because they lacked the knowledge to develop their own independent distribution channels. However, my research showed that access to the internet—in order to become acquainted with other companies and to advertise their own—is now changing distribution patterns, although many traditional craft businesses have been slow to put their own services online. Initially this tardiness might have had to do with the development of the Japanese telecommunications system; until the 1990s telephone land lines (*kenri*) had to be purchased at considerable expense and were closely regulated by Nippon Telegraph and Telephone (NTT); running the phone and internet through the same line caused congestion problems for businesses. This ceased to be an issue with the lowering of landline costs due to competition from other phone providers, and the introduction of broadband networks and wireless technology. It might also be because production in traditional craft industries did not necessitate the use of computers or the internet, and therefore the potential of an online presence was not apparent. An additional factor may be that artisans such as weavers are older; as mentioned in Chapter Two, my informant estimated the average age for weavers was between 60 and 70 years old, and he suggested that because of their age they were not as familiar with the technology, although this is a large and problematic assumption. Now, more wholesalers and retailers are putting their services online, which means that the manufacturers can more easily see the distribution possibilities and make contact with relevant companies. They are also able to keep up with consumer trends, such as e-commerce. Sou Sou was the only company I interviewed in 2012 that had online shops that offered international delivery (this has changed and now more of them have online shops, including Pagong and Tabata Shibori). Kameda established a Pagong website not long after he started the business in 2001, although there was no online shop when I did my fieldwork in 2012—online shops in Japan have been slower to take off than in other countries because Japanese prefer to use cash rather than credit cards (Fitzpatrick 2013). In fact, most of the people I interviewed had some kind of online presence (see Table 5.1). Of the twenty-five individuals and companies listed in the table, three did not have an online presence at all, but twelve had a domestic online shopping service.

Between 2005 and 2010, the increased online presence of wholesalers and retailers has had an impact on distribution channels in Nishijin. Yamada drew a diagram to explain the changing nature of the distribution system, which I have reproduced as two diagrams to illustrate the traditional system and the new one (Diagrams 5.1 and 5.2). Yamada explained that now Nishijin weaving manufacturers like himself are able to bypass the wholesalers if they wish, and even deal directly with retailers. This is an enormous change for a system that has been operating in the same way for centuries. It means that not only can he supply *obi* at a more reasonable price, but he can also get direct feedback from retailers regarding consumer trends, thus speeding up the response to demand. Mori has also stated that the lack of contact between manufacturers and consumers is a problem when gauging consumer trends (2012). Mori's response has been to create doll-sized kimono costumes and sell them directly to consumers online in internet auctions, allowing him to gather data on the popularity of his designs.

Older artisans, however, tend not to have an online presence—I met those listed in Table 5.1 through the companies or associations that employed them. The younger designers I interviewed were highly protective of the older artisans to whom they outsourced work and refused to pass on their information or introduce me (as mentioned in Chapter Three). The reason for this was not explained to me but I surmise that it is because, in part, protecting the industry is historically typical of the Japanese arts, and in part because they do not want their relationships jeopardized in any way. Moon has noted that it is a feature of the textile industry that artisans are secretive, competitive, and protective of potential leakages of information regarding their products (2013: 77). This barrier no doubt also causes difficulties for younger designers entering the field who do not already have contacts in the industry. They might want to employ artisans with traditional skills, or even learn directly from established artisans, but the average age of artisans being older, and relationships between designers and

Table 5.1 *The Online Presence of Kyoto-Based Artisans*

Company	Product	Online presence	Online shop	International shipping
A.N.T. Words	Apparel from recycled kimono	Website	Yes	No
Aizenkōbō	Indigo-dyed goods	Website	No	No
Bunzaburo Shōten	*shibori* scarves, apparel	Website, blog,	Yes	No
Eirakuya	*furoshiki*, bags	Website, blog, Facebook, Twitter	Yes	No
E-Shibori-An	*tsujigahana* kimono	Website, blog, Facebook, Twitter	No	No
Japan Style System	Digital *yūzen* kimono, apparel	Website, blog, Twitter	Yes	No
Karakusaya	*furoshiki*	Website, Facebook (2013)	Yes	No
Kyoto Denim	*Kyō-yūzen* jeans	Website, blog, Facebook, Twitter	Yes	No
Kyoto Montsuki and BL-WHY jeans	*kuromontsuki* kimono, black jeans	Website, Facebook (2014)	Yes (for jeans)	No
Kyoto Shibori Kōgeikan	*shibori* kimono, accessories	Website, Facebook (2013)	Yes	No
Mori (ian kimono, Tocomarimo)	*furisode*	Website, blog	No	No
Nishijin Ori Kōgei Bijutsukan	*obi*, wall hangings, small accessories	Website	No	No
Nishijin Textile Weaving Center	*Kimono*, *obi*, *accessories*	Website, Facebook (2014)	No	No
	Weaver	No	No	No
Yamasaki Sayo Kawabe Zenji[a]	*Kyō-yūzen*	No	No	No

Orinasukan	kimono and *obi*	Website, Facebook (2015)	No	No
Nojiri Shūichi	*obi* weaver	no	No	No
Kamedatomi Co. Ltd. (brand: Pagong)	*kata yūzen* apparel	Website, blog, Facebook	No	No
Saeki Akihiko and Kayoko	*Kyō-yūzen* kimono	Facebook	No	No
Seisuke88	*kata yūzen* bags, accessories	Website, Facebook	Yes	No
Sou Sou	*furoshiki, jikatabi*, kimono, fabric, clothing	Website, blog, US website, Facebook	Yes	Yes
Tabata shibori	*shibori* bags, apparel	Website, Facebook, Twitter,	Yes	No
Yamada	*obi* manufacturer	Website	No	No
Tatsumura Kōhō	*obi* manufacturer	Website, Facebook (2013)	Yes	No

Note: [a] Kawabe Yūnosuke (Japan Style System) is the son of *kyō-yūzen* artisan Kawabe Zenji.

Source: Jenny Hall.

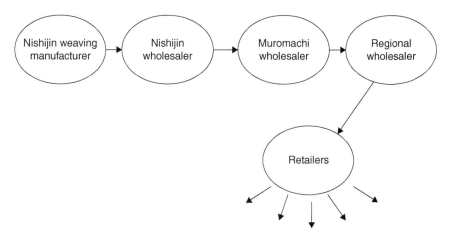

Diagram 5.1 Traditional Nishijin distribution system.
Source: Jenny Hall.

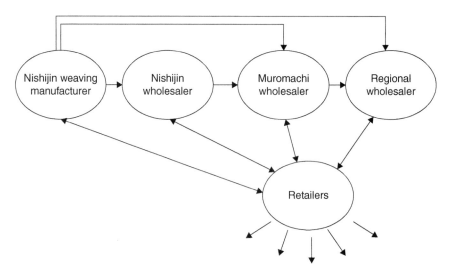

Diagram 5.2 Changing Nishijin distribution system.
Source: Jenny Hall.

artisans already firmly established, this could prove almost impossible. Hanada Keiichi, a traditional Japanese hairdressing artist found this to be the case when he returned from working in New York in the early 1990s and wanted to learn *nihongami* (Edo-period Japanese hairstyles, mainly worn by brides and *maiko*). He told me that he approached one of the five Kyoto hair stylists able to do *nihongami* forty times before he finally agreed to teach him (personal interview September 20, 2012). Although Hanada now has the skills, he is still not called upon to do the hair of *maiko* because the existing relationships within the Kyoto *hanamachi* (geisha quarters) are so tightly knit.[4]

While older artisans are largely absent from online media, younger designers are not only present through websites, but are engaging with social media and this allows them to gauge the popularity of new products. "Likes" on Facebook and comments on websites and blogs can give the producers an indication of the items that might sell well. In addition, the way in which these companies and individuals market their goods through their websites—for example, through use of video and images of current artisans at work, or through vintage images and text—invoke "the legacy of the craftsman" and transmit the notion of *kokoro* in their products. For example, Kyoto Denim featured images on its blog showing its "Shinobi" men's jeans and the pattern from a pattern book that inspired them (Figure 5.18a and b). This pattern is a common one in Japanese design, called "Bishamon Kikkō" and was often found on helmets.[5] The blog states that the interlaced hexagonal shapes mimic that of tortoise shell and signified longevity (Kyoto Denim 2007–2014a). By supplying such information to customers, the company draws direct connections between its contemporary clothing and traditional techniques and designs.

Figure 5.18a Kyoto Denim's men's jeans featuring the pattern called "Bishamon Kikkō." Photo: © Kyoto Denim. Reprinted with kind permission.

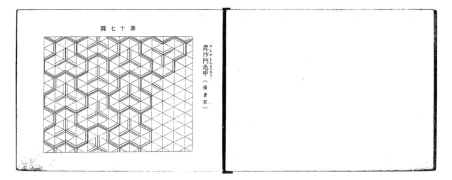

Figure 5.18b A pattern book similar to the one used by Kyoto Denim designer Kuwayama for the Bishamon Kikkō pattern on his jeans (Yoshikawa 1903). This example is from a publication called *Moyōga Shoho* (Basics of Design).
Source: National Diet Library Digital Collections.

However, as can be seen from Table 5.1, Nishijin weavers are still lagging behind other Kyoto artisans in utilizing social media: traditional craft associations such as the Kyoto Shibori Kōgeikan and the Nishijin Textile Weaving Center have only started utilizing it in the period since my fieldwork, and galleries such as the Nishijin Ori Kōgei Bijutsukan; and *obi* manufacturers such as Yamada as yet do not engage in social media.

Innovation in Marketing

Finally, a further response to the decline in demand for kimono has been through innovative ways to engage with consumers, such as creating new contexts in which to wear their products, or through various hands-on activities that serve to connect the consumer to the brand in a personal way. In the past, kimono makers did not need to do as much in terms of "marketing" in the sense of engaging new consumers: they had a very well-established, long-term clientele, which was often passed on through the generations. Therefore, previously, the Kyoto textile companies relied on the connections and marketing efforts of their industry organizations, such as the Nishijin Ori Kaikan, the Kyoto Shibori Kaikan, and the Kodai Yūzen Kaikan. Of these the former is the most successful in Kyoto, pulling in busloads of tourists, especially Chinese, while the other two barely rate a mention in tourist information. The industry organization marketing largely consists of providing galleries for products, demonstration sessions, simple museums, and *taiken* (workshops). Even with the introduction of e-commerce and new distribution systems, Kyoto artisans continue to utilize "traditional approaches" as a strategy to promote their products. However, some of the companies used as case studies in this book also adopt what can be termed "multisensory" marketing concepts, which make their brands more than merely a consumer item and add to the consumer's personal experience.

I have already mentioned *taiken* as one such marketing tool. There are various kinds of *taiken*, but in the heritage industries it primarily involves learning the basics of a technique such as weaving, *yūzen* or *shibori*. Some of the retail companies—those linked directly to a factory such as Kamedatomi—have *taiken* workshops (although these may not be on offer all of the time). Such hands-on experiences bring the consumer and the artisan closer, enabling the consumer to appreciate the skills the artisan brings to the manufacturing of their products through a multisensory experience. Kamedatomi holds two kinds of *taiken*— printing patterns onto fabric in their factory, and flower making using their fabric. In the former, *katagami yūzen taiken*, participants learn about the *yūzen* process, mixing dyes, and color selection for a pattern (a different pattern is offered each month and they vary in difficulty). Participants print a section of material with help from the artisans. The material they create can be custom-made into a garment and sent to their home after completion (Hall 2018a: 300). In the flower-making *taiken*, participants choose a fabric and make a flower by stretching the fabric over a wire frame, and then mounting it on a hair or brooch clip.

This sampling of *yūzen* production can be viewed as a "speeding up" of what is considered a "slow" manufacturing method in today's terms. The process is condensed into a one-day package because participants do not have the time to learn the skills in depth. By doing the workshop they are offered a package of nostalgia, a period before high-tech gadgets and incomprehensible digital machines, where products were made by hand. This experience of production in a day is, of course, ultimately a marketing exercise so that consumers appreciate the products and buy more.

In addition to *yūzen taiken* in their factory, Kamedatomi has offered a number of other unique experiences: a factory tour (Figure 5.19), a Spring and Fall fashion show, a haunted house and a manga. The aim is to create a Kamedatomi experience as well as to sell clothing. The two more unusual experiences are the haunted house, the "Kyō-yūzen Obake Yashiki," and the online manga. The haunted house, no longer on offer, was in an unused part of the factory decorated with *yūzen* fabric. Kameda collaborated with the famous detective film director and screenwriter, Hayashi Kaizō (b. 1957), on its design. Customers started at the entrance (which symbolized heaven) and exited via hell. According to some customers it was quite scary (Baxter 2009). Entrance to the house was free but for Kamedatomi brand Pagong members only and reservations were required. Kameda created the haunted house in order to help his customers cool-off by sending chills down their spines in summer, following an old Japanese belief.

Kamedatomi's manga can be viewed online and tells the story of the founding of the Pagong brand. It was done in collaboration with a Kyoto Seika University

Figure 5.19 Kamedatomi's factory tour, 2010. Photo: Jenny Hall. First published in *Fashion Theory*, Vol. 22:3, pp. 283–307 (2018), https://doi.org/10.1080/1362704X.2017.1319175.

student and depicts the factory and how the fabric is printed, including the staff and their roles. The most recent issue of the manga comes with a *kamishibai* (a traditional picture story show, in this case an online video of Kameda telling the story using the manga images). This mix of contemporary and traditional storytelling illustrates an innovative use of an older form of media. The manga tells of the latest Kamedatomi recruit, a female student from Kyoto Zōkei Geijutsu Daigaku (Kyoto University of Art and Design) who is now a dye apprentice at the factory. When I asked Kameda why he created the manga, he said,

> Why manga? My company gives this to customers. Customers become interested, and ask, "What is Pagong?" They want to find out, so bit by bit people talk about us and find us interesting. Customers are able to view the manga on the Internet and come to our shop. A usual company, a standard apparel maker, a typical Japanese textile maker would definitely not do this, right? (Personal interview September 24, 2012)

Kameda has a reputation in Kyoto for being eccentric. A Kyoto writer told me that he used to be the lead member of a motorbike gang in his teens and that he has been known to hold parades in the main streets of Kyoto dressed in unusual clothes. In 2014, he started the Kyō-shishimai Project, creating five lion dance costumes using Pagong fabric. He had staff perform a lion dance for customers in Sanjo-dōri and along Teramachi near his Sanjo store, and also near his Gion store. In addition, the lion dancers offered a dance of oblation for Kyoto 2014 marathon runners at a local temple. Kameda's marketing strategies reflect his eccentricity; he is trying a variety of different approaches to get his brand known and it is succeeding. In January 2011, Kameda was invited to collaborate with Paris-based designer Ji Haye in creating two dresses with patterns from Pagong's catalog, and these were part of the Paris haute couture fashion show that year and again in 2014. Fashion designer Yumi Katsura used Pagong *yūzen* fabric for her Paris 2016 collection (Pagong Kamedatomi Co. 2016). Kameda's stores and events also receive both national and international media coverage.

Sou Sou's marketing strategies are slightly different to Kamedatomi but are also aimed at a multisensory experience for consumers. Sou Sou now has nine stores within a small area of Kyoto near Shijo-dōri, which give the sense of an aesthetically themed village: Sou Sou Tabi (*jikatabi*), Sou Sou Kikoromo (women's wear), Sou Sou Kei-i (men's wear), Sou Sou Isemomen (accessories and *tenugui*), Sou Sou Warabegi (children's wear), Sou Sou Hotei (*furoshiki*, bags), Sou Sou Someori (fabric, paper, cushions, *noren*, furniture), Sou Sou Le Coq Sportif (a range of sports clothing in collaboration with Le Coq Sportif), and Sou Sou Zaifu (sweets, tea, and books).[6] This clustering of stores creates a community feel—even the potted plants in the street near the stores are patterned with Wakisaka's designs (Figure 5.20). Many of the shops feature elements of Kyoto

Figure 5.20 The potted plants in the street near the stores feature Wakisaka's designs. Designs © Sou Sou. Photo: Jenny Hall.

machiya such as sliding wooden doors, *tokonoma*, *shoji* screens, and *noren* (Figure 5.21), and each store features a special design. For example, Sou Sou Warabegi has wooden walls and floor reminiscent of children's building blocks and the small changing room feels like a child's playhouse (Figure 5.22). When I visited in 2012, Sou Sou Hotei had a feature wall by the artist Kimura Hideki.[7] Sou Sou Kei-i and Sou Sou Zaifu have a tea counter where customers can order tea that is prepared for them by a tea master following the methods of tea ceremony (Figure 5.23) (visit https://www.youtube.com/watch?v=yONsXoDglJ w&feature=youtu.be for a video of Kei-i's interior with tea counter). In Sou Sou Kikoromo (downstairs from Sou Sou Zaifu) there is a changing room that feels aesthetically like a teahouse (visit https://www.youtube.com/watch?v=HGaFHh_ n6qs&feature=youtu.be for a video of Kikoromo), and upstairs in Zaifu, there is a *tokonoma* decorated with a tea set, fan, and *kakijiku* (hanging scroll) all patterned with Wakisaka's designs. Takahashi Osuni, the tea master, wears Sou Sou's clothing while preparing the tea. *Wagashi* (Japanese sweets) are served with the tea. Sou Sou collaborated with a *wagashi* maker to create sweets especially for

Figure 5.21 Sou Sou Tabi has *machiya*-like wooden shelves, sliding door, and *noren*. Photo: Jenny Hall.

Figure 5.22 Sou Sou Warabegi has wooden walls and floor reminiscent of children's building blocks, and its changing room feels like a child's playhouse. Photo: Jenny Hall.

Figure 5.23 Sou Sou Kei-i's tea counter. Photo: Jenny Hall.

Figure 5.24 A collaboration with a *wagashi* maker means that sweets are specifically designed to match a platter patterned with distinctive Wakisaka textile designs. Designs © Sou Sou. Photo: Jenny Hall.

their store and each sweet is specifically designed to match a platter patterned with distinctive Wakisaka textile designs (Figure 5.24). Wakabayashi told me the concept for the *wagashi* was to create something pretty and tasty that observed the change in the seasons, a philosophy that is typically heeded in Japanese food. He said, "For example, now it is October so the *wagashi* uses October's food and flowers as inspiration" (personal interview October 5, 2012). The innovative point is the direct link between the *wagashi* and the textiles, putting the textiles into an experience at the place of sale. Rather than just produce clothing, Wakabayashi says he wants to produce what people would do. "I want to see people wearing Sou Sou clothes and doing Japanese cultural activities like tea ceremony," he told me (ibid.). He believes that tea ceremony contains the Japanese essence of beauty and hospitality and it would be a shame if such a tradition disappeared. Traditionally the upper classes practice tea ceremony as a leisure pursuit because they have the time and money to participate in the costly lessons, to buy the accoutrements, and so on. By offering a casual version of tea ceremony, Sou Sou is making it more accessible to more classes, and in this way, whether consciously or not, the company is eroding the traditional leisure boundaries.

In addition, all of Sou Sou's staff in every store wear Sou Sou apparel, and also serve as the models for Sou Sou's online catalog, which adds a sense of familiarity when customers visit the stores. And as you enter each store there is a particular fragrance and music that are obviously carefully chosen to enhance the overall sensory effect. Many retail stores in Japan and around the world use smell and sound for marketing purposes but Sou Sou have appealed to all of the senses in a highly sophisticated manner. Sou Sou collaborated with an Osakan-based candle maker, Kameyama, by doing the packaging designs for some of their products, including their incense, which Sou Sou in turn burns throughout their stores. Le Coq Sportif and Sou Sou celebrated their 10th anniversary in 2014 so have been collaborating for some time creating sports-style apparel with Wakisaka's designs. As part of this collaboration Sou Sou supports Le Tour de Kyoto, a tour of Kyoto where participants can do various *taiken* in *shibori*, *wagashi*, and textile dyeing. They also collaborated with Kyoto football team Kyoto Sanga; they used Kyoto Sanga's colors and motifs on their *tabi* socks and other apparel. I asked the sales assistant whether or not the footballers wear the *tabi* but he replied that he did not think so—it was mainly the fans that were interested in the apparel. This kind of marketing is setting up a context for the product because the original context does not exist so they are creating new contexts in which to experience their products such as at tea ceremony, or football games.

It is clear that companies such as Kamedatomi, Kyoto Denim, and Sou Sou use "tradition" as a lens through which to market their contemporary goods. They constantly play with past and present, and see no contradiction in this because, as I argued in Chapter One, emic concepts of tradition have always incorporated innovation and change. By highlighting "traditional" aspects of their production techniques or design, they tap into consumers' nostalgia for a romantic past or an idealized view of Japanese culture, and in turn reinterpret it for the future. But they also use contemporary culture to market their clothing. Although Kamedatomi and Sou Sou know of each other but are not linked in any way, they have both been involved in another innovative project, the "Kyoto Manga Girls Collection," or MaGiC for short. This project, established by the Kyoto Manga Museum in 2011, aims to develop a new fashion industry in Kyoto inspired by *shōjo manga* (girl's manga). In 2012 Sou Sou created five kimonos and fifteen garments based on illustration artist Nakahara Junichi's work, and in 2013 Kamedatomi made twelve items using their *kata yūzen* fabric, inspired by Anno Moyoko's series *Sugar Sugar Rune*. The project involved exhibitions and fashion shows of the clothing (Kyoto International Manga Museum 2006–14). Concurrently, Kyoto Denim produced a manga designed by Kyoto illustrator Baron Ueda, for their menswear range that was included in their website. They stated that they were "following tradition" by producing the manga, and that

this is why we have turned our denim into manga illustrations. By drawing our denim, we have given it new life. It allows the Japanese aesthetics in our blood to be materialized in a 2D art form. It is completely modern, but also traditional in the sense that we are trying to create something beautiful. That is something no time in the world can change, our soul. Kyoto Denim will continue to put our soul into the work and create beautiful apparel by linking tradition and the future, as our ancestors have done since the beginning of time. (Kyoto Denim 2014b)

Therefore, all three companies use manga as both a link to the past and "tradition" as well as a way to contextualize their products as "modern" and contemporary. By using the format of manga they are attempting to piggyback on the success of this medium to advertise their products.

Conclusion

The Kyoto textile industry is undergoing changes in all aspects of production, and these changes are having various outcomes. There is a speeding up of the industry, in the application of technology that enables faster production, in the changes from a linear distribution system to a networked one, new versions of *wafuku* that take less time to don and allow for a speeding up of the body, and marketing that gives consumers a condensed and therefore speedier version of the production process in *taiken.* It is natural that these changes result in questions about legitimacy and authenticity, and participants in the Kyoto textile industry demonstrate a complex use of tradition and authenticity to imagine and reimagine their artistic tradition.

In the case of Nishijin *obi*, the markers used here for rendering authenticity reveal the sometimes precarious cultural nationalist grounds on which cultural identity is based. Since the Meiji era (1868–1912) in particular, those involved in the Japanese heritage industries have used the construction of a "national style" to authenticate products and render them uniquely "Japanese" (Taylor Atkins 2000: 32). In regard to Nishijin *obi*, this gives an added twist to what Taylor Atkins has termed "authenticity anxiety" because the strategies for rendering the products authentic do not stand up (ibid.: 31). These examples have shown that the methods of production or the physicality (where and who makes the items) is not important—it does not matter if the weavers making Nishijin *obi* are based elsewhere—what is important is who decides what is "traditional" and "authentic." Nishijin is a label put on after production, so the decisive moment of authentication is after the fact, and decided by the main stakeholders—the artisans, the Nishijin Textile Industrial Association, and METI. As long as the stakeholders retain legitimacy in the eyes of the consumers then the authenticity of such goods is accepted. It is the certification seal that is shrouding the true processes and relationships. Resorting to the national cultural heritage line is a way of resolving the authenticity anxiety because it is more simplistic to say that rather than unpicking all of the complexities. In addition, very few challenge this line of argument because certification as an unassailable mark of authenticity is particularly powerful.

However, the real issue about outsourcing Nishijin weaving is that these shaky foundations of national cultural heritage are in danger of being exposed. Globalization is often seen as a threat to authenticity in this regard, but perhaps transnationalism can help us redefine authenticity. Curator and writer Kevin Murray is coordinator of a transnational textile project involving Australia and India. The Sangam project is promoting "honesty about origins and outcomes of product development (the right to know)" and "respect for creative contributions (the right to be known)" (Sangam Australia India Design Platform 2013). Such approaches tie in with the "slow fashion" movement, in that they "challenge existing hierarchies of designer, producer, and consumer" and "highlight collaborative/cooperative work providing agency especially to women" (Clark 2008: 428). The Nishijin industry on the one hand seeks to highlight the fact that production of *obi* is contingent on the local community, but at the same time wants to obscure the actual location (and community) of production. Such obfuscation is usually a feature of mass-produced fast fashion (Clark 2008: 434) where

> the metaphor of speed serves as a smoke screen for the harsh realities of the sourcing of materials, means of production, conditions of workers, distances traveled for distribution, and other less than acceptable factors. A slow or more sustainable approach focuses greater attention on valuing and knowing the object, and demands design that generates significant experiences, which are not transformed into empty images for rapid consumption. (Ibid.: 440)

A slow/sustainable approach discussed here has been described as "sustainable sensoriality" (ibid.: 440) because it focuses on "sensorial aspects that acknowledge the existence of the many abstract and emotional factors that underpin the choices of what people wear" (ibid.: 441–2). I concur with Clark that this approach changes the sensory aesthetic "from one that prefigures sight and 'senses of distance,' to favor the 'senses of proximity,' taste, touch, and smell" (ibid.: 441–2). In addition, as Clark further notes, "Referencing local cultural practices provides for more transparent production systems, often using hand skills, which can address a contemporary search for authenticity" (ibid.: 435). Promoting the origins of Nishijin *obi* transparently, including all who worked on producing them, would give those involved in the industry a new way to render authenticity.

6
CONCLUSION

During my first week of staying in Nishijin for fieldwork, I could hear thumps and knocks from the house next door which were not the rhythmic sounds of a loom that I had heard on previous visits. I asked the owners what the noises were. *Obi* weavers Hamada (aged 81) and his wife (aged 77) decided that it was time to retire, but since they had no heir for their business they had to close the studio and sell the equipment. The noise I heard was the dismantling of the looms after over sixty years of weaving *obi*. Hamada said that the industry had been hit hard by the Fukushima disaster—they had relied on many buyers from northeastern Honshu but the disruption of the Tohoku economy had filtered down even to *obi* sales. This story lends a certain irony to this book, which strives to document the way in which young artisans are taking the traditional textile-making techniques into the future. Here was a story of an elderly couple giving up their weaving business in the face of lack of interest. This anecdote served to remind me of the diversity of experiences of people involved in the traditional textile industry: while there are success stories via designers I interviewed, there are also stories of defeat.

However, labelling Kyoto textiles as an industry in decline does not account for its complexities, or for traditional techniques being used to produce contemporary apparel. Young people are taking on heritage skills, as I have demonstrated: these include *kanoko shibori* artisan Tabata Kazuki, the young female *kata yūzen* dye apprentice at Pagong, *tsujigahana* artisan Fukumura Takeshi, and *tegaki yūzen* artisans Saeki Akihiko and his wife Kayoko. In addition, young people are also working in the heritage industry sphere, such as *yūzen* jeans designer Kuwayama Toyoaki at Kyoto Denim, digital *yūzen* designers Mori Makoto and Kawabe Yūnosuke, and the *obi* designer at Yamada's *obi* manufacturing company (Yamada's son), to name a few mentioned in this research. I have shown how these contemporary Kyoto designers and artisans are adapting and adopting *wafuku* and how their new designs act as a vehicle for designers' and consumers' expressions of Japanese culture. This book has documented social change in regard to heritage industries in Kyoto but it would not be complete without some discussion about the future of such industries.

The Evolution of Tradition

Central to any discussion of the future of traditional textiles in Japan is the concept of "tradition" because this term is often invoked by those in the industry as a means for dealing with social change. Tradition and change are not necessarily antithetical; it is important to recognize that Japanese ideas of tradition include revitalization and change. As discussed in Chapter One, this enables artisans to frame their work, even those products made using modern technology such as digital printing, as "traditional," and consumers to accept it as such. Bestor, in his discussion of "traditional" practices such as the community work of neighborhood associations in Tokyo, argued that "in the minds of many Japanese and foreign observers alike, culture is history, culture is not something affected, changed, or generated by the lives of living people" (1989: 10). However, artistic traditions are represented in a variety of vital and changing ways that involve the artists and creators in continual interpretation and reproduction of what has gone before them—through their creations, they repeatedly connect the past with the present and the future. It is also clear that certain individuals within the industry view themselves as a contemporary link between the past and the future by demonstrating the conscious way they think about "tradition" and utilize "tradition." Miyamoto clearly made this point, stating, "If you don't sharpen the tradition, it doesn't survive. Tradition has to be honed again and again. By combining kimono and denim, now he [Kuwayama] is shaping the tradition" (personal interview November 2, 2012).

When asked about the role tradition plays in design inspiration and his view of history, Sou Sou's designer, Wakabayashi, said,

I sit and draw quickly from library books, or look at clothing in the Jidai Matsuri parade or in museums. I haven't taken part in Jidai Matsuri. It was only three years ago that the Shōwa section was established [in the parade]. One day, when the Heisei section is set up, it would be nice to have Sou Sou clothes in the parade. (Personal interview October 5, 2012)[1]

These observations reprise discussion of history and tradition made in Chapter One. With reference to change as a complementary aspect of cultural history and tradition, I cited the ritual reconstruction of Ise Shrine every twenty years as representative of the Japanese artisans' ongoing connection of things past to the present, and the idea that "tradition" intrinsically includes renewal, adaptation, and change enables Japanese society to legitimize and authenticate "Japanese culture." Scholars such as Bestor (1989) and Moeran (1997) have already noted the inclusion of change in Japanese concepts of tradition and my findings are in line with this. An analysis of the Kyoto textile industry showed how "new" technologies such as digital weaving and digital *yūzen* have become accepted alongside more traditional forms of production. This is particularly remarkable in the case of digital *yūzen* because it appears to differ so greatly from traditional processes. This is a noteworthy case in which tradition is "used to imbue ideas, things and practices with the appearance of historicity and thereby legitimate them as authentic and right" (Robertson 1997: 98).

Artisans also legitimize their crafts through the invocation of *kokoro* (heart). Representing their work as embodying *kokoro* emphasizes the connection between production and consumption because consumption is assumed to encompass not only the physical connection through use of the product but also an appreciation and interaction with the artisan's *kokoro*. As Kondo states, "In Japan, objects in general are not considered atomistic entities, but extensions of people" (2005: 202) and therefore the products are seen as an extension of the artisan and embody the care and attention that the artisan has taken in creating them. In addition, as noted earlier, *kokoro* is imbued from the consumer's side through both their reinterpretation of the garment's use and through the appreciation of it. It also links them to a larger image of the "heart" or "spirit" of the nation as imagined community (Anderson 2006[1983]) through their investment in garments that are made by what are recognized as part of Japan's intangible cultural heritage and representative of Japanese cultural identity. Even though the majority of Japanese do not wear kimono, as Goldstein-Gidoni notes (2005), the essentialized and idealized views of Japan (including the practices of kimono wearing, ikebana, tea ceremony, martial arts, origami, and calligraphy) that emerged in the postwar period are officially and unofficially endorsed by mainstream Japanese media such as NHK and Japanese government departments such as METI as "Japanese culture." The existence of the idealized culture in material form adds further legitimacy to my informants' products and their means of production. It is this carefully constructed view of "traditional" Japanese culture that METI and MEXT have aimed to preserve and utilize with various programs. As Goldstein-Gidoni states, "Japanese formal authorities have been vigorously involved in protecting and in fact in reproducing 'traditional' (*dentō-teki*) cultural properties (*bunka zai*). From the 1950s the Japanese government has been protecting intangible cultural properties such as traditional craft techniques and even the people who make them, who were designated by the government as 'human' or 'national' treasures" (2005: 159). This recognition of not only the technique or skill, but the human element as part of intangible cultural heritage, a "Living National Treasure" (*Ningen Kokuhō*),[2] acknowledges the embodiment of art through a living person and also substantiates the Japanese belief that the spirit of the creator is transmitted to the tangible property, as discussed in Chapter Two.

A discussion of the institutionalization of the Living National Treasures trope is a useful way to connect and consolidate different ideas regarding the preservation of culture presented throughout the book by my informants. Becoming a Living National Treasure is both an honor and a burden, according to one artisan, who was offered an individual certification but refused it. The artisan explained to me that those who accept certification

> are completely controlled by the government. They are told what they can do, and whether or not they can go overseas for exhibitions. They are only given 30,000 yen [about AUD$300] a year,[3] and the government dictates how this money is spent. They have about forty appointees and if one dies they promote someone else, irrespective of their talent. It's also very political—you are encouraged to affiliate yourself with a particular artistic school. I don't have the support or contacts to become well known but at least I'm free artistically to do what I want. (Personal communication 2011)

One example of this control, albeit outside my formal fieldwork period in Kyoto, was observed at a *tsutsugaki yūzen* workshop I attended which was held at the Australian Academy of Design in Melbourne in 2011. If the *tsutsugaki yūzen* artisan had been a Living National Treasure, he believed that he would not have been able to run the workshop. This is because the institute was not considered prestigious enough by MEXT to host a Living National Treasure, demonstrating the seriousness with which the Japanese government promotes "Japanese culture," both domestically and internationally. This official promotion may help to preserve culture, but acts as a double-edged sword because it serves to freeze culture rather than allowing for change. This recalls Daliot-Bul's observation that, with regard to the "Cool Japan" policy, government agencies "produce their own politically motivated and carefully reinvented imagery which thus becomes a competing sterilized version of the original" (2009b: 262). In regard to the Nishijin weaving industry, Moon has concluded that "once incorporated into the realm of culture it will be the end of the industry" (2015).

According to art historian Michele Bambling, many Living National Treasures have expressed they feel the burden of their title in other ways: there is an expectation from the public that every work produced will be "traditional" and an exemplary model of its type (2005: 163). Because of this, artisans feel their creativity is stifled, they are reluctant to innovate, and they become tense and nervous about producing work (ibid.). Their "creativity becomes institutionalized" (ibid.: 163) because they are expected to create "traditional" works that are modeled on earlier works and adhere to the aesthetic expectations of the Living National Treasures program. Aikawa-Faure has also noted this issue, stating, "As these forms of art, which are strictly formatted, stylized and documented and leave little room for change, are selected under criteria requiring the maintenance of authenticity at the time of inscription, artists and practitioners are not allowed to express their creativity, and some have argued that creative renewal should also be allowed to the holders of the title" (2014: 44). Furthermore, "the ACA [Agency for Cultural Affairs] regularly monitors the work of the Living National Treasures in order to ensure that they are able to transmit their know-how or techniques" (ibid.: 44) and the way they pass on their knowledge is changing. The Living National Treasures program sponsors video productions, publications, and exhibitions and expects artisans to take on a mentor. Mentors today have less time to invest in their own development and maintenance of their craft, and devote less time to memorizing *kata*. As a result, there are various attempts to speed up training. Artisans are encouraged to stop and explain rather than show through working. There is increasing reliance on written instruction, textbooks, or video, and there has been a shift from "bodily to cognitive approaches to skill acquisition," from "proactive self-motivated observation to passive absorption of knowledge" (Bambling 2005: 163). Ironically, this shift has refocused training from that of intangible methods to tangible ones (ibid.: 166); because young artisans no longer "learn and remember by body" (*karada de oboeru*) (ibid.: 155) the skills do not become second nature and the *kokoro* of younger artisans is not developed. This view was reiterated by ikebana master, Ishido, who told me regarding flower arrangement, "If you take a short course it is like fast food—it isn't good for you. You have to learn slowly. If you learn slowly, then the ikebana becomes a part of you" (Hall 2004: 84). The succession of skills is a key point to any discussion of the future of such crafts, and one that was cited by many of the artisans I interviewed. Wakabayashi at Sou Sou stated, "Probably in ten to twenty years the artisans will die or stop and there will be only individual artisans in certain districts who will also eventually disappear. Education is important to preserve the skills. People should learn from a young age. Artisans have to be respected, but these days not many people do" (personal interview October 5, 2012). The Living National Treasure trope therefore shows the difficulties facing artisans who must navigate through the interplay between their own and the community's or nation's ideas and expectations of tradition while satisfying their own creative imagination, how to pass on or acquire skills, as well as how to market their products in a fast-changing "mediascape" (Appadurai 1990). And while the idea that government involvement ends up freezing development and stifling creativity in such industries may not be unexpected, more research into the changing nature of skill acquisition would aid understanding of developments in the textile industry because it might give an indication of what skills are passed on and how quality can be maintained.

Using the Past to Weave the Future

Since completing this research, I have found that young designers and artisans are continuing to use and learn various traditional techniques and processes alongside new technologies. This investigation has also flagged opportunities for further research in the viability of heritage material culture in Japan. Although my research found revitalized activity in this area, there is still the distinct possibility that the industry may decline due to the lack of successors for auxiliary skills such as the tools needed for *orimono*, *yūzen*, and *shibori*. *Tegaki yūzen* artisan Saeki Kayoko told me,

> As far as kimono makers and dyers are concerned, there are young artisans but there are few that can make the materials or ingredients for their work. It is a problem. For example, *itome*, *tsutsu*, *kinzoku* [thread, piping cones and metal items]. Machines can make some things but handmade tools—there are only one or two people who can make them. There are no more people who can make the *shinshi* [bamboo poles] that are used to stretch out the kimono fabric. (Personal interview November 7, 2012)

When I asked how the scarcity of tools affects their future, Kayoko's husband Akihiko told me that he had collected many of the tools so that he had them in reserve for the future. This is obviously not a sustainable option. However, there is also a trend toward an artisan working alone, doing all of the steps in processes rather than the collaborative division of labor that has been a characteristic of these industries until recently. My interviews with sole artisans such as Saeki Akihiko, Tabata Kazuki, and Fukumura Takeshi confirm this movement from collective/collaborative work to solitary production but this is another potential area of further research. In these cases, often the artisans learn to make their own tools. *Tegaki yūzen* master Kobayashi Shumei not only does all of the processes such as sketches, applying the paste-resist, dyeing, and steaming himself, but he also shapes his own *tsutsu* nozzles for dye resist paste, selects wood and boils up the pieces to make his own dye, and built his fabric steamer himself. He even made an airtight nail-less paulownia wood box to protect his *noren* crafts, the pottery dishes used to mix dyes that included specialized indents for his brushes, and a large wooden frame on which he stretched his handcrafted material for display. He said that to call it his own work, he feels he has to do all of the processes, even though in the past every process would have been done by different individuals. He asserted that he needs many different skills that involve both knowledge of science and design (personal communication 2011). He learned from studying old documents and through trial and error, repeating processes hundreds of times before he was successful; I surmise that artisans such as Kobayashi are rare.

It also became evident from my research that not only do contemporary artisans require a wider knowledge base in these areas, but they also require new skills in communication technologies. The impact of social media on cultural heritage industries is another potential area for future research. My inquiries found that communication technology is starting to impact on the Kyoto textile industry in both positive and negative ways. In Chapters Two and Five, I demonstrated that artisans and manufacturers were able to use the internet for both marketing and distribution for positive results. The internet provides industry visibility, which is vital for success—especially for those artisans with a high degree of specialization such as Tabata, the fabric dyer. Tabata's website gives his specialty as *kanoko shibori*, which allows manufacturers searching for this particular form of *shibori* to find him and to view examples of his work. The internet enables artisans and designers to do market research for particular products, as well as serving to expand distribution networks, as discussed in Chapter Five, but the impact in terms of sales and further developments in the industry are difficult to analyze without additional data. Such data could be gathered through the usual means of surveys as to how customers discovered companies and their products, and these might easily be procured through website analytics as well as in store. However, judging by the fact that many of my informants only established a website presence during the period since my fieldwork, and also by admissions such as Miyamoto's in Chapter Three regarding his lack of factual data of his company's customer base, it is difficult to assess the impact of any technological change, especially in an industry where customer analysis and market research are not common practice.

Weaving Social Change

The changes occurring in the Kyoto textile industry are indicative of wider social changes in Japan. For example, the relatively recent phenomenon of fashion *taiken*, discussed in Chapter Four, has arisen in conjunction with an increasing atmosphere of nostalgia and cultural nationalism throughout the country, no doubt spurred by general social malaise related to Japan's environmental disasters and continuing economic woes. As Robertson states, "Nostalgia is a barometer of present moods. It figures as a distinctive way of relating the past to the present and future" (1997: 105) by "juxtaposing the 'uncertainties and anxieties of the present with presumed verities and comforts of the … past'" (Robertson 1997: 105). Reflexive questions of who the Japanese are, what constitutes "Japaneseness," and the relationship between "tradition" and cultural identity have become national obsessions (see Goldstein-Gidoni 2005 for an insight into how Japan packages itself for the global market[4]) but early postwar and contemporary consumers' experience with kimono varies. For many young people in Japan, the customs and cultural artifacts believed to symbolize the timeless Japanese past have become exotic, as per Mathews' discussion of traditional Japanese dance, music, and calligraphy (2000). When I first went to Japan in 1998, I was disappointed to find that most young Japanese I spoke to had little knowledge of some traditional decorative objects which intrigued me, such as *inro* (small wooden or lacquer boxes often used for pills or seals, worn hanging off the *obi* as a substitute pocket) or *netsuke* (miniature carvings used as toggles to secure the *inro*). This was also apparent from my fieldwork interviews. Kawabe Yūnosuke conducted marketing research in the early 2000s for his digital *yūzen* company, Japan Style System. He told me that he anticipated that his customers would be middle-aged women but he found that those interested in his products were primarily teenagers. Kawabe explained that "it was the first time they had seen such products and designs because they had mostly grown up with American culture" (personal interview October 9, 2012). Accordingly, Mathews makes a similar point that the traditional arts in Japan are often not experienced firsthand by the mainstream, stating, "If we define 'Japaneseness' as a matter of how Japanese live today—how Japanese people actually experience the cultural world that surrounds them—then it seems that pizza and jazz are Japanese, while *no* [*nō*] theater is not Japanese, but foreign" (2000: 34). Of course, just because individuals have no direct experience of something in their culture does not make it "foreign"—rather, it is more the case that a lack of familiarity has rendered some cultural facets distant to consumers. In regard to clothing, Japanese have a specific expression for this: *kimono-banare*. This refers to the separation of young Japanese from traditional attire such as kimono (Wada 1996: 158). Creighton supports this argument, stating that "as material goods and customs associated with the once-exotic West have become a routine part of life, the customs, goods, and habits believed to symbolize the timeless Japanese past have been embraced as the new exotica" (1992: 53).

I saw this in my fieldwork many times. For example, young Japanese visit Kyoto in particular in their search for their understanding of the "Japanese past" and this search is played out in various ways. *Obi* manufacturer Yamada gave an example of one of the ways their imaginings are implemented; "When young people come to Kyoto, they have a yearning, an aspiration about Kyoto. They want to walk around wearing kimono, see the sights while wearing kimono" (personal interview November 1, 2012). This sentiment has led to the growing popularity of *kankō taiken* in Kyoto as discussed in Chapter Four, allowing domestic and foreign tourists to experience "Japanese culture" through various activities including textile-related activities such as *shiborizome, aizome, kyō-yūzen,* and kimono *taiken.* As previously discussed, Pagong offers *katagami yūzen taiken* at their factory as part of their marketing strategy to bring in new consumers, generate alternate income and raise sales. These short experiences serve to give individuals a bodily (and sensory) encounter of the activity and the complexities involved with it, which highlights the skill of the master craftspeople as well as addressing Japanese notions about learning through action. These activities also make immediate (and therefore more "real") past "traditions" even if they are idealized versions of those traditions, and participants become personally connected to them. This firsthand sensory experience is the reason *taiken* is popular in Japan, but it is also vital to the ethnographer, as Tessa Morris-Suzuki pointed out in a recent presentation (2015). She spoke of the importance of being present to do research because the sensory experience can change the researcher's ideas. This was certainly the case in terms of my fieldwork. Merely exploring Kyoto's streets gave me a clearer idea of the number of artisans and designers attempting to produce contemporary items using traditional techniques, and, through participation in various *kankō taiken*, I was able to obtain an idea of why or why not certain artisanal skills might be popular and therefore taken up by younger individuals.

In addition, it seems as if the artisans and designers' attraction to cultural identity and "tradition" was a decision affected by experiences they had outside of Japan. This can lead to what has been termed "self-orientalizing"—non-Western designers internalize the Western gaze to create "Asian-style" fashion by uprooting cultural and ethnically specific designs and textiles from their original contexts (Nakatani 2015: 35). Many of the artisans I interviewed, such as *tegaki yūzen* artisan Saeki Kayoko, did not become interested in the heritage industries until they had travelled overseas and were asked about Japanese traditional culture—questions for which they had no answers. This was a story repeated by many interviewees, even if those artisans had grown up in families involved in such industries. Japanese sociologist Kurita Isamu has noted this phenomenon, stating, "The very international-ness of the life-style makes the traditional Japanese arts appear quite alien and exotic. We look at our tradition the way a foreigner does, and we are beginning to love it" (Kurita 1983: 131). In the process of learning their craft, Japanese artisans become preservers, interpreters, and creators of Japanese identity. By choosing this personal as well as cultural identity, they become promoters, who like the traditional musicians, dancers, and calligraphy practitioners studied by Mathews, "must convince at least some of their fellow Japanese—their prospective and present students—to pursue the cultural identities and adhere to the conceptions of Japaneseness that they proffer" (2000: 41). To do this, they emphasize these arts as being the essence of Japaneseness[5] and promote the notion that if Japanese traditions are lost, then Japanese identity as a whole is lost. *Kata yūzen* brand owner Takahashi Seisuke confirmed this view, telling me, "Traditional crafts are part of our [Japanese] identity so we can't lose them, we have to save them. For example, the current generation doesn't understand the meaning of *kabuki* or the traditional Japanese show business world but those who have studied the past can see that it is important. They are interested and those people want to see more" (personal interview November 2, 2012). It is these concepts that companies such as Sou Sou, Pagong, and Kyoto Denim, as well as Nishijin weavers and *yūzen* artisans draw on to promote their products. They not only draw on the concept of "tradition" to do this but also on essentialist ideals about Japanese culture. However, the success of such products is reliant on a receptive audience. As Wakabayashi told me, "It is not only craftsmen; we need someone to use such items to preserve them" (personal interview Octtober 5, 2012). Tabata echoed this viewpoint, defining tradition as,

> of course, handmade, but in addition, daily necessities (*nichiyōhin*). We have to be able to use items. If we have no use for them, it is not tradition. For example, when you go to a museum, the decorative things are only for looking at with your eyes (*me de miru mono*). You say it is beautiful, it is an excellent thing, but of course you cannot use them. (Personal interview October 5, 2012)

This receptive audience is both willing to consume such revised versions of Japanese tradition and culture and to reinterpret it themselves. This need for a receptive audience is intertwined with that of the need for a "market" but the Japanese government has made a point of distinction in this regard. Hareven states that "Nishijin weaving is defined not as an art but as a traditional industry (*dentō sangyō*)" (2002: 96) and therefore Nishijin weavers "are considered craftspeople (*shokunin*) rather than artists" because they are not independent or self-employed and cannot chose designs or colors (ibid.). In terms of production, artists will create art for reasons other than market demand, such as their own gratification, whereas according to Hareven's distinction, artisans will not. However, the trend toward sole artisans discussed above shows that this distinction between artist and artisan is becoming blurred. Dalby makes the same point in regard to *mingei* (2001: 173). The original definition of *mingei* folk crafts was that of "materials brought together according to tradition by an anonymous craftworker" (ibid.: 173) but those involved in contemporary *mingei* are now seen as cultural "heroes." Dalby states that "it could even be argued that the social conditions of the modern industrial age render true mingei impossible. We can have artists who create 'in the style of mingei,' but their relationship to their materials and the consumer is now market-directed" (ibid.: 173). Moeran has also recognized such blurring of categories in regard to Onta pottery, stating that "the media have tended also to make 'artists' out of craftsmen" (1997: 168). Therefore, while the government has delineated the difference between these categories on a practical level, in reality it is not feasible to isolate the artist from the commercial process, or isolate the commercial process from ideals about Japanese culture. It is likely also the case that artists/designers and manufacturers wish to identify and represent themselves as "artisans" as a way of increasing their appeal to nostalgia-seeking consumers.

Despite various views of the creative process, the wearing of kimono—the sensory experience, and its motives, meanings, and pleasures—is also an important part of understanding the place contemporary kimono holds in Japan today. Chapter Four demonstrated how individuals are challenging conventional ways of wearing kimono by deviating from the standard modes of donning and wearing. Examples of this are front-tied *obi*, or combining kimono with Western accessories. They are also creating their own new, more casual and playful, contexts for wearing kimono through organizations such as Kimono Jack. In performing such actions, they are repeating history in that they are using kimono as a form of subversion, challenging how it is "read." Kimono in the postwar period has become symbolic of the nation's cultural identity, but an identity shaped in the form of "good wife, wise mother": individuals from the upper classes who perform ikebana and tea ceremony in their leisure time. Through nonconformism to this ideal, individuals subvert this image and what it stands for in terms of identity. This is taken to extremes via an increasing focus on *asobi* (play) and self-expression that is bringing the world of cosplay into the world of the kimono, as discussed. This aspect of the consumption of kimono and *wafuku* demonstrates that "socially, consuming is both a bonding and an individuating experience" (Stevens 2010: 202), and the concept of cosplay explicates this because by wearing both kimono and contemporary *wafuku*, consumers create and participate in a community. Chapter Four demonstrated how various forms of fashion *taiken*, such as *maiko henshin*, can be viewed as forms of cosplay, and where these forms might sit within the context of the nation as imagined community. The popularity of kimono *taiken*, in particular, illustrates the Japanese public's desire for not only new contexts in which kimono can be worn that are outside the accepted formal occasions but also index a desire for nostalgia that has existed in Japan for many decades. It demonstrates that nostalgia has in fact become "a natural(ized) frame of mind shaping desires and motivating patterns of consumption" (Robertson 1997: 105).

Chapter Five elucidated how companies are using this desire for nostalgia to sell their products, such as Sou Sou's referencing of *kabukimono* on its netshop website, Pagong's provision of Taishō-era explanations for its patterns, or Kyoto Denim's linking of its jeans to the "romantic" and "chivalrous" Warring States period. These retailers are also challenging conventional ways of wearing kimono, as seen in Chapter Five, by making both the kimono and the contexts, in which it is worn, less formal. For example, they are creating casual clothing with the "essence" of kimono—new forms of *wafuku*. In their retail outlets, Sou Sou is merging these new forms with alternative contexts in which to wear them, such as wearing *jikatabi* to support a football team, or wearing contemporary *wafuku* (other than kimono) for a casual form of tea ceremony. The companies are not only doing this through the use of multisensory marketing techniques, creating sensory experiences for customers but also through the use of social media to directly target and inform their customers about new products, including their imbued (constructed) meanings. Such marketing practices help deliver their concepts of a Japanese "essence" or "feeling" to customers, and are resulting in a revitalization of the Kyoto textile industry. In a sense, they are creating culture, which "is every bit as much an ongoing production as it is a constantly transforming product" (Robertson 1997: 98). These retailers willingly evoke tradition to market their products because this concept gives them "the appearance of historicity" and legitimates them as "authentic and right" (Robertson 1997: 98). Kameda's comment in Chapter Five demonstrates his insight concerning the current zeitgeist in Japan surrounding nostalgia, when he says that Pagong's products are ideal for the current time, "when people are longing for more connection to tradition and a by-gone world" (Pagong Kamedatomi Co. 2014).

This yearning for by-gone eras has ironically resulted in a "speeding up" of the process of donning kimono, through kimono *taiken* and ready-to-wear *obi*, in order to experience wearing a "slow" apparel. Throughout this book I have noted both a simultaneous speeding up and slowing down of various aspects of *wafuku*. Chapter Two described a speeding up in production of kimono through technology such as digital *yūzen* and digital weaving. Chapter Five detailed a speeding up in distribution channels online that allow for faster turnaround and supply as well as a speeding up of *wafuku* in that designers are creating kimono-like clothing that is easier and faster to put on and allows more freedom of movement for fast-paced urban lifestyles. However, there is also a rising interest in "slow fashion" in terms of demand for handmade, inherited, and recycled clothing (Hall 2018a: 287), and in the thinking surrounding clothing such as the Japanese concept of *mottainai*. This increasing interest in slow fashion appears to be antithetical to the speeding up of production because usually handcrafted products involve "slow" production. Of course, in comparison to mass-produced goods, this industry is still relatively small scale, and artisans still have a high degree of contact with the items they are creating. Many of the companies I researched still claim that their products have *kosei* (unique characteristics) and *kokoro* (heart), defining qualities of traditional handicrafts. Not only the handcrafted nature of the products, and the physical energies and contact that artisans use to create them, but also the knowledge accumulated by years of learning through *kata*, and the *kodawari* (obsession) necessary to pursue such learning, are all important facets of this claim. As White states, "At an exalted level, a traditional item, made by a traditional craftsperson, will almost automatically have *kodawari*" (2012: 68).

So the artisan's spirit in terms of *kodawari* also becomes part of what is consumed, "*Kodawari* is embedded in the thing produced—it is not only in the attitude or practice of the maker but is consumed by the recipients or buyers of the goods themselves" (ibid.: 67–8). In this regard, we can see a link between sensory experience and the perception of authenticity. By telling the stories behind the creation of such products (or allowing consumers to experience the making of goods through *taiken*), the designers create an "emotional attachment between human beings and clothes" that provide models for more "socially aware design" and also make consumers want to cherish them (Clark 2008: 441). This way of thinking is not limited to Japan but is occurring in other countries, so that, "What is emerging here is the potential of 'slow products' to inculcate a 'new beauty' in fashion, based not purely on the visual, but also including sensorial aspects that acknowledge the existence of the many abstract and emotional factors that underpin the choices of what people wear" (ibid.: 441–2).

Viewed more broadly, the Kyoto textile industry can be seen as participating in an emerging global community that Kawlra has termed a "transnational craftscape" (2015). The relationship between the artisanal community and concepts of cultural heritage and the nation engage with the local/global dichotomy through the lens of craft as a cultural practice and identity. The shared characteristics of craft forge for its creators a sense of a cultural affinity and a shared identity between participants. The significance of analyzing the Kyoto textile industry in terms of a "craftscape" is that it helps us to understand such developments as declines in certain markets, changes in production, or shifting consumer tastes. With market (or other) information we might be able to gauge or at least anticipate the effects of these dimensions on the craftscape. For example, technological developments mentioned in Chapter Five that have enabled Chinese weavers to sell Nishijin *obi* online directly to customers at reduced prices will of course have an impact on manufacturers and retailers in Japan. Examining the Kyoto textile industry within this "craftscape" context serves to highlight the transnational nature of the industry. More importantly, it demonstrates the constructed nature of values and meanings embedded in the practices, and how these are used to achieve objectives such as identity, power, and authenticity in the field of heritage industries.

I have already discussed the value of collecting research using a sensory ethnography approach, and shown how this approach results in data that might otherwise be hidden or overlooked. But it is also important to view my book in terms of its interdisciplinary nature. Entwistle argues that the study of fashion in itself usually fails to acknowledge the dual nature of the subject as both a cultural phenomenon and as an aspect of manufacturing, resulting in parallel histories of consumption and production (2000: 2). By focusing on the ideological debates about fashion and tradition, as well as social, political and economic aspects of production and consumption, I have bridged the gap between these arenas, using the point of intersection between traditional textiles, Japanese studies, and sensory anthropology to provide a more comprehensive idea of the textile industry and its place in Japanese society. Addressing "tradition" and the textile industry in relation to modernization and globalization in Kyoto has enabled me to explicate the relationship between global, national, and local practices in that region. My research highlights the tensions and opportunities that arise in the process of imagining, interpreting (or reinterpreting) cultural identity, and practicing tradition in a context of changing cultural values.

NOTES

Historical Dates

1   Varley (2000: x).

CHAPTER ONE

1   I discuss this statement later in this chapter.

2   For example, see Demetriou (2010) regarding kimono as a "dying art."

3   Western here refers to European, North American or any other country culturally or linguistically influenced by these two areas. Western (in Japanese the term *ōbei*, or the prefix *yō-*) is used primarily to distinguish between these cultures and those of Asia, specifically Japanese culture. Other uses include *yōshoku* (Western food), *yōshiki* (Western style) or *yōsho* (Western books).

4   I am aware that the world of traditional artisans (*shokunin*) and that of the newly emerging artists (*sakka*) have been considered separate, both historically and culturally in Japan. To that end I have tried to maintain a distinction between "artisan" and "artist" or "designer" but this distinction is becoming blurred in contemporary Japan, discussed further in Chapter Six.

5   It is interesting to note that in *kōdō*, the smelling of incense was typically referred to as "listening to incense" (Liddell 2011).

6   *Kyō* stands for Kyoto, and *mono* is object, so this literally means Kyoto product.

7   According to Smith, the "old saying is *Kyō no ki-daore Ōsaka no kui-daore*: Kyoto people's financial ruin is clothes; Osaka people's financial ruin is food," meaning that Kyoto people are often thought of as preferring to spend money on clothing rather than food (1995: 25).

8   The "Conference on Authenticity" held in Nara in 1994, the UNESCO Intangible Cultural Heritage Convention of 2003 held in Paris, and the "International Conference on the Safeguarding of Tangible and Intangible Cultural Heritage: Towards an Integrated Approach" of 2004 also held in Nara.

9   Meaning revival, revitalization, refresh, regeneration.

10   *Boro* has now become a huge (and arguably overpriced) global collector's item.

11 *Tsutsugaki* is a form of rice-paste resist dyeing, the same as *tegaki yūzen* (discussed in more detail in Chapter Two).

12 The Edo period has become "a repository of traditions (*dentō*) associated with Japanese distinctiveness," according to Gluck (1998: 263).

13 The title of this book came from a cartoon of a mother and child in which the mother says, "Eat your broccoli, dear," to which the child responds, "I say it's spinach—and I say to hell with it." At the end of the book, Hawes expresses the hope that American women will have the same response in regard to fashion.

14 See Cameron (2000), Davis (1992), Edwards (2011), Entwistle (2000), Slade (2009).

15 A "costume" is "an ensemble" of clothing items, accessories, and makeup, which is worn for a special occasion and helps the wearer realize a specific identity or role (Eicher 2005: n.p.).

16 This statement refers to a period following the Heian period (794–1185).

17 Here Kawakami is referring to *tsujigahana*, a stitch resist tie-dyeing.

18 Milhaupt provides detailed evidence of the relationships between fashion leaders, *ukiyo-e* artists, the publishing industry, kimono retailers, kimono producers, and customers in the Edo era in her book, *Kimono: A Modern History* (2014: 31–55).

19 Sumptuary laws were also used for the same purpose in Europe during the medieval and renaissance periods (Benhamou 2005).

CHAPTER TWO

1 In Japanese, "-dōri" means street or avenue.

2 The *jūnihitoe* was worn by women of rank during the Heian period, and literally means "twelve-layered robe" although the actual number of robes could vary and sumptuary laws limited the basic set to five layers early in the eleventh century, as mentioned in Chapter One.

3 *Mottainai* means wasteful, but in this context it means it is a shame for something to go to waste without making use of its full potential.

4 Interestingly, discussions of color perception can bring up *Nihonjinron*-type arguments (such contentions typically focus on the uniqueness of Japanese culture in comparison to others). Kyoto Montsuki makes the claim that Japanese people are better able to perceive the different shades of black because the high amount of melanin in their dark irises regulates the amount of light entering their eyes more effectively (Kyoto Montsuki Co. Ltd., n.d.: 12). In a recent study on whether or not iris color is associated with visual functions, researchers found that contrast sensitivity (CS) was lower in participants with light-blue pigmented irises than in the other groups (the groups were light-blue, blue-grey, green-hazel, and brown), but the difference between light-blue and brown irises was only statistically significant for persons aged 40–80 years so the researchers conclude that "we do not think that the small difference in regard to CS is clinically important" (Nischler et al. 2013: 200). They also tested for intraocular stray light (IOSL), which can cause hazy vision, and loss of contrast and color in certain situations such as night driving.

They found that light-blue pigmented individuals were statistically different from the other groups. However, very few studies have been done in this area so the impact on visual perception is debatable.

5   Although apparently *polygonum tinctorium* is easy to grow, I surmise that the decline in demand for naturally dyed products, and the increase in easy-to-use chemical dyes has meant it is not economically viable for farmers to grow it any longer.

6   These are the Mimaki TX200 and the Epson PM-10000 (Mori 2012: 129).

7   Even the well-known food market in Kyoto is called Nishiki Ichiba—literally "brocade market"—because of the trade in fabric that initially occurred there in the Enryaku era (782–805).

8   Kondo defines the "*ura*" as the back or intimate side as opposed to the "*omote*," which is the front or formal side (1990: 31). As Kondo makes clear, these Japanese terms are contextually constructed and used in regard to social relations for describing "a complex series of gradations along a scale of detachment and engagement" (ibid.: 31).

9   A pseudonym has been used for this interviewee.

10   Yamada also told me that in the past it was even more expensive to get a pattern designed for an *obi*—about 100,000 yen (AUD$1,000) using the traditional methods rather than computer (Hall 2015: 65).

11   The Nishijin Ori Kōgei Bijutsukan closed in 2013 and the parent company, manufacturer Nishijin Asagi, filed for bankruptcy. I have been unable to ascertain the reason for their bankruptcy, but I have to acknowledge that it adds to the impression of a declining industry.

12   This is supported by the Cultural Foundation for Promoting the National Costume of Japan website which states that for *Kyō-kanoko shibori*, the number of points tied ranges from forty-five to seventy in one *shaku* (about 30 cm). A *heko-obi*, a soft sash often worn by children, of 36–38 cm width and 380 cm length, requires eight thousand to nine thousand points. For a whole kimono, about 250,000 points would be needed (the usual size for a bolt of kimono cloth is 36 cm width and about 114 cm length) (2014a).

13   This association was established by *kitsuke* schools (kimono academies where students learn how to don and wear kimono) in 1977 to promote and hand down the knowledge and techniques of kimono with approval from the Ministry of Education, Culture, Sports, Science and Technology (MEXT).

14   Paste is applied to the fabric so that dye will not penetrate that area. Detailed designs can be applied to the fabric in this way, and fabric can be dyed several times, applying the paste to different areas each time to protect different colors. In Indonesia, wax is used as the resist substance.

15   In fact the ratio of female to male students in university art faculties (which includes visual art, design, music) in Japan is 5:2. The ratio of female to male university students across the board is 3:4. Source: MEXT Basic Schools Survey 2012, http://www.e-stat.go.jp/SG1/estat/List.do?bid=000001044883&cycode=0 (no. 16).

16   Chapter Five will discuss how the heritage industries and those claiming affiliation with them draw on this concept to promote their products.

CHAPTER THREE

1 Some of Sou Sou's production line is manufactured abroad but this will be discussed in more detail as part of innovation strategies in Chapter Five.

2 The name "Pagong" is Tagalog for a sea turtle that conveys happiness because of the beauty of the ocean. The family name, Kameda, means turtle field.

3 Kameda Kazuaki is now the chairman of Kamedatomi Co. Ltd and his son, Tomihiro, has taken over the directorship of the company.

4 According to Chinese legend, Kikujidō was a favorite attendant of Emperor Mu. He accidentally stepped over the imperial pillow and was exiled to a valley of blooming chrysanthemums, where he mixed the spring water of the valley stream with the dew of the chrysanthemum leaves and produced an elixir of immortality (JAANUS 2001).

5 Homay only produces Kyoto Denim jeans. It does not produce any other product lines but this appears to be a common way of establishing a business, perhaps because it allows scope for product lines in other directions.

6 It was also fortunate that the original color of denim fabric, indigo, is a color closely associated with Japanese textiles, discussed in the previous chapter.

7 All three of the case study companies have internal marketing staff members.

8 Miyamoto admitted that he had not actually calculated the number of customers from Hokkaido, but that he estimated there were many based on his interactions with customers that had visited the store.

CHAPTER FOUR

1 Fans of Malice Mizer do adopt Mana's style as cosplay, and Mana has his own Gothic Lolita fashion label called Moi-Même-Moitié (Mackie 2009), which demonstrates the intertwined nature of these concepts.

2 The Yano Research Institute, founded in 1958, is an independent private marketing research company and its statistics are often quoted in newspapers and academic papers.

3 It is acceptable and expected to wear hand-me-downs from within a family but wearing second-hand kimono from outsiders is discouraged because of bad karma that might be associated with the former owner. Also, a number of second-hand kimono are exported overseas for foreign consumption where ideas about bad karma are not pervasive.

4 This serves a practical purpose as the wide opening allows wearers to use it as a sort of pocket for small objects (fans, handkerchiefs, etc.).

5 Dalby (2001) gives a detailed analysis of these intricacies and I do not deem it necessary to so here.

6 Courtesans and prostitutes became known for wearing their elaborately tied *obi* in the front rather than the back to assist with speedier disrobement and redressing. In fact, originally everyone tied the *obi* in front but as it gradually changed through

the centuries from a cord to a 10-inch wide belt, and because of this fashion trend, it became too cumbersome to have in the front so was pushed out of the way to the back. By the late seventeenth century, it was generally tied in the back (Dalby 2001: 52).

7   A similar organization was started several years earlier in Tokyo and it is likely that Akagi replicated this group's format. Kimono de Ginza encourages participants at monthly gatherings to "be creative, to play with different identities, and to experiment with gender boundaries" when wearing kimono (Assmann 2008: 365). Kimono de Ginza was established in 2000 by a group of male friends and has grown in popularity, drawing an average of fifty participants ranging in age from 20 to 80 (Sasaki 2009). Kimono de Ginza provides an event in which participants can dress in kimono as formally or casually as they wish. Their website states that they have no sponsor, political, or religious affiliation, and no membership fee; their purpose is to simply enjoy wearing kimono and anyone who likes kimono can join them and participate in a light-hearted or carefree (*kigaru*) way (Kimono de Ginza 2015). Images of the monthly gatherings show that the men appear to experiment more than the women in regard to what and how they wear kimono, often combining other forms of *wafuku* in playful ways. The kimono has been gaining popularity across Japan since 2002, according to writer Ima Kikuchi (who has published several books on kimono), with internet communities hosting real-life gatherings and second-hand kimono shops increasing in number (Sasaki 2009).

8   It is worth noting that dressing in period costume is a global phenomenon that has gained popularity at various museums and events.

9   In fact, when I asked them how it felt to wear kimono their response was "*kitsui*" (tight or close).

10 It is now also available as an app, according to the Kyoto Kimono Passport website, http://kimono-passport.jp/ app/ (accessed January 15, 2016).

11 Here I use the word scopophilic to refer to a love of looking or of being looked at, without its sexual connotations.

12 This information was viewed in 2015 but has since been removed with the website's renewal (Maiko-Henshin Studio Shiki 2015).

13 Sakamoto Ryōma was a low-ranking samurai who led a movement to overthrow the Tokugawa Shogunate during the late Edo period in Japan and is considered a hero by many Japanese today.

14 As of 2015 the website no longer states this. The only people that are excluded from service are pregnant individuals (at any stage of pregnancy) or those who are intoxicated (Maiko-Henshin Studio Shiki 2015).

15 The primary setting for Japanese to view *yoroi* today is when it is paired with *kabuto* (helmets) in miniature for *kodomo no hi* (Children's Day) displays. There are specialist shops that create these, but Nagatoshi is one of only five people in Japan that can create full-size *yoroi*.

16 Again, the broadening of the museum experience to include not just viewing but interaction and direct experience has been a global phenomenon over the past decades.

17 The *kozane* are now made of layers of paper rather than leather.

18 It is worth noting that there are many other festivals held throughout the year, such as those organized by local neighborhoods, in which participation is more accessible.

19 Note that I have limited this to Kyoto-specific examples, rather than include cosplay or Gothic Lolita because their transnational nature would have added an extra layer of complexity that I did not deem useful for this discussion. Although kimono *taiken* is available in other cities such as Tokyo and Kanazawa, the majority of rental outlets are in Kyoto (e.g., a basic websearch shows six outlets in Asakusa, three in Kanazawa, and nineteen in Kyoto). In addition, from my observation of both Kyoto and Asakusa streets in 2015, the number of customers utilizing this service is much greater in Kyoto.

CHAPTER FIVE

1 According to Japanese media and other informants, under the "cool biz" campaign government office workers have been encouraged not to wear neckties and to wear short-sleeved shirts so that they do not need to have their air conditioners on such a cool setting, with the aim of reducing electricity use.

2 It has another subsidiary called Ihee that sells bags with many of the same patterns as its *tenugui* and *furoshiki*.

3 Manami Okazaki substantiates this in her book, *Kimono Now* citing another Kyoto recycling atelier, Fuji Kōbō (2015: 150–2).

4 Sadly, my informant and dear friend Hanada-san passed away in May 2017. His legacy lives on through his studio, Arms Hair & Make-up, which he established to teach other hairdressers the art of *nihongami*.

5 Bishamonten was the god of war.

6 Sou Sou also has stores in Tokyo and San Francisco.

7 According to their website they now have a new Sou Sou Hotei shop.

CHAPTER SIX

1 See historical dates table on p. xxiii.

2 Under Japan's Law for the Protection of Cultural Properties (*Bunkazai Hogōhō*, enacted 1950).

3 In fact, according to Aikawa-Faure, since 1964 individuals have received an annual grant of 2 million yen to help train successors, further develop skills and make records of techniques (2014: 41).

4 This has been a long tradition in postwar Japan (see Befu 1984; Dale 1986; Mouer & Sugimoto 1986).

5 Mathews is mainly discussing arts such as *shakuhachi* (bamboo flute), *nihonbuyō* (Japanese dance), and *shodō* (calligraphy) in which case he argues that throughout Japanese history only the elite practiced them and therefore their "traditional" status is questionable. A much wider percentage of the population was involved with the production and consumption of heritage industries such as weaving and *yūzen* and therefore this is less of an issue.

GLOSSARY

aizome 藍染	indigo dye
aobana 青花	a fugitive (or non-permanent) blue dye made from the dayflower (*Commelina Communis*—also known as spiderwort)
asa 麻	linen
asabura zōri あさぶら草履	straw sandals
asobi 遊び	play
aya-ori 彩織	twill weaving; crossing points of warp and weft form a diagonal
Bishamon kikkō 毘沙門亀甲	a common design pattern featuring interlaced hexagonal shapes that mimic tortoise shell; Bishamon is the god of war, and tortoise shell symbolizes longevity
bokashi ぼかし	gradations of colors shading into each other
chadō 茶道	tea ceremony
cha dōgu 茶道具	specialized tea utensils
cha-kaiseki 茶懐石	tea ceremony cuisine
chashitsu 茶室	teahouse
chijimi ちぢみ	ramie crepe
chirimen 縮緬	crepe silk
daimyo 大名	feudal lord
darari-no-obi だらりの帯	a style of wearing the *obi* originating in the Edo period that is popular with Kyoto *maiko* now—*darari* means loosely, or languidly, referring to how the long *obi* hangs down the back.
dekasegi 出稼ぎ	going out to work
dentō kōgei 伝統工芸	traditional crafts
dentōteki 伝統的	traditional
digital *yūzen* デジタル友禅	a form of *yūzen* where designs are created on a computer and printed onto fabric using an inkjet printer
fudangi 普段着	everyday wear

fukuro obi 袋帯	casual and colorful *obi*
furisode 振袖	long-sleeved formal kimono worn by unmarried women
furoshiki 風呂敷	wrapping cloth
fusuma 襖	paper sliding doors
geiko 芸子	Kyoto geisha
geta 下駄	wooden clogs
gōjiru 豆汁	a soybean juice mixture (also referred to as soybean milk) used in *yūzen* dyeing to stabilize and smooth the resist paste prior to coloring
habutae 羽二重	light-weight silk fabric often used as lining
hadajuban 肌襦袢	the simple white cotton under-robe that crosses the chest, named because *hada* means skin in Japanese
han-katsura 半鬘	half wig for *maiko*
hanten 半纏	folk equivalent of a *haori*—a short winter coat
haori 羽織	short formal coat
hare ハレ	sacred
haregi 晴れ着	best clothes, Sunday best
hataya 機屋	weavers
hatsumōde 初詣で	the first shrine visit of the New Year
hikizome-shi 引き染め師	the person who applies the dye for *yūzen*
hira-ori 平織	plain weaving
hirogata mompe 広形もんぺ	wide-legged *mompe* (trousers)
hōmongi 訪問着	literally "visiting wear," a ceremonial kimono for public or social occasions, distinguished by asymmetrical patterning that continues without break across the kimono
hozon 保存	preservation
iki 粋	a kind of "understated chic" (Dalby 2001: 8) of subdued hues, fine patterns, restrained eroticism—a combination of restraint and dandyism (Ikegami 2005); also "urbane chic," an aesthetic taste, attitude or, sensibility that "suggests the ability to convey an attitude of playful delight in an understated, subtle manner" (Milhaupt 2014: 126)
iro muji 色無地	the highest level of the formal kimono (as opposed to ceremonial), an unpatterned kimono with one, three, or five crests
irosashi 色さし	dyeing

itajime shibori 板締め絞り	shaped-resist technique of tie-dyeing created by sandwiching cloth between two pieces of wood
jakādo ジャカード	jacquard component of a weaving loom
jikatabi 地下足袋	split-toed shoes
jinbei 甚平	informal short jacket that crosses left over right with a tie fastening, and matching loose-fitting shorts or trousers
jinrikisha 人力車	rickshaw
kabukimono 歌舞伎者	young men in the Tokugawa era who expressed their frustration with the rigid political regime by subverting the government's sumptuary laws
kadō 華道	the way of flowers, ikebana
Kaga-yūzen 加賀友禅	Kanazawa-style paste-resist dyeing
kankō taiken 観光体験	personal experience tourism
kanoko shibori 鹿の子絞り	fawn-spot tie-dyeing; the tiny tie-dyed dots are said to look like the spots on a fawn's back
kantōi 貫頭衣	Yayoi period clothing (300 BCE–300 CE); a simple garment made from a rectangle of cloth with a hole for the head
kanzashi 簪	decorative hair ornaments
kasane no irome 色目の重ね	literally "layers of colors," a combination of colors created by layering garments, especially during the Heian period
kasuri 絣	Japanese ikat or resist dyeing
kata 型	patterns of movement; patterning
katagami 型紙	the Japanese art of making paper stencils for kimono printing
kataginu 肩衣	sleeveless ceremonial robe for samurai
kata yūzen 型友禅	stencil-based dyeing (see also *katazome*)
ke ケ	profane
kidaore 着倒れ	dress to destruction
kimono 着物	literally "object of wear" (Dalby 2001: 65); usually referring to *wafuku* (defined in opposition to *yōfuku*); also used to refer to the robe that has come to represent Japanese national dress
kindami-shi 金彩師	person who applies the gold leaf to *yūzen*
kodomo no hi 子供の日	literally "children's day," a Japanese national holiday that occurs on May 5 each year to celebrate children
kōdō 香道	the way of incense

komon 小紋	this refers to both the least formal style of kimono and the repeat pattern that covers this style of kimono
kosei 個性	unique characteristics
kosode 小袖	the ankle-length robe with flowing sleeves that the world now recognizes as Japanese dress
kosupure コスプレ	cosplay; usually refers to the practice of dressing in the clothing of a manga, anime, video game or movie character, and role-playing that character
kozane 小札	lacquered rectangles of leather used to make *yoroi* armor
kumihimo 組紐	braid or plaited cord for clothing
kumo shibori 蜘蛛絞り	spider web tie-dyeing
kurozome 黒染め	dyeing fabric black
Kyō- 京	a prefix that refers to crafts done in the Kyoto style
kyūchūsuso 宮中裾	imperial court-cuffed trousers
kyūchūsuso ayui 宮中裾挙脚結	imperial court-cuffed trousers with leg bindings
maiko 舞子	apprentice geisha
maiko henshin 舞子変身	transformation into an apprentice geisha
mamasan ママさん	bar, brothel, or geisha house owner
maru obi 丸帯	formal kimono sash
mizushōbai 水商売	night entertainment business
mofuku obi 喪服帯	mourning kimono sash
mompe もんぺ	loose-fitting trousers that come in at the ankle
mottainai もったいない	wasteful, a shame for something to go to waste without making use of its full potential
nerinuki 練貫	a fabric that was woven with raw silk as the warp threads, and scoured silk as the weft, making it lustrous
nihonga 日本画	Japanese-style painting
Nishijin 西陣	district located in the northwest of Kyoto renowned for weaving
Nishijin *ori* 西陣織	Nishijin weaving; the technique of Nishijin weaving
noragi 野良着	regional work clothing
noren のれん	split entrance curtains
nori 糊	paste
norioki-shi 糊置き師	the person who applies the paste-resist for *yūzen*
nui shibori 縫い絞り	stitched tie-dyeing

obi 帯	kimono waist sash
okobo おこぼ	clogs that taper nearer the ground
oiran 花魁	courtesan
omote 表	public face
rinzu 綸子	woven damask
ro 絽	silk gauze
ryōsai kenbo 良妻賢母	good wife, wise mother
sadō 茶道	(or *chadō*) the way of tea
saisei 再生	revitalization
samue 作務衣	traditional monk's working clothes
sankin kōtai 参勤交代	alternative attendance of *daimyō* on Shogun during the Tokugawa era
seijin shiki 成人式	the coming-of-age ceremony
sensu 扇子	fan
shibori 絞り	tie-dyeing
shinsengumi 新撰組	shogunate police
shinshi 伸子	narrow bamboo dowels used to stretch *yūzen* taut
shishū-shi 刺繍師	embroiderer
shitae-shi 下絵師	design sketcher for paste-resist dyeing
shitamachi 下町	neighborhood
shodō 書道	calligraphy, the way of writing
shokunin 職人	artisans, craftspeople
shōji 障子	paper-sliding screens
shusu-ori 繻子織	satin weaving; crossing points of warp and weft are positioned at regular intervals, with the warp being thicker than the weft
sobyō-shi 素描師	specialist who copies the design outline onto the cloth for paste-resist dyeing
some-iro 染め色	dye pigment
sorabiki-bata 空引き機	draw loom
tabi 足袋	split-toed socks
taiken 体験	personal experience
takabata 高機	treadle looms
takageta 高下駄	tall wooden clogs
tasuki-kikubishi 襷菊微	diamond patterns that are a traditional design from the Heian period
tatami 畳	Japanese straw floor coverings
tegaki yūzen 手描き友禅	rice-paste resist dyeing in which the rice paste is piped on by hand
tenugui 手ぬぐい	hand towel made of cotton

tōketsu hozon 凍結保存	"freezing preservation," retaining the structure as unaltered as possible
totei 徒弟	live-in apprentice system
tsujigahana 辻が花	stitch-resist tie-dyeing (*c.* 1570s)
tsukesage 付け下げ	a kimono for formal occasions (as opposed to ceremonial), distinguished by a diagonal pattern on the left shoulder and hem (*tsukesage* can be made more formal if crests are added)
tsumugi 紬	pongee, a low-quality silk made from the floss of wild silk cocoons or from the leftovers of a cultivated crop
tsutsugaki yūzen 筒描友禅	hand-painted rice paste-resist dyeing
uchiwa 団扇	fan
ukiyo-e 浮世絵	Japanese woodblock prints
umezome 梅染め	plum dye
ura 裏	private face
urushinuri 漆塗り	Japanese lacquer
wafū 和風	Japanese-style
wafuku 和服	Japanese dress, including kimono
wagasa 和傘	Japanese umbrella
wagashi 和菓子	Japanese sweets
ware shinobu 割れしのぶ	*maiko* hair style
yōfuku 洋服	Western dress
yōmō 羊毛	wool
yoroi 鎧	samurai armor
yukata 浴衣	lightweight summer kimono
yukata-mitate 浴衣見立て	dresses with features of the *yukata*
yūzen 友禅	rice-paste resist dyeing
zen-katsura 全鬘	full wig for *maiko*
zōri 草履	flat thonged sandals
zundō 寸胴	style of wearing kimono that mimics a cylindrical container

REFERENCES

Aikawa-Faure, N. (2014), "Excellence and authenticity: 'Living National (Human) Treasures' in Japan and Korea," *International Journal of Intangible Heritage*, 9: 37–51.

AMUSE Museum (2015), "Life cloth—Bodo" [wall text], 2nd Exhibition Gallery, Miraculous Textile Art, Boro—Chizaburo Tanaka Collection (permanent collection).

Anderson, B. (2006 [1983]), *Imagined Communities: Reflections on the Origin and Spread of Nationalism*, London: Verso.

Appadurai, A. (1990), "Disjuncture and difference in the global cultural economy," *Theory, Culture & Society*, 7: 295–310.

Asai, R. (2011[1667]), *Shinsen Ohiinagata* [Newly Compiled Pattern Book], Digitised edition, National Diet Library [Kokuritsu Kokkai Toshōkan]. Available online: http://dl.ndl.go.jp/info:ndljp/pid/2541138 (accessed February 14, 2015).

Assmann, S. (2008), "Between tradition and innovation: the reinvention of the kimono in Japanese consumer culture," *Fashion Theory*, 12(3): 359–76.

Bambling, M. (2005), "Japan's Living National Treasures program: the paradox of remembering," in Tsu Yun Hui, Jan Van Bremen, and Eyal Ben-Ari (eds.), *Perspectives on Social Memory in Japan*, 148–72, Kent: Global Oriental.

Baudrillard, J. (1996), *The System of Objects*, trans. J. Benedict, London: Verso.

Baxter, M. (2009), "Beautifully frightening: Kyoto Aloha shirt marker Pagong's Haunted House PR Coup," *Open Kyoto*, web log, August 7. Available online: http://openkyoto.com/stores/pagong-haunted-house.html (accessed February 15, 2016).

Befu, H. (1984), "Civilization and culture: Japan in search of identity," in T. Umesao, H. Befu, and J. Kreiner (eds.), *Japanese Civilization in the Modern World*, A Special Issue of Senri Ethnological Studies, 16: 59–75.

Benhamou, R. (2005), "Sumptuary laws," in V. Steele (ed.), *Encyclopedia of Clothing and Fashion* (Vol. 3 Occult Dress to Zoran), 238–40, Farmington Hills, MI: Charles Scribner's Sons.

Bestor, T. (1989), *Neighborhood Tokyo*, Stanford, CA: Stanford University Press.

Billig, M., (1995), *Banal Nationalism*, London: Sage.

Bourdieu, P. (1984), *Distinction: A Social Critique of the Judgement of Taste*, trans. R. Nice, Cambridge, MA: Harvard University Press.

Bourdieu, P. (1993), *Sociology in Question*, trans. R. Nice, London: Sage.

Bowring, R. (2005), "Introduction," *The Diary of Lady Murasaki*, trans. R. Bowring, Kindle edition, London: Penguin Books.

Brumann, C. (2010), "Houses in motion: the revitalisation of Kyoto's architectural heritage," in C. Brumann and R. Cox (eds.), *Making Japanese Heritage*, 149–70, London: Routledge.

Brumann, C., and R. Cox, eds. (2010). *Making Japanese Heritage*, London: Routledge.

Cameron, D. (2000), "Off-the-rack identities: Japanese street fashion magazines and the commodification of style," *Japanese Studies*, 20 (2): 179–87.

Carlyle, T. (2008 [1831]), *Sartor Resartus: The Life and Opinions of Herr Teufelsdröckh*, E-book. Available online: http://www.gutenberg.org/ebooks/1051 (accessed April 16, 2012).

Carr, L. (2008), *Taisho Chic: Japanese Modernity, Nostalgia and Deco*, Sydney: Art Gallery of NSW.

Caruso, H. (2012), "Sakai Hoitsu: the aesthetics of Japanese Rinpa paintings," *International Journal of Multicultural Education*, 14(3): 1–7.

City of Kyoto, (2011), "Topics of city government—Kyoto tourism survey results released," *Kyoto City Web*. Available online: https://www2.city.kyoto.lg.jp/koho/eng/topics/2011_8/index.html (accessed February 6, 2016).

Clark, A. (1997), *The Struggle for the Breeches: Gender and the Making of the British Working Class*, Berkeley: University of California Press.

Clark, H. (2008), "Slow + fashion—an oxymoron—or a promise for the future…?," *Fashion Theory*, 12(4): 427–46.

Classen, C. (1993), *Worlds of Sense: Exploring the Senses in History and Across Cultures*, London: Routledge.

Classen, C. (1997), "Foundations for an anthropology of the senses," *International Social Science Journal*, 49(153): 401–12.

Cliffe, S. (2017), *The Social Life of Kimono: Japanese Fashion Past and Present*, London: Bloomsbury.

Clifford, J., and G. Marcus, eds. (1986), *Writing Culture: The Poetics and Politics of Ethnography*, Berkeley: University of California Press.

Craik, J. (1993), *The Face of Fashion: Cultural Studies in Fashion*, London: Routledge

Creighton, M. (1992), "The depato: Self-exoticising and the marketing of Japaneseness," in J. Tobin (ed.), *Re-Made in Japan: Eeveryday Life and Consumer Taste in a Changing Society*, 42–57, New Haven, CT: Yale University.

The Cultural Foundation for Promoting the National Costume of Japan (2014a), "Kyo Kanoko." Available online: http://www.kimono.or.jp/dictionary/eng/kyoukanoko.html (accessed February 20, 2016).

The Cultural Foundation for Promoting the National Costume of Japan (2014b), "Nishijin Ori." Available online: http:// www.kimono.or.jp/dictionary/eng/nishijinori.html (accessed February 6, 2016).

Dalby, L. (2001), *Kimono: Fashioning Culture*, London: Vintage.

Dale, N. (1986), *The Myth of Japanese Uniqueness*, Oxford: Routledge and Nissan Institute for Japanese Studies.

Daliot-Bul, M. (2009a), "Asobi in action," *Cultural Studies*, 23(3): 355–80.

Daliot-Bul, M. (2009b), "Japan brand strategy: the taming of 'Cool Japan' and the challenges of cultural planning in a postmodern age," *Social Science Japan Journal*, 12(2): 247–66.

Davis, F. (1992), *Fashion, Culture and Identity*, London: University of Chicago Press.

Demetriou, D. (2010), "Kimono making in Japan is a dying art," *The Telegraph*, 23 October. Available online: http://www.telegraph.co.uk/news/worldnews/asia/japan/8082875/Kimono-making-in-Japan-is-a-dying- art.html (accessed February 14, 2016).

Dentō kōgeihin sangyō shinkō kyōgai (2015), Dentō kōgeihin wo sasu [Search for traditional crafts]. Available online: http://kougeihin.jp/crafts/ (accessed January 5, 2016).

The Devil Wears Prada (2006), [Film] Dir. D Frankel, US; France: Fox 2000 Pictures, Dune Entertainment, Major Studio Partners.

Diamond, J. (1992), *The Rise and Fall of the Third Chimpanzee*, London: Vintage.

Dickens, P. (2012), "The craftsmen of Kyoto," in M. Adkins and P. Dickens (eds.), *Shibusa: Eextracting Beauty*, 107–16, Huddersfield: University of Huddersfield Press.

Durston, D. (2005 [1986]), *Old Kyoto: A Guide to Traditional Shops, Restaurants and Inns*, Tokyo: Kodansha International.

Dusenbury, M. (2010), "Snapshot: archaeological evidence: Japan, Part 1: overview of dress and fashion in East Asia," in J. Eicher (ed.), *Berg Encyclopedia of World Dress and Fashion* (Vol. 6 East Asia), online, Oxford: Berg. Available online: http://www.bergfashionlibrary.com/viewencyclopedia/bewdf/BEWDF-v6/EDch6006.xml (accessed March 2, 2012).

Edwards, T. (2011), *Fashion in Focus*, Abingdon: Routledge.

Eicher, J. (2005), "Clothing, costume, and dress," *A–Z of Fashion*, the Berg Fashion Library online. Available online: http://www.bergfashionlibrary.com/view/bazf/bazf00129.xml (accessed February 10, 2016).

Entwistle, J. (2000), *The Fashioned Body: Fashion, Dress and Modern Social Theory*, Cambridge: Polity Press.

Fitzpatrick, M. (2013), "Death of cash? Maybe, but not quite yet in Japan," *The Fortune* [magazine], February 20. Available online: http://fortune.com/2013/02/20/death-of-cash-maybe-but-not-quite-yet-in-japan/ (accessed February 25, 2016).

Francks, P., and J. Hunter (2012), "Introduction: Japan's consumption history in comparative perspective," in P. Francks and J. Hunter (eds.), *The Historical Consumer: Consumption and Everyday Life in Japan, 1850–2000*, 1–23, New York: Palgrave Macmillan.

Fu, Z. (2006), "Pigmented ink formulation," in H. Ujiie (ed.), *Digital Printing of Textiles*, 218–32, Cambridge: Woodhead Publishing.

Gagne, I. (2007), "Urban princesses: performance and 'women's language' in Japan's Gothic/Lolita subculture," *Journal of Linguistic Anthropology*, 18(1): 130–50.

George, B., D. Wood, M. Govindaraj, H. Ujiie, M. Fruscello, A. Tremere, and S. Nandekar (2006), "Integration of fabric formation and coloration processes," in H. Ujiie (ed.), *Digital Printing of Textiles*, 123–43, Cambridge: Woodhead Publishing.

Gluck, C. (1998), "The invention of Edo," in S. Vlastos (ed.), *Mirror of Modernity: Invented Traditions of Modern Japan*, 262–84, Berkeley: University of California Press.

Gn, J. (2011), "Queer simulation: The practice, performance and pleasure of cosplay," *Continuum: Journal of Media and Cultural Studies*, 25(4): 583–93.

Goffman, E. (1959), *The Presentation of Self in Everyday Life*, London: Allen Lane.

Goldstein-Gidoni, O. (1999), "Kimono and the construction of gendered and cultural identities," *Ethnology*, 38(4): 351–70.

Goldstein-Gidoni, O. (2000), "The production of tradition and culture in the Japanese wedding enterprise," *Ethnos: Journal of Anthropology*, 65(1): 33–55.

Goldstein-Gidoni, O. (2005), "The production and consumption of 'Japanese culture' in the global cultural market," *Journal of Consumer Culture*, 5(2): 155–79.

Goldstein-Gidoni, O. (2008), "Fashioning cultural identity: body and dress," in J. Robertson (ed.), *A Companion to the Anthropology of Japan*, 153–66, Blackwell reference online: Blackwell Publishing.

Guiches (2015), *Kyoto de kimono rentaru* [Kimono rental in Kyoto]. Available online: http://guiches.co.jp/rental/odekake (accessed March 7, 2015).

Hahn, T. (2007), *Sensational Knowledge: Embodying Culture through Japanese Dance*, Middletown CT: Wesleyan University Press.

Hall, J. (2004), "An Ikebana Journey," *Kyoto Journal*, 58: 84–5.

Hall, J. (2008), "Kameda Kazuaki: Textiles," *Kyoto Journal (Kyoto Lives* Issue), 70: 96–7.

Hall, J. (2014), "The spirit in the machine: Mutual affinities between humans and machines in Japanese textiles," *Thresholds 42: Human* (Journal of the MIT Department of Architecture), Spring, 170–81.

Hall, J. (2015), "Re-fashioning kimono: How to make 'traditional' clothes for postmodern Japan," *New Voices* 7: 59–84.

Hall, J. (2018a), "Digital kimono: Fast fashion, slow fashion?," *Fashion Theory: The Journal of Dress, Body and Culture* 22(3): 283–307.

Hall, J. (2018b), "Digital traditions: The future of the kimono," *TAASA Review* 27(3): 15–17.

Hareven, T. (2002), *The Silk Weavers of Kyoto: Family and Work in a Changing Traditional Industry*, Berkeley: University of California Press.

Harootunian, H. (1998), "Figuring the folk: History, poetics, and representation," in S. Vlastos (ed.), *Mirror of Modernity: Invented Traditions of Modern Japan*, 144–60, Berkeley: University of California Press.

Hashimoto, M. (1998), "Chiho: Yanagita Kunio's 'Japan'," in S. Vlastos (ed.), *Mirror of Modernity: Invented Traditions of Modern Japan*, 133–43, Berkeley: University of California Press.

Hawes, E. (1938), *Fashion Is Spinach*, New York: Random House.

Hendry, J. (1993), *Wrapping Culture*, New York: Oxford University Press.

Hirahara, S., ed. (2012), *Kyoto Toraberakko* [Little Kyoto Traveller], October–November, Kyoto: JTB.

Hiramitsu, C. (2005), "Japanese tradition in Issey Miyake," *Design Discourse*, 1(1): 35–43.

Hobsbawm, E., and Ranger, T., eds. (1983), *The Invention of Tradition*, Cambridge: Cambridge University Press.

Howes, D. (2003), *Sensual Relations: Engaging the Senses in Culture and Social Theory*, Ann Arbor: University of Michigan Press.

Howes, D. (2005a), "Introduction," in D. Howes (ed.), *Empire of the Senses: The Sensual Cultural Reader*, 1–18, Oxford: Berg.

Howes, D. (2005b), "Hyperesthesia, or, the sensual logic of late capitalism," in D. Howes (ed.), *Empire of the Senses: The Sensual Cultural Reader*, 281–303, Oxford: Berg.

Ikegami, E. (2005), *Bonds of Civility: Aesthetic Networks and the Political Origins of Japanese Culture*, New York: Cambridge University Press.

Inoue, S. (1998), "The invention of the martial arts: Kano Jigoro and Kodokan Judo," in S. Vlastos (ed.), *Mirror of Modernity: Invented Traditions of Modern Japan*, 163–73, Berkeley: University of California Press.

Iwabuchi, K. (2009), "Complicit exoticism: Japan and its other," *Continuum: Journal of Media and Cultural Studies*, 8(2): 49–82.

JAANUS (2001), Terminology of Japanese Architecture and Art History. Available online: http://www.aisf.or.jp/~jaanus/ (accessed December 9, 2015).

Jackman, S. (2014), "Flash mobs put spotlight on kimono," *Japan Times*, January 6. Available online: http://www.japantimes.co.jp/news/2014/01/06/national/flash-mobs-put-spotlight-on-kimono/ (accessed November 25, 2015).

James, A., J. Hockey, and A. Dawson, eds. (1997), *After Writing Culture: Epistemology and Praxis in Contemporary Anthropology*, London: Routledge.

The Japan Craft Forum (1996), *Japanese Crafts: A Complete Guide to Today's Traditional Handmade Objects*, Tokyo: Kodansha International.

Japan Style (2011), "How to distinguish between real and fake maiko (geisha)," Web log. Available online: http://www.japanstyle.info/04/entry16099.html (accessed December 11, 2015).

Japan Style System Co. Ltd. (2015), *Meido in yūzen* 4 [Made in *yūzen*]. Available online: http://www.jss-kyoto.jp/home/madeinyuzen4.html (accessed March 16, 2015).

Johnson, D., and Foster, H. (2007), *Dress Sense: Emotional and Sensory Experiences of the Body and Clothes*. Oxford: Berg.

Jokilehto, J. (2009), "The complexity of authenticity," *Kunstiteaduslikke Uurimusi*, 18(3/4): 125–35.

Kawakami, S. (1997), "Clad in beautiful colors and myriad motifs," in M. Morrison and L. Price (eds.), *Classical Kimono from the Kyoto National Museum: Four Centuries of Fashion*, 21–30, San Francisco, CA: Asian Art Museum.

Kawamura, Y. (2005), *Fashion-Ology: An Introduction to Fashion Studies*, Oxford: Berg.

Kawamura, Y. (2012), *Fashioning Japanese Subcultures*, London: Berg.

Kawlra, A. (2015), "Craft conversations: India-Japan and the making of an Asian modern textile aesthetic," paper presented at the *9th International Convention of Asian Scholars (ICAS) Conference*, July 5–9, Adelaide.

Kensinger, K. (1991) "A body of knowledge, or the body knows", *Expedition*, 33(3): 37–45.

KIC (Kyoto Foreign Investment Promotion Committee) (2009), *KIC Report 2009*. Available online: http://www.kic-kyoto.jp/eng/kyoto/pdf/09/kic_report_all.pdf (accessed June 21, 2012).

KIC (Kyoto Foreign Investment Promotion Committee) (2014), 'Key Industries of Kyoto'. Available online: https://www.kic-kyoto.jp/industries/key_industries_of_kyoto/ (accessed July 14, 2014).

Kimono de Ginza (2015), "Kimono de Ginza to wa?" [What is Kimono de Ginza?]. Available online: http://www.kimono-de-ginza.net/sub1.htm (accessed February 14, 2016).

Kimono Hearts Corporation (2014), "Furisode katarogu" [Furisode catalogue]. Available online: http://portal.kimono-hearts.co.jp/coordelabel/coordelabel.html (accessed November 13, 2014).

Kimono Hime [Kimono Princess] (2003), issue 1, Tokyo: Shōdensha.

Kimono Hime [Kimono Princess] (2009), issue 9, Tokyo: Shōdensha.

Kimono Jack (2015), "Kimono Jakku konseputo" [Kimono Jack concept]. Available online: http://www.kimonojack.com/concept/ (accessed December 9, 2015).

Kobayashi, K. (1998), "Recreating a warp-faced compound weave with the Jacquard mechanism—considering Heizo Tatsumura," Textile Society of America Symposium *Proceedings*, Paper 181. Available online: http://digitalcommons.unl.edu/tsaconf/181 (accessed February 26, 2013).

Kobayashi, S. (2011), *Japanese Traditional Craft Workshop: Reviving a Dyeing Art— tsutsugaki yuzen with Master Shumei Kobayashi*, course notes from a professional development course, April 16–21, Sydney: Australian Academy of Design; Japan Foundation.

Koho Tatsumura Corp. (n.d.), "Nishiki weaving: textile fine arts of Koho Tatsumura." Available online: http://www.koho-nishiki.com/en/about/ (accessed July 10, 2013).

Koide, Y., and K. Tsuzuki, (2008), *Boro: Rags and Tatters from the Far North of Japan*, Tokyo: Aspect Corp.

Kondo, D. (1990), *Crafting Selves: Power, Gender and Discourses of Identity in a Japanese Workplace*, Chicago, IL: University of Chicago Press.

Kondo, D. (1992), "The aesthetics and politics of Japanese identity in the fashion industry," in J. Tobin (ed), *Re-Made in Japan: Everyday Life and Consumer Taste in a Changing Society*, 176–203, New Haven, CT: Yale University.

Kondo, D. (2005), "The way of tea: A symbolic analysis," in D. Howes (ed), *Empire of the Senses: The Sensual Cultural Reader*, 192–211, Oxford: Berg.

Kurita, I. (1983), "Revival of the Japanese tradition," *Journal of Popular Culture*, 17(1): 130–4.

Kyoto Denim (2012), "Kyoto Denim." Available online: http://kyoto-denim.jp/en/h (accessed January 2, 2013).

Kyoto Denim (2007–2014a), "Bishamon kikkō." Available online: http://blog.homay.jp/5-kyotodenim/8538/ (accessed March 14, 2016).

Kyoto Denim (2007–2014b), "Iki to iu wakugumi no denim" [the *iki* concept within the framework of denim]. Available online: http://blog.homay.jp/3-design/74/ (accessed January 9, 2016).

Kyoto Denim (2014a), "Kyoto denimu kōshiki saito" [Kyoto Denim formal site]. Available online: http://kyoto-denim.jp/ (accessed September 20, 2014).

Kyoto Denim (2014b), "Kyoto Denim." Available online: http://kyoto-denim.jp/en/ (accessed July 17, 2015).

Kyoto Denim (2015), "Kyoto Denim men." Available online: http://kyoto-denim.jp/men/ (accessed July 17, 2015).

Kyoto Foreign Investment Promotion Committee (2014), "Kyoto today." Available online: http://www.kic-kyoto.jp/eng/kyoto/index.html (accessed February 6, 2016).

Kyoto International Manga Museum (2006–14), "Magic—cuteness magic spells from shojo manga." Available online: http://www.kyotomm.jp/english/event/exh/kyotomagic_2013eng.php (accessed February 15, 2016).

Kyoto Kimono Passport 2011–12, Kyoto: Kyoto Foundation for Promotion of Japanese Dress (kimono) Industry (84-page passport-sized book).

Kyoto Kimono Passport 2012–13, Kyoto: Kyoto Foundation for Promotion of Japanese Dress (kimono) Industry (80-page passport-sized book).

Kyoto Montsuki Co. Ltd. (n.d.), *The Culture of Black*. Available online: http://www.kmontsuki.co.jp/pdf/THE_CULTURE_OF_BLACK_EN.pdf (accessed September 18, 2012).

Kyoto Prefecture (2010), "City and municipal populations" (according to the national census). Available online: http://www.pref.kyoto.jp/en/01-01-02.html (accessed January 5, 2016).

Kyoto Prefecture (2011), "Traditional industries," *Kyoto Prefecture Web Site*. Available online: http://www.pref.kyoto.jp/en/01-02-01.html (accessed February 6, 2016).

Laskow, S. (2012), "A better way to dye," *Conservation: Creative Ideas for a Greener Future*. Available online: http://conservationmagazine.org/2012/05/a-better-way-to-dye/ (accessed November 28, 2015).

Lehmann, U. (2000), *Tigersprung: Fashion in Modernity*, Cambridge, MA: MIT Press.

Liddell, C. (2011), "Art in the realm of the sense of smell," *Japan Times*. May19. Available online: http://www.japantimes.co.jp/culture/2011/05/19/arts/art-in-the-realm-of-the-sense-of-smell/ (accessed June 4, 2011).

Mackie, V. (2009), "Transnational bricolage: Gothic Lolita and the political economy of fashion," *Intersections: Gender and Sexuality in Asia and the Pacific*, Apr (20). Available online: http://intersections.anu.edu.au/issue20/mackie.htm (accessed January 11, 2013).

Mackie, V. (2010), "Reading Lolita in Japan," in T. Aoyama and B. Hartley (eds.), *Girl Reading Girl in Japan*, 187–201, New York: Routledge.

Maiko-Henshin Studio Shiki (2015), *Flow of the Maiko Experience*. Available online: http://www.maiko-henshin.com/en/flow/ (accessed December 11, 2015).

Maiko-Henshin Studio Shiki (2018), *Promotional Campaigns*. Available online: http://www.maiko-henshin.com/en/campaign/ (accessed November 22, 2018).

Masangkay, M. (2013), "Okayama uniqueness in its jeans?" *Japan Times*, November 26. Available online: http://www.japantimes.co.jp/news/2013/11/26/national/okayama-uniqueness-in-its-jeans/ (accessed January 24, 2016).

Mathews, G. (2000), *Global Culture/Individual Identity: Searching for Home in the Cultural Supermarket*, London: Routledge.

Matsui, T. (2015), "Textile as an external/transformative commodity," *Paper Presented at the* 9th International Convention of Asian Scholars (ICAS) Conference, July 5–9, Adelaide.

Mauss, S. (2006), "Techniques of the body," in N. Schlanger (ed.), *Techniques, Technology and Civilization*, 77–96, Oxford: Durkheim Press.

METI (Ministry of Economy, Trade and Industry) 2013, *Traditional Crafts of Japan*. Available online: http://www. meti.go.jp/english/policy/mono_info_service/ creative_industries/pdf/Traditional_Crafts_of_Japan. pdf (accessed March 11, 2015).

MIC (Ministry of Internal Affairs and Communications) 2015, *Statistical Handbook of Japan 2015*. Available online: http://www.stat.go.jp/english/data/handbook/pdf/2015all.pdf#page=17 (accessed September 3, 2016).

Milhaupt, T. (2002), 'Flowers at the crossroads: The four-hundred-year life of a Japanese textile,' Ph.D. thesis, Missouri: Washington University. ProQuest Dissertations Publishing. Available online: http://search.proquest. com.ezproxy.lib.monash.edu.au/docview/275913062/ (accessed January 5, 2016).

Milhaupt, T. (2014), *Kimono: A Modern History*, London: Reaktion Books.

Miller, L. (2003), "Youth Fashion and Changing Beautification Practices," in Gordon Mathews and Bruce White (eds.), *Japan's Changing Generations: Are Young People Creating a New Society?*, 83–98, London: Routledge.

Miller, L. (2004), "Those naughty teenage girls: Japanese kogals, slang, and media assessments," *Journal of Linguistic Anthropology*, 14(2): 225–47.

Miller, L. (2006), *Beauty Up: Exploring Contemporary Japanese Body Aesthetics*, Berkeley: University of California Press.

Ministry of the Environment (2006), "In focus: Minister Koike created the 'Mottainai Furoshiki.'" April 3. Available online: https://www.env.go.jp/en/focus/060403.html (accessed February 19, 2016).

Moeran, B. (1997), *Folk Art Potters of Japan: Beyond an Anthropology of Aesthetics*, Surrey: Curzon Press.

Monden, M. (2008), "Transcultural flow of demure aesthetics: Examining cultural globalisation through Gothic & Lolita fashion," *New Voices*, 2: 21–40.

Monden, M. (2014), *Japanese Fashion Cultures: Dress and Gender in Contemporary Japan*, London: Bloomsbury.

Moon, O. (2013), "Challenges surrounding the survival of the Nishijin silk weaving industry in Kyoto, Japan," *International Journal of Intangible Heritage*, 8: 71–86.

Moon, O. (2015), "From a viable industry to protected heritage: The fate of Nishijin silk weaving in Kyoto, Japan," *Paper Presented at the* 9th International Convention of Asian Scholars (ICAS) Conference, July 5–9, Adelaide.

Mori, M. (2012), "History and techniques of the kimono," in M. Adkins and P. Dickens (eds.), *Shibusa—Extracting Beauty*, 117–34, Huddersfield: University of Huddersfield Press.

Morris-Suzuki, T. (2015), "The frontiers of Japanese Studies: crossing geographical and conceptual borders," *Paper Presented at the Japanese Studies Centre Postgraduate Symposium,* Exploring Japan through New Lenses: Emerging Themes in Japanese Studies, Monash University, September 26.

Moshi Moshi Nippon (2014). [TV programme], Ep17 'K' Kyo-yuzen. Japan International Broadcasting Inc. Aired December 12, 2014. Available online: http://www.jibtv.com/programs/moshimoshinippon/20141212.html (accessed February 15, 2016).

Mouer, R., and Sugimoto, Y. (1986), *Images of Japanese Society: A Study in the Social Construction of Reality*, London: KPI.

Murasaki, S. (2005), *The Diary of Lady Murasaki*, trans. R. Bowring, Kindle Edition. London: Penguin Books.

Murayama, M., ed. (2011), *Fashion Snap Magazine Untitle* [sic], No. 25 (Spring), The Faculty of Fine Arts student publication, Osaka: Osaka University of Arts.

Nakamura, A. (2004), "Kimono makes comeback—in used form. Female shoppers search for a cheap, elegant reminder of yester-year," *Japan Times Online*, April 30. Available online: https://www.japantimes.co.jp/news/2004/04/30/national/kimono-makes-comeback-in-used-form/ (accessed October 15, 2018).

Nakaoka, T., K. Aikawa, H. Miyajima, T. Yoshii, and T. Nishizawa (1988), "The textile history of Nishijin (Kyoto): East meets West," *Textile History*, 19(2): 117–42.

Nakatani, A (2015), "Dressing Miss World with Balinese brocades: the 'fashionalisation' and 'heritagization' of handwoven textiles in Indonesia," *Textile*, 13(1): 30–49.

Nischler, C., R. Michael, C. Winterstellar, P. Marvan, L. van Rijn, J. Coppens, T. van den Berg, M. Emesz, and G. Grabner (2013), "Iris color and visual functions," *Graefes Archive for Clinical and Experimental Ophthalmology*, 251: 195–202.

Nishijin Textile Center (2004), *Guide to Nishijin Textile Center*. Available online: http://www.nishijin.or.jp/eng/brochure/ (accessed June 20, 2013).

Nishijin Textile Industrial Association (2011), *Nishijin seisan gaikyō* [A survey of Nishijin textile production], Kyoto: Nishijin ori kōgyō kumiai.

Nishijin Textile Industrial Association (2015), "The history of Nishijin weaving." Available online: http://www.nishijin.or.jp/eng/history/history.htm (accessed January 5, 2016).

Nishikawa, S. (1716), *Hiinagata Miyako Fūzoku* [Rare and Popular Kimono Patterns of the Capital], Kyoto: Tanimura Shinbei. Digitised edition. National Diet Library [Kokuritsu Kokkai Toshōkan]. Volume 1, frame number 8. Available online: http://dl.ndl.go.jp/info:ndljp/pid/2551566 (accessed March 13, 2016).

Norris, C., and J. Bainbridge (2009), "Selling otaku? Mapping the relationship between industry and fandom in the Australian cosplay scene," *Intersections: Gender and Sexuality in Asia and the Pacific*, April (20). Available online: http://intersections.anu.edu.au/issue20/norris_bainbridge.htm (accessed December 16, 2012).

Notebook on Cities and Clothes (1989), [Documentary] Dir. Wim Wenders, France: Centre Pompidou, Centre de Creation Industrielle, Road Movies Filmproduktion.

Okazaki, M. (2015), *Kimono Now*, Munich: Prestel.

Otowa, R. (2009), "Mirka: Nishijin harmonies," *Kyoto Journal*, 73: 10–16.

Pagong Kamedatomi Co. (2014), "Pagong brand and history." Available online: http://www.pagong.jp/en/about/ (accessed September 20, 2014).

Pagong Kamedatomi Co. (2016), "Pagong Yuzen fabric used by Fashion Designer Yumi Katsura for Paris 2016 collection." Available online: https://pagong.jp/en/news/yum-katsura-grand-paris-collection-2016/ (accessed November 20, 2018).

Pettersson, M. (2014), "Seeing what is not there: pictorial experience, imagination and non-localization," *British Journal of Aesthetics*, 51(3): 279–94.

Pink, S. (2009), *Doing Sensory Ethnography*, Los Angeles: SAGE.

Piotti, S. (2014), "Fibres and fabrics," in R. Menegazzo and S. Piotti (eds.), *Wa: The Essence of Japanese Design*, 215–19, London: Phaidon Press.

Powell, S., and A. Cabello (2014), "Jidai Matsuri: Sad-eyed lady at the festival of the ages," *Japan Times*. October 4. Available online: http://www.japantimes.co.jp/life/2014/10/04/travel/jidai-matsuri-sad-eyed-lady- festival-ages/ (accessed December 11, 2015).

Pratchett, T. (1999), *The Fifth Elephant*, London: Corgi Books.

Ragalye, R. (2012), "(Cos)playing culture: reimagining the kimono in modern-day Kyoto," Unpublished Honors thesis. Department of Sociology and Anthropology. MA: Mount Holyoke College. Available online: https://ida. mtholyoke.edu/xmlui/handle/10166/993 (accessed December 13, 2012).

Rahman, O., L. Wing-sun, E. Lam, and C. Mong-tai (2011), " 'Lolita': Imaginative self and illusive consumption," *Fashion Theory*, 15(1): 7–28.

Rahman, O., L. Wing-sun, and B. Hei-man Cheung (2012), " 'Cosplay': Imagining self and performing identity," *Fashion Theory*, 16(3): 317–42.

Redick, S. (2013), "Surprise is still the most powerful marketing tool," *Harvard Business Review*. May 10. Available online: https://hbr.org/2013/05/surprise-is-still-the-most-powerful/ (accessed September 5, 2014).

Reisinger, Y., and C. Steiner (2006), "Reconceptualizing Object Authenticity," *Annals of Tourism Research*, 33(1): 65–86.

Robertson. J. (1997), "Empire of nostalgia: Rethinking 'Internationalization' in Japan today," *Theory, Culture and Society*, 14(4): 97–122.

Robertson. J. (1998), "It takes a village: Internationalization and nostalgia in postwar Japan," in S. Vlastos (ed), *Mirror of Modernity: Invented Traditions of Modern Japan*, 110–30, Berkeley: University of California Press.

Sangam Australia India Design Platform (2013), *Code of Practice for Partnerships in Craft and Design: Draft—31 October 2013*, Available online: http://sangamproject.net/code (accessed January 22, 2016).

Sasaki, S. (2009), "All for the love of wearing kimono," *Japan Times*, December 31. Available online: http://www.japantimes.co.jp/news/2009/12/31/national/all-for-the-love-of-wearing-kimono/ (accessed December 14, 2012).

Sato, C. (2010), "Regarding fashions in 20th century women's kimono," MA thesis. Melbourne: RMIT. Available online: https://researchbank.rmit.edu.au/view/rmit:10880 (accessed January 16, 2015).

Schoeser, M. (2012), *Textiles: The Art of Mankind*, London: Thames & Hudson.

The Secret World of Comiket (2015), [Documentary]. Japan: NHK World.

Seidensticker, E. (2010), *Tokyo from Edo to Showa 1867–1989: The Emergence of the World's Greatest City*, Hong Kong: Tuttle.

The September Issue (2009), [Documentary] Dir. R. J. Cutler, US: A&E IndieFilms, Actual Reality Pictures.

Sharp, L. (2011), "Maid meets mammal: The 'animalized' body of the cosplay maid character in Japan," *Intertexts*, 15(1): 60–78.

Simmel, G. (1957), "Fashion," *American Journal of Sociology*, 62(6): 541–58.

Slade, T. (2009), *Japanese Fashion: A Cultural History*, Oxford: Berg.

Smith, K. (1995), "Introduction," in M. Nakano (ed.), *Makiko's Diary: A Merchant Wife in 1910 Kyoto*, trans. K. Smith, 1–39, Stanford, CA: Stanford University Press.

Smith, S. (2010), "The wrapped, the rapt, and the rapped: Considerations on models of Japanese society, 'Japanists,' and stigmatized Japanese hotrodders," *Reviews in Anthropology*, 23(1): 21–34.

Sou Sou (2013), "About Sou Sou." Available online: http://www.sousouus.com/aboutsousou (accessed October 10, 2010).

Sou Sou (2015), "Sou Sou Kei-i." Available online: http://www.sousounetshop.co.jp/ (accessed June 13, 2015).

Sou Sou (n.d.), "Sou Sou Kei-i." Available online: http://www.sousounetshop.jp/?no=0&mode=cate&cbid=146645&csid=0 (accessed March 2, 2016).

Sou Sou US (2014), "Why split-toe?" Available online: http://www.sousouus.com/about/why-split-toe/ (accessed February 4, 2014).

Sou Sou US (2015), "About Takashima Chizimi cotton." Available online: http://www.sousouus.com/about-chizimi/ (accessed December 5, 2015).

Sou Sou US (2016), "About Ise cotton." Available online: http://www.sousouus.com/our-products/about-ise-cotton/ (accessed February 19, 2016).

Stavros, M. (2014), *Kyoto: An Urban History of Japan's Premodern Capital*, Honolulu: University of Hawai'i Press.

Stevens, C. S. (2008), *Japanese Popular Music: Culture, Authenticity and Power*, London: Routledge.

Stevens, C. S. (2010), "You are what you buy: Postmodern consumption and fandom of Japanese popular culture," *Japanese Studies*, 30(2): 199–214.

Stinchecum, A. (2010), "Cloth and identity in Yaeyama," in C. Brumann and R. Cox (eds.), *Making Japanese Heritage*, 124–48, London: Routledge.

Stoller, P. (1997), *Sensuous Scholarship*. Philadelphia: University of Pennsylvania Press.

Tabata Shibori (2015), "Tabata shibori." Available online: http://kyoshibori.jp/ (accessed February 24, 2015).

Takahashi, M. (2008), *Kyō no kimono hajime* [Let's start wearing kimono today]. Raku tabi bunko series no.031 [Kyoto journey paperback series no. 31]. Kyoto: Kotokoto.

Takasago Sangyō Corp. (2015), "omoi • tsuyomi" [hope and strength]. Available online: http://takasago-sangyo.com/ strength.php (accessed December 5, 2015).

Taylor Atkins, E. (2000), "Can Japanese sing the blues?" in T. Craig (ed.), *Japan Pop! Inside the World of Japanese Popular Culture*, 27–59, New York: M.E. Sharpe.

Thompson, L. (1998), "The invention of the Yokozuna and the championship system, or, Futahaguro's revenge," in S. Vlastos (ed.), *Mirror of Modernity: Invented Traditions of Modern Japan*, 163–73, Berkeley: University of California Press.

Tsunoda, R., W. de Bary, and D. Keene (1958), *Sources of Japanese Tradition*, New York: Columbia University Press.

Tsurumi, E. (1990), *Factory Girls: Women in the Thread Mills of Meiji Japan*, New Jersey: Princeton University Press.

UNESCO World Heritage Centre (1992–2016), "Historic monuments of ancient Kyoto (Kyoto, Uji and Otsu Cities)." Available online: http://whc.unesco.org/en/list/688 (accessed February 11, 2016).

Urry, J., and Larsen, J. (2011), *The Tourist Gaze 3.0*, 3rd edition. Los Angeles: SAGE.

Varley, H. P. (2000), *Japanese Culture*, 4th edition. Honolulu: University of Hawai'i Press.

Veblen, T. (2008 [1899]), *Theory of the Leisure Class*. E-book. Available online: http://www.gutenberg.org/ebooks/833 (accessed April 16, 2012).

Vlastos, S., ed. (1998), *Mirror of Modernity: Invented Traditions of Modern Japan*, Berkeley: University of California Press.

Wada, Y. (1996), "The history of the kimono: Japan's national dress," in R. Stevens and Y. Wada (eds.), *The Kimono Inspiration: Art and Art-to-Wear in America*, 131–57, Washington, DC: The Textile Museum.

Wakisaka, K. (2012), *Wakisaka Katsuji no dezain: Marimekko, Sou Sou, tsuma he ateta ichiman-mai no aidea* (Katsuji Wakisaka: Japanese textile designer: Marimekko, Sou Sou, and 10,000 postcards to his wife). Tokyo: PIE Books.

Webb, M. (2005), "In skeptical quest of a boom," *Japan Times*, September 18. Available online: http://www.japantimes.co.jp/life/2005/09/18/to-be-sorted/in-skeptical-quest-of-a-boom/ (accessed December 14, 2012).

White, M. (2012), *CoffeeLlife in Japan*, Berkeley: University of California Press.

Woodson, Y. (1997), "Forming the national style: Classical kimono in historical review," in M. Morrison and L. Price (eds.), *Classical Kimono from the Kyoto National Museum: Four Centuries of Fashion*, 9–21, San Francisco: Asian Art Museum.

Yamamoto, Y. (1999), "An aesthetics of everyday life: Modernism and a Japanese popular aesthetic idea, 'iki,'" (Master of Arts MA), University of Chicago, Chicago.

Yanagizawa, M. (2011), "Old-style looms weave contemporary chic," *Highlighting Japan*, 4(9): 30–1.

Yano, C. (2002), *Tears of Longing: Nostalgia and the Nation in Japanese Popular Song*, Cambridge: Harvard University Press.

Yano, C. (2005), "Covering disclosures: Practices of intimacy, hierarchy, and authenticity in a Japanese popular music genre," *Popular Music and Society*, 28(2): 193–205.

Yoshikawa, Y. (1903), *Moyōga Shoho* [Basics of Design], Dainippon Books, Digitised edition, National Diet Library [Kokuritsu Kokkai Toshōkan]. Available online: http://dl.ndl.go.jp/info:ndljp/pid/854661 (accessed July 16, 2019).

Yume Koubou (2011), "Oiran plan." Available online: http://www.kyoto-oiran.com/plan/ (accessed March 2, 2014).

Yun Hui, T., J. van Bremen, and E. Ben-Ari (2005), "Memory, scholarship and the study of Japan," in T. Yun Hui, J. van Bremen, and E. Ben-Ari, (eds.), *Perspectives on Social Memory in Japan*, 1–22, Kent, UK: Global Oriental.

INDEX